# MARRIED TO THE AMADEUS

---

After graduating from Oxford University with a degree in philosophy, politics and economics, Muriel Nissel worked in the Civil Service until she married Siegmund Nissel in 1957. In the early years when she was at home looking after their two young children, she carried out research into the economics of the arts for a study based at Princeton University. She was also appointed a magistrate. When the children went to school, she joined the Central Statistical Office and was the first editor of *Social Trends*, a highly successful annual government publication, now in its twenty-eighth year. She left the Civil Service in 1976 and in the following year joined the Policy Studies Institute, researching mainly into the family and the arts. She was a member of the Gulbenkian Enquiry into the Training of Musicians, which reported in 1977. She is now retired but still works on a freelance basis.

# Married to the Amadeus

## LIFE WITH A STRING QUARTET

*by*

MURIEL NISSEL

**dlm**

First published in 1998
by Giles de la Mare Publishers Limited
3 Queen Square, London WC1N 3AU

Typeset by Tom Knott
Printed in Great Britain by
Hillman Printers (Frome) Limited
All rights reserved

A CIP record of this book is available
from the British Library

ISBN 1-900357-12-7

# Contents

# Illustrations

## LINE ILLUSTRATIONS

## ACKNOWLEDGMENTS FOR PHOTOGRAPHS
*(where photographer known)*

### PLATES

# Acknowledgments

---

Many people have helped in the writing of this book. Above all it would not have been possible without the help of my family and the close collaboration of my husband, Siegmund Nissel. Not only did he have in his diaries the basis for the story of the Amadeus Quartet, but he was always ready to talk about specific incidents, check drafts and discuss the details of each chapter.

Several friends read drafts of the book and my thanks go particularly to my daughter Claire, and to George Bluestone, David Hapgood, Derek Kartun, Michael MacLeod, Terry Maher, Susan Pattie, Daniel Snowman and Rosamund Strode. Pauline Del Mar not only read the draft but compiled the index with admirable skill.

Norbert Brainin and Martin Lovett were an invaluable support throughout, as were Katinka Brainin, Susi Lovett and Margit Schidlof and their families. Amongst the large number of people with whom I discussed the book, I would particularly like to single out John Amis, Mariedi Anders, Robin Anderton, Emile Cantor, Imogen Cooper, Milein Cosman-Keller, Brigitte Eisner, Kenneth Essex, William and Anne Glock, Emmie Hess, Claus and Mary Moser, Bill and Maggie Pleeth and Dick Stoltzman.

My thanks also go to my editor and publisher, Giles de la Mare, for his kindness and his great care in preparing the manuscript.

# *Preface*

---

A string quartet is a fragile creation. Many are born but few survive. The myriad factors that came together to make the Amadeus Quartet one of the world's great chamber-music ensembles and then enabled it to survive for forty years with its original four members unchanged form an absorbing story. Although the success of the group was mainly due to the exceptional qualities of its players, these four people all married and had children, and the family support that sustained them played a critical part. This book takes a close look at the impact of quartet life on the everyday activities of the individuals within these families, in particular the Nissel family.

Norbert Brainin, Siegmund Nissel and Peter Schidlof were all born in Vienna at the beginning of the 1920s. They never met in that city but, having come to Britain to escape Nazi persecution, they were brought together in internment camps in 1940 during the Second World War as 'friendly enemy aliens'. This was a small miracle. When they were released, in spite of their daily jobs as part of the war effort, they were able to take part in the very active musical life in London, and it was here that they found a sympathetic cellist, Martin Lovett, a few years their junior. Like them he was Jewish, which perhaps helped to establish the strong bond that grew up between them.

The personalities in a quartet must be compatible. The players may fight and argue but on the platform they must have resolved their differences and join forces in a united musical endeavour. However gifted they may be individually, they have to develop a group feeling and sense of purpose to carry them forward.

It has been said that a great and successful performer needs not only talent but endless stamina. This is specially true of a string player in a quartet in the present century, with its continual round of concerts the world over. Touring was fundamental to the Amadeus Quartet's existence, and the tensions it produced pervade the book. The pattern of touring changed over time but it remained a matter of different countries, different towns, different hotels, upset stomachs, long journeys, maybe fear of flying, separation from home and family and the ordeal of the concert itself. However badly you may have slept, or however difficult your personal life may be, you have to walk onto the platform and face the audience looking good and prepared to give of your best.

To flourish, a string quartet needs to be in the right place at the right time. The musical climate in Britain after the war was sympathetic to chamber music, and the rest of Europe was eager to rebuild its concert halls for a population starved of musical entertainment during the devastation of the war years. The British Government was helpful, with grants being given to the Council for the Encouragement of Music and the Arts – CEMA was the precursor of the Arts Council – and to the British Council. In those days of post-war austerity, the cost of putting on full-scale symphony concerts was formidable and chamber music had the advantage of being much cheaper. The record industry was booming. Building a record library was every music-lover's ambition.

Times change and people change. Although the members of the Quartet continued to develop and to search for deeper meaning in the interpretation of the repertoire throughout their career, their forty years together can broadly be divided into ten-year periods. The first decade from 1948 to 1957 was a period of building repertoire and reputation. When the Nissels married in 1957, the Quartet was busy making records and extending its audiences worldwide. In the ten years from 1968 to 1977, it was an 'established' quartet. During the final phase up to Peter Schidlof's death in August 1987 it was concerned with staying at the peak of the profession musically and played mainly in the world's major cities and concert halls rather than to audiences in music clubs and other smaller venues.

For the Nissels the last three phases more or less coincided with changes in their own family life and economic circumstances. For the first ten years of their marriage, with none too much money, they were setting up home and raising a family. During the next decade, in addition to looking after two children both parents had full-time jobs and were often away from home travelling. This brought with it the benefit of two incomes and a sense of achievement from the work they were doing. At the same time, there were additional strains, particularly on the mother of the family who was more likely to be at home. In the last period, when the children were changing into young adults and family life was entering a different phase, the pressure was more on Siegmund Nissel. The world expected the famous quartet always to be on top form.

The interaction between work and family life affects nearly all of us. Professional couples in particular find that the demands of their jobs conflict with their personal commitments to each other and, if children are born, new problems arise. It is even harder for musicians whose need to travel brings with it separation and isolation. This can easily lead to the break-up of a quartet, especially when a player, whether a man or a woman, starts a family. The players in the Amadeus Quartet all had children of fairly similar ages. Two of their wives had full-time jobs outside the home and two did not. The juggling of demands on the time and affection of all those involved plays a prominent part in the book.

Its structure is broadly chronological, but certain topics stand by themselves and have been slotted into the unfolding story. The Aldeburgh Festival and the Dartington Summer School are two examples. The buying of instruments is also given a chapter to itself. In the early stages of the Quartet's life it was, as so many musicians know, in direct conflict with such things as buying houses and bringing up families. The Nissels' holiday homes in Tuscany and Sussex both played a significant part in their lives and are also given a chapter to themselves. The description of my own professional life, which I pursued for twenty out of the thirty years I was 'married to the Amadeus', is mainly concentrated in two chapters.

Although my book is primarily about musicians and their families, the problems that arise are not perhaps so different from those facing many other families. As travel and communications shrink the world, more and more people find they may have to work away from home. Developing careers may involve a change of location and conflicts can arise, particularly if both partners are concerned about their job prospects. Society changes and attitudes to marriage and family life change with it. The four members of the Amadeus Quartet and their wives and children lived through forty years of such change. Their experience thus has general relevance and I hope that their story will interest musicians and non-musicians alike.

*Muriel Nissel*
*March 1998*

# CHAPTER ONE

# Forty Years
# Playing Quartets

———————

The Amadeus Quartet gave their last concert on 5th July 1987. As my husband, Siegmund Nissel, and I drove from our house in north London through the summer countryside, we did not know that it was to be the culmination of those forty years of friendship and collaboration between the members of this unique group of four musicians.

The concert was part of the Summer Festival in Cheltenham organized by John Manduell,* who was Principal of the Royal Northern College of Music, and a long-standing friend. The Quartet had arranged to meet a good hour before the start of the concert to warm up and try out the acoustics of the hall, something they never took for granted. Sigi, who played second violin, and I arrived at much the same time as Norbert Brainin, the first violinist, and Martin Lovett, the cellist. Uncharacteristically, Peter Schidlof, the viola player, was late because he had mistaken the time of the concert. The programme consisted of two Beethoven string quartets, Opus 18, no. 4, and Opus 74, and Benjamin Britten's third and last quartet. Concerts were never routine and tension was always present, but the works were familiar and unlikely to produce problems. The Quartet was on peak form. The wives of the other members, Katinka Brainin, Margit Schidlof and Susi Lovett, were all coming, for whenever we could we accompanied our husbands to concerts within easy reach of our homes. We were looking forward to this concert, especially as there would most likely be old friends in the audience with whom we could enjoy and share this musical experience. On this occasion we – the Nissels – were expecting two friends from Canada who were staying in Oxford to take part in Rhodes Scholars' celebrations, and also our son, Daniel, who was stage-managing at the Old Vic Theatre in Bristol.

Our expectations were not disappointed and even by Amadeus standards it was an excellent concert, warmly acclaimed. It was a fine summer evening and they were wearing white dinner jackets. The stage in the Pittville Pump Room was festooned with flowers. The Quartet played the final chords and

———————

* Later Sir John Manduell.

two balding and two greying heads bowed to the audience to acknowledge the applause.

Six weeks later, on 15th August, Peter Schidlof died following a heart attack shortly after his sixty-fifth birthday. This tragedy meant the end had come for the Amadeus Quartet, for there had been a tacit understanding that, if any one of them could no longer play, they would not try to find a substitute. Time had moulded them into one body, and their musical sensitivity to each other was such that once a limb had been torn off, any attempt to graft on a new one would only be rejected.

Our last meeting with Peter was at the end of July at our house in Tuscany when he and his wife Margit, who were staying nearby, visited us for a pro-longed and wonderfully Italian lunch of melon and smoked ham, peaches and *dolcelatte* cheese, washed down by the local Montecarlo white wine.

By the beginning of August the members of the Quartet were all back in England ready for the start of the 1987–8 season. We ourselves were briefly visiting our Sussex cottage and Peter was in his cottage in the Lake District. He was having pains in his chest and several times telephoned Sigi, who had had a heart attack some years earlier, to discuss the symptoms with him. The telephone rang again at breakfast one morning, and I heard Sigi give a cry followed by the unearthly wail of a stricken animal. He was beside himself with grief, for Peter's death meant the loss of his closest friend. We walked out of the cottage, over the stile down the lane, and in silence crossed the stubbled field, away from the excited family staying with us who had just been to Gatwick airport to collect their father from Hong Kong. A lifetime had passed and no words could express the anguish we felt.

The Quartet's first concert had taken place nearly forty years before on 10th January 1948. Sigi had just had his twenty-sixth birthday, Peter was twenty-five, Norbert twenty-four and Martin twenty. Martin had been born in London but the other three, who had come from Vienna as refugees, had arrived in England less than twelve months before war broke out in September 1939.

Although the three refugees came from the same city, they had not known each other there. Their meeting had to wait until the Second World War when they were interned in Britain in the summer of 1940 as 'friendly enemy aliens'. France had fallen to the Germans and Britain was being threatened with invasion. An anxious government rounded up all who were 'enemy aliens' irrespective of their origins and put them into camps surrounded by soldiers and barbed-wire. It is difficult to imagine how these three Viennese teenagers, two of whom had escaped to England on children's transports, could possibly have been a security risk. Indeed, Norbert, who was only seventeen, was released after a month because, as a result of revised regu-lations, he was under age. Peter and Sigi, who were already eighteen, had to stay inside. Sigi was freed on 14th May 1941, and Peter some three months afterwards.

Fifty years later Sigi returned to the Isle of Man, where he had been interned at the camp in Onchan, to take part in a television programme called 'His Majesty's Most Loyal Enemy Aliens'. Standing once again in the room in the peeling stuccoed boarding-house on the sea-front where he had lived, he recalled how when he arrived and looked through the double barbed-wire fence surrounding them, he had felt it the darkest moment in his life. There was a grave possibility of invasion followed by a German holocaust in this closely packed island. 'I never experienced such a fear, such a foreboding. The danger was that if the Germans succeeded in invading Britain, we would be handed over to the Nazis on a plate with very little chance to escape or go underground. But, in retrospect, all the good things that have happened to me since then started there.'

The camp was Sigi's university. It contained many cultured and talented people. Amongst the musicians were Franz Reizenstein, the composer and pianist, and Max Jekel, previously a member of the Vienna Philharmonic Orchestra, who gave Sigi violin lessons. Not only were they fed and housed, but there were lectures and concerts and companionship. One of the houses in the camp was given over to music for practising and concert-giving, and Sigi recalls playing the Bach E major concerto with Reizenstein at the piano. It was here that he began to believe that he might after all be able to develop his talents as a violinist and become a professional musician, something he had never dared to dream could happen.

Peter was first interned at Prees Heath in Shropshire, where he briefly met Norbert. One day a small crowd had gathered round Norbert to listen to him practising the Mozart A major concerto. In the crowd was a tall, slim good-looking youth with a mop of thick brown hair who said diffidently, 'I also play the violin.' Norbert, short and stocky with unruly dark hair, handed him his fiddle. 'Here, play something.' So young Hans Schidlof, as he was then known, started playing the Bach E major concerto. Norbert was spell-bound. Here was this teenager with little musical training but a most extraordinary talent playing in the middle of nowhere, in a camp, in the open air. A few days later Stephanie Hess, who had befriended Peter when he first arrived in England, sent him his own violin. From the piano version that he happened to have with him, Norbert arranged the Mendelssohn concerto for two violins so that he and Peter could play it together. To everyone's delight they gave a camp concert with Peter playing the solo part and Norbert's single violin rendering the whole orchestra. 'When I wrote it down it was more or less unreadable, so I played it myself and let Peter have the more familiar solo part,' Norbert said. It demonstrated Norbert's exceptional gift of being able to hear themes and harmonies and somehow adapt them for one fiddle.

Later Peter was transferred to the Isle of Man, and Peter and Sigi found themselves in the same camp. They too played chamber music and, during their months together, there grew up between them a deep friendship that was to last a lifetime. Reminiscing many years later in a huskily sentimental voice during his television interview on the Isle of Man, Sigi went on to say that if anyone had told him then what the next fifty years would bring, he would have refused to believe it. And yet it happened. 'It was only because I was here in this camp that I met people who recognized that Peter and I had talent and recommended us to the best teacher in Europe, Max Rostal, who said he would teach us without taking any money. He kept his word and that was the beginning of the good things.'

Amongst the camp's musicians was Ferdinand Rauter, the pianist who for many years accompanied and arranged song-settings for Engel Lund, the well-known singer from Iceland. He had many friends who were eminent musicians and he told them of the remarkable gifts of the two young Austrian refugees who had delighted the camp with their recitals. Through the intervention of these musicians and Bloomsbury House,* Sigi and Peter were eventually released under the category of 'Persons of Eminent Distinction who have made Outstanding Contributions to Art'. Their outstanding contributions had been made within the barbed-wire of internment, but that enabled them to be fitted into the Home Office specifications.

Unless there were reasons for exemption, everyone during the war was required to do war work. After they were released Sigi worked in a scrap-metal smelting foundry and Peter trained as a dental mechanic. Norbert was already working as an unskilled machine-tool fitter.

As soon as they were free, Sigi and Peter began taking lessons with Max Rostal. Norbert was already studying with him and there was soon a close friendship between the three students. Max had a profound influence on them all and subsequently on the Amadeus Quartet itself. Their debt to him is inestimable. He was a little man, with glasses and a squint, but what they remember him for was his excellence as a teacher and his generosity, friendliness and humour. He also was born in Central Europe, in Teschen (at that time in Poland, but after the war to be transferred to Czechoslovakia). He had made his mark as a child prodigy before going on to have a distinguished career both as a performer and as a violin teacher. At the Musikhochschule in Berlin he became an assistant to Carl Flesch and then a professor himself. When he came to London in 1934, he and the pianist Franz Osborn soon achieved fame as a duo. His playing marvellously expressed his personality through the colours he could evoke, with never a wrong accent or a clumsy division of the bow. In Mozart and Schubert, he conveyed all the lilt and

---

* This was the name by which it was commonly known. It comprised a number of organizations concerned with helping refugees from Germany and Central Europe.

charm of his mid-European background. Sigi remembers in particular the way he played the first phrase of the Schubert *Fantasia* – it was slightly irregular with a smile in it.

Whilst on the Isle of Man, Sigi had struck up a friendship with Hans Berge, who was not Jewish but had left Germany for humanitarian reasons because he was nauseated by the Nazi regime. Hans and his wife, Kristin, had invited Sigi and Peter to stay with them when they were released from internment. They gratefully accepted the offer, but as the Berges lived in south London it meant a long journey for Sigi to the factory in the East End, and also to his lessons with Max Rostal in Belsize Park in north-west London. But he was already showing the stamina he was going to need as a member of an internationally famous string quartet. Much of the musical life of the Jewish refugees was concentrated in the Swiss Cottage and Hampstead areas of London, and at weekends Sigi and Peter joined in many musical evenings at houses of people such as Eddie May and Martin Cahn. At these gatherings they played with musicians like Maria Lidka and with Norbert, who was living nearby in Hampstead Garden Suburb with his aunt Dora. Whenever they could, they took part in recitals in London and elsewhere. They often had to do this surreptitiously because, being immigrants, they were not allowed to take paid work as musicians. Once when they gave a concert for Alec Sherman's New London Orchestra in a security-restricted area, the organizer, without telling Norbert and Sigi, went so far as to put them down under the anglicized names of Norman Brown and Sydney Mitchell. At one point Norbert began to take his alien card out of his pocket and was hastily told to put it away!

When the war ended things were easier. All three began playing in various orchestras and small ensembles. They played in Fistoulari's London International Orchestra and also in a small orchestra conducted by Arnold Goldsborough which was the forerunner of the English Chamber Orchestra. There were problems, however, because they were still Austrians by nationality. Sigi and Peter were both to be granted British nationality in April 1948. But Norbert's naturalization was deferred until 1956, because his relatives had had associations with the Communist Party.*

Martin's story was different. In 1942, at the age of fifteen, he had won a scholarship to the Royal College of Music. It was there that he had met a gifted young violinist, Suzanne Rozsa, who later became his wife. After the war Suzanne took lessons with Max Rostal at the Guildhall School of Music, and it was through her that Martin was introduced to Max. He joined the Rostal Chamber Orchestra, a group consisting mainly of Rostal's pupils

---

* Harry Brainin, the son of Norbert's uncle Solomon, was a considerable intellectual with very left-wing views. He returned to Vienna at the end of the war together with Norbert's brother Hugo to try and rebuild Austria in accordance with their ideals.

which gave occasional concerts. Norbert, Sigi and Peter, who were a few years older than Martin, were already in the orchestra so that all four members of the future Amadeus Quartet were thus playing together in the same ensemble. From Max Rostal they learnt how to work, an experience which was to imprint itself indelibly on their approach to music. It was studying with him that taught them how to take a whole movement to pieces, analyse it, break it down into its parts, and discuss and argue amongst themselves how to approach it. Martin has described the thoroughness with which each aspect of a performance was tackled in the orchestra. He thought that the secret of the working success of the Amadeus Quartet was that in a similar way they were prepared to confront every problem and 'stick at it until we reached some sort of conclusion. We worked as though we had infinity in front of us. We would, for example, spend the whole morning on the opening of *Death and the Maiden*.'

A little later, in 1946, Martin and Peter both played together in the Glyndebourne production of Britten's *The Rape of Lucretia* under Ansermet. When Martin arrived the small orchestra had already been rehearsing for some while, and he describes how the ever-critical Peter kept on turning round and telling him that he was playing too loudly or too softly. Martin grudged the interference, regarding it as the conductor's job, not Peter's. 'To be honest,' he said, 'we didn't get on too well at that point.' What Peter thought of this somewhat cocky nineteen-year-old with his bow-tie we do not know.

In 1946 Peter and Martin played together at the Wigmore Hall in the first performance in Britain of Honegger's duo for violin and cello. Martin had intended to perform it with Suzanne Rozsa but Max Rostal had decided she ought to not play in public concerts at that particular stage of her development, and he had recommended Peter Schidlof in her place. Martin went to the Berges' flat to rehearse with Peter and afterwards Sigi would join them to perform Beethoven trios with Peter on the viola. For Martin it was a new experience. 'This was real chamber-music playing; I hadn't really done it quite like that before.' He had always wanted to play quartets, and the thought crossed his mind that the string trio he was taking part in could, with the collaboration of Norbert, be the genesis of a quartet.

Meanwhile Dartington Hall began to have a role in the lives of both Norbert and Sigi. Well before the Amadeus Quartet was formed, they had both visited this incredibly beautiful estate established by Leonard and Dorothy Elmhirst on the banks of the Dart near Totnes in Devon. Sigi had gone there during the war to take part in Bach cantatas and other works under Hans Oppenheim, Director of the Dartington Hall Music Group, and again later when he led a quartet with Edward Bor playing the second violin, his sister Sylvia Bor the cello and Hans Berge the viola. Norbert also performed Bach cantatas with Hans Oppenheim, who on one occasion took the group to perform in a concert in Cambridge. This was the first time Imogen Holst, then in charge of the music courses at Dartington, had heard Norbert play. In a radio interview* she recollects how, when she visited the Blue Boar Hotel in Trinity Street where Norbert was staying, she was walking down the corridor with a message for one of the guests when she heard somebody practising in a hotel bedroom 'very slowly, two notes of a scale – I had never heard anything so beautiful.' Imogen then went to the concert and was introduced to Norbert. Soon afterwards she invited him to stay for a few days at Dartington to help with her young students. She describes how, enraptured, they listened to Norbert playing the Bach *Chaconne* and how she herself had learnt from him too, particularly his 'extraordinary power of continuity of rhythm going through'. Norbert's zest for performance was such that he loved playing to groups of people of all kinds, but especially to young students like those he met at Dartington.

Norbert went back to Dartington several times, gaining knowledge and experience of chamber music whilst playing with various members of the staff. It seemed natural that, during one of these visits, plans were made for him to give a concert together with Sigi, Peter and Martin in memory of Christopher Martin who had died in 1944 and had been the first arts administrator there from 1934. In the summer of 1947, under the name of the Brainin Quartet, the four of them performed an exacting programme consisting of Mozart's quartet in D major, Schubert's *Death and the Maiden* and Beethoven's third Rasumovsky quartet.

Imogen Holst was so impressed by their performance that she personally offered to underwrite their professional début at the Wigmore Hall in London the following January. What should they call themselves? Many quartets, such as the Busch, the Griller and the Hurwitz, were still being named after their leaders, but the practice was beginning to lapse. London audiences were already familiar with names such as the Aeolian, the Pro Arte, the Quartetto Italiano and the Budapest. Moreover, in all fairness to Peter, whose original instrument was the violin and who changed from violin to viola to make the Quartet possible, some more impersonal name seemed appropriate. The London-Vienna Quartet? No: too much like a railway train. Sigi suggested 'Amadeus'. It was a name that gave them divine protection.

The concert, which took place on 10th January 1948, is legendary. Imogen Holst once described it thus. 'I offered to do what I could to put it on and got the hall for them and the agent and all that but they, bless them, saved up to do the posters on the London Underground because it was quite a business to get an audience. I had had quite a bit of experience in organizing concerts but never at a distance of several hundred miles for a group who

---

* In an interview with Norbert, Sigi and Martin and other musicians on Radio 3 in December 1987, David Wheeler started with a recording of these remarks made by Imogen Holst.

# WIGMORE HALL
WIGMORE STREET, W.I

## THE

# AMADEUS

# STRING QUARTET

**NORBERT BRAININ** *(Violin)*      **PETER SCHIDLOF** *(Viola)*

**SIEGMUND NISSEL** *(Violin)*      **MARTIN LOVETT** *('Cello)*

## SATURDAY AFTERNOON

## JANUARY 10th, 1948

## at 3 p.m.

TICKETS (including Tax):   Reserved 9/- and 6/- ;   Unreserved 3/-
(All bookable in advance)

May be obtained from BOX OFFICE, WIGMORE HALL (WEL. 2141), usual Ticket Offices and

**IBBS & TILLETT LTD.**, 124, Wigmore Street, W.I

Telephone: Welbeck 2325 (3 lines)                    Hours: 10—5. Saturdays, 10—12
Telegrams: "Organol, Wesdo, London."                  Ticket Office: Welbeck 8418

Vail & Co., Ltd., E.C. (1947)                              For Programme P.T.O.

Programme for the Quartet's first concert, the Wigmore Hall, 10th January 1948 didn't yet exist, so to speak, and I remember wondering, "Well, I suppose there will be an audience." I couldn't leave my work in Dartington till that very morning and I got to the Wigmore Hall as soon as I could. To my astonishment there was a queue stretching down Wigmore Street and people were being turned away. I, in my greed, thinking well dammit this is my concert, I'm going to have the privilege, like the Emperor Ludwig, of sitting in that little box in the darkness over the stage all by myself – that will be lovely. All by myself, my dear: they crammed in all the real musicians who couldn't bear not to get into the auditorium – they crammed them in on top of me, so I never saw the first performance at all!' Their reputation amongst people they had played with was such that musicians were clamouring to hear them. Kenneth Essex, the viola player in the Hurwitz Quartet, managed to get into the hall and he relates how they went along to see what their 'buddies' were going to do. 'I must say it was really quite impressive. Although they had been playing together for only a comparatively short time they had achieved a very impressive homogeneous sound which of course has been one of the things you have been able to identify the Amadeus Quartet with over the years.'*

The Quartet were elated by their success and they could hardly believe the good fortune that had enabled them not only to pay the expenses Imogen had underwritten but also to pocket a small surplus. The concert marked the beginning of a remarkable career. From then on they knew that the Quartet was to be a full-time commitment.

Both Norbert and Peter could have had successful careers as soloists, but they chose differently, believing that it was in the quartet repertoire that lay the summits of musical experience. Sigi had never had the ambition to be a soloist. When he started playing quartets at the camp on the Isle of Man, he knew what he wanted. From the early days, when he played with amateurs, Martin too knew that that was the career he wished to follow.

Norbert, however, had trained as a solo violinist and when he started to play quartets he was not necessarily thinking of it as a job for life. He describes how he had played extensively and got to know a lot of quartet music. But, he said, 'I had never really worked properly at it with anybody.' When he came together with Sigi, Peter and Martin, his attitude changed. 'After a short time it blotted out everything that I had done before. It just took over – I couldn't think of anything else. At the end, when Peter died, people asked me: "What are you going to do now?" I said, "I am going to continue my solo career where I left off forty years ago – I never gave it up – it just happened."'

Although Peter's first instrument had been the violin, he had already played the viola on many occasions, such as with Max Rostal's Chamber Orchestra

---

* This description is quoted by David Wheeler in the Radio 3 interview referred to above.

in Bach's third Brandenburg Concerto. For a brief period, when they played Mozart piano quartets, Peter and Norbert changed roles with Peter playing the violin and Norbert the viola; but once they settled down to serious rehearsals as a quartet in 1947, they knew that if they were to achieve the high standards they had set themselves, this could not last. In the Amadeus Quartet, Norbert always played the first violin and Peter the viola. With his beautiful, silken carrying tone, Peter went on to become one of the great viola players of his day. Both he and Norbert were fine instrumentalists and in some magic moments they would inspire one another. The music critic and broadcaster, John Amis, once described how, when the viola had an equal part with the violin, such as in the slow movement of the Mozart C major quintet, K515, the way Peter 'would howl on the viola was just amazing and would inspire Norbert to go even further. That is what made the Quartet tick – those moments of high inspiration.' If asked about his decision to renounce a career as a soloist, Peter would say that when he realized the potential of the Quartet, the tremendous range and quality of the repertoire, and the calibre of the people with whom he was to play, he had no hesitation in wishing to devote his life to it.

Sigi, who as second fiddle played a role which people might regard as subsidiary, has explained how in a string quartet you play one quarter of the music and 'when you are actually playing it you are not aware that you are playing either the viola, cello or first or second fiddle. Each one has his role to play and each is important because he is a quarter of the whole.' Norbert, Peter and Martin similarly identified with the other players. 'When I play the viola,' Peter said, 'I don't think particularly about my part only, I think much more about the other parts. I imagine I am playing the first fiddle or the cello, and one just fills in.'

In the years after their first concert the Amadeus Quartet began performing widely in Britain and most countries in Europe, and in North America as well. Many of their tours were supported by the Arts Council and the British Council. There were regular broadcasts for the BBC and also for RIAS (Radio im Amerikanischem Sektor) in Berlin and the local German stations in Cologne, Munich and Baden-Baden. As early as 1949 they began recording for various companies. They played at summer schools and festivals too. The work poured in and they took on whatever they could. At their first concert in the Wigmore Hall in 1948, they only had a handful of works that they knew really well, and they had to rehearse phenomenally hard to get the standard repertoire under their fingers and keep up with their broadcasts and recitals. Nonetheless, however busy they may have been, the early stages of a career for a chamber-music group are always lean ones, and the Amadeus were no exception. Touring meant travelling as cheaply as possible, sharing third-rate hotel rooms, and – dare it be said about the Amadeus? – eating frugally.

At the time of their début at the Wigmore Hall, John Amis wrote a critique in *The Scotsman* both of the Amadeus concert and of one given a week earlier by the Hurwitz Quartet. He pondered on the prospects for the two quartets. Which would last the longer? A question people often ask is what factors determine whether a chamber-music group stays together. Mutual musical understanding combined with shared ability and fierce determination to make their vision a reality is of overwhelming importance. This the Amadeus certainly had.

Their exceptional though dissimilar musical gifts enabled them to blend their ideas into a whole, and the intensity of the musical experience overcame personal rivalries and differences. John Amis remembers some of their early rehearsals: 'You really thought they wouldn't last out without one of them killing the other or smashing a violin or doing something horrific.' Sigi did indeed once smash his bow when in anger he brought it down violently on a music stand. As time went by experience taught them the futility of taking it out on each other with such vehemence and, although there were plenty of arguments, their rehearsals became less stormy. They remembered with regret the occasion in 1959 when they played with the pianist Mieczyslaw Horszowski, who was by then already an old man. At the rehearsal he asked them to be nice and kind to each other. But to his dismay there were outbursts of temper, with them all going for each other angrily.

The fact remains that not only did fortune bring the four members of the Amadeus together to form a quartet but they stayed together for close on forty years. Nobody was replaced. However promising a young chamber-music group may be, many factors can blow apart fragile beginnings. Relationships with other people and the ensuing emotional tensions can be severely testing. Like other human beings, musicians develop differently. Some marry and have children and so their material needs change. The attractions, real or imaginary, of branching out into a different musical career may be overwhelming; or perhaps ill-health, physical and mental, may undermine the stamina that life within a quartet demands. My book describes some of the problems the Amadeus had to face. The chapter which follows sets the scene by giving a brief snapshot of the family background of its various members and their wives.

# CHAPTER TWO

# *Early Years*

---

In contrast to the ephemeral existence of so many quartets and so many marriages, not only did the original four members of the Amadeus Quartet themselves remained unchanged but they also stayed married to the same four wives. As people we were a cosmopolitan group and all very different. Only Martin Lovett and I were born in England, and only I myself and Margit Schidlof, who came from Stockholm, had a Christian upbringing. Siegmund Nissel, Norbert Brainin and Peter Schidlof came from Vienna; Katinka Brainin from Breslau; Susi Lovett from Budapest. Their stories poignantly illustrate the problems and agonies facing so many Jews in central Europe before the war.

Although Norbert, Sigi and Peter were all from Vienna, they had diverse backgrounds. The Brainins had had a thriving fur business in the centre of the city. The Schidlofs had been shopkeepers in a small village outside the city near the Czech border. Sigi was born in Munich where his father had been the managing director of a cutlery firm, and his mother had had a prosperous tailoring business. After his mother died from cancer when Sigi was nine, his father returned to his native Vienna. There was no strong musical tradition in any of these three families. Martin's background was different. He was born in London and his father was a musician, playing the cello professionally in an orchestra.

Norbert Brainin was born in 1923. His father died in 1930 when he was seven, and his mother in 1938 when he was fifteen, just before the Brainin family left for England. Originally his father had been a Kachelofen or tiled-stove builder in Poland, but after they moved to Vienna he and his brothers successfully built up a business as furriers. After his father's death Norbert and his younger brother and sister were brought up by his three uncles. They lived in Leopoldstadt, the Second District of Vienna. This area included the termini of all the mainline stations from Poland, Russia and Czechoslovakia and was thus the first stopping place for Jewish refugees arriving in Vienna before and during the First World War. It contained the only Jewish school in the city – and this is where Norbert went. The Brainin furrier business prospered and the family opened a branch in London in Bond

Street. This stood them in good stead after the Anschluss in March 1938 when the Nazis marched in and annexed Austria. The whole of this immense family was able to take refuge in London and settle in Hampstead Garden Suburb.

Norbert was seven when he had his first lesson on the violin. It was with cousin Max, who was at that time making a living by giving violin and maths lessons to children by day and playing in night-clubs in the evening. Max ultimately put enough money together to train as an architect/surveyor, but when Norbert had lessons with him he was very much a jack-of-all-trades. He had a great sense of humour and once described himself on the phone to a pompous cousin as a Zitzesmacher – or a person who used to make the fringes on the ends of traditional Jewish prayer-shawls. When it became clear that young 'Bertschi' had outstanding talent, his uncles sent him, at the age of ten, to Ricardo Odnoposoff. Odnoposoff was the gifted young leader of the Vienna Philharmonic Orchestra and went on to gain second prize at one of the early Queen Elizabeth violin competitions in Belgium; the first prize went to David Oistrakh. He was also a teacher at the Vienna conservatoire where Norbert learnt to play the piano (badly, he says) as well as studying harmony and counterpoint. Norbert then had lessons from a teacher whom he both adored and admired, Rosa Hochmann-Rosenfeld. She happened to come into his uncle's shop to order furs, and when she was told about Norbert she suggested he might like to come and play to her. She not only taught him the violin but introduced him to string quartets and, together with a viola and a cello, they worked their way through some of the repertoire. According to Norbert, although she was not very good technically, she conveyed to him the essence of Viennese music-making.

When Norbert came to London, an introduction from Rosa Hochmann led to his studying with Carl Flesch. He had a tremendous respect for Flesch and regarded him as something of a father figure. At that time Norbert was at a boarding-school in Leigh-on-Sea and he used to travel up to Canfield Gardens in Swiss Cottage every week for his nine o'clock lesson. He would stay for the rest of the morning listening to fellow students like Yfrah Neaman, Ida Haendel, Josef Hassid and Suzanne Rozsa. Then he would have lunch at Balsam's, a German restaurant in the Finchley Road. It was subsequently renamed the Dorice and became the 'Stammlokal' or regular meeting place of the Amadeus Quartet. Norbert's three-course meal cost one shilling and sixpence. 'I had a glass of wine with it for 3d and with a 3d tip I spent two shillings. It was my weekly treat. Then back to boarding school.'

In June 1939, Flesch left England to spend the summer at Knocke in Belgium. Before he could return war had broken out and, as already mentioned in the previous chapter, Norbert began lessons with his assistant, Max Rostal, an outstanding violinist and brilliant teacher. A year later, after his brief internment, Norbert had to do war work. He continued to play whenever he could, at musical evenings in private houses and at recitals in London and elsewhere, and he soon made his mark as a young violinist of exceptional quality. However, he found the tension between war work and playing the violin demoralizing and depressing. His job as a machine-tool fitter was making his fingers stiff, and it was not until the end of the war that he made a determined effort to get back into top form. By 1946 he was appearing all over the place, full of dynamism and vitality. Partly as homage and in gratitude to Flesch, who had died in 1944, he set himself the task of competing for the much coveted Carl Flesch Gold Medal Award at the competition established in memory of the great teacher. In 1946 he won first prize. Gradually his ambition to become a soloist was eclipsed by his love of chamber music. He started playing trios with the cellist William Pleeth and with the composer Edmund Rubbra at the piano. It was a very satisfying experience, and it seemed at one point as if his loyalty to the trio might conflict with establishing the quartet in which he was now regularly rehearsing with Sigi, Peter and Martin.

Norbert was the first to marry. When the Amadeus Quartet gave its first recital at the beginning of 1948, its members were all bachelors; but shortly afterwards Norbert married Katinka Kottow and they set up house in Edgware. Their daughter Ann was born in 1950. Katinka came from West Prussia but her family later moved to Breslau. Her father died when she was nine and her mother, who was a supervisor in a shop, was left to bring up Katinka and her older brother. In 1934 they went to Tel Aviv in what was then known as Palestine. Katinka studied dressmaking and at the end of 1938, speaking scarcely a word of English, she came to London to train at the Ryman School of Design. Her mother at first sent her money, but when war broke out this soon became impossible. Katinka, like so many others, had to live on the £1 per week given to her by the Jewish Relief Organization in Bloomsbury House. She finally got a work permit and a job soldering radio-sets. Later she became a full-time dressmaker.

Although in the early days of her marriage Katinka continued to earn money from dressmaking, in later years she came to regard it as a hobby. When asked what else she did with herself during the long weeks when the Quartet was away, she laughingly said, 'That's the question I am always asked and I hate to answer! I don't know; I must be a very disorganized person. If I had really wanted to work, I don't suppose Norbert would have minded; I am sure he would have let me, but he would not have been that keen and I just didn't have the urge.' It was her lively sense of humour and her kindly, well-balanced personality that made it possible for her to live with such a volatile character as Norbert. 'Only Katinka could have done it,' is a comment I have so often heard. She loved music but did not herself play an instrument, nor did their daughter Ann.

Peter Schidlof was also born in 1922, a few months earlier than Norbert.

Apart from their both being Jewish, their backgrounds were quite different. Peter spent his childhood in Goellersdorf, a tiny village between Vienna and the Czech border, where his parents ran their small general-purpose shop. His first lessons on the violin were given to him by the village blacksmith. He went to a Roman Catholic boarding-school to the south of Vienna. After the Anschluss in 1938, the shop was closed down and the family, being Jewish and conspicuous in such a tiny community in the country, moved to Vienna. Peter then had lessons with Pichler, the leader of the Vienna Symphony Orchestra.

It was a terrifying time for the Schidlofs and they took immediate steps to get Peter and his sister out of the country. When he was sixteen, Peter – like Sigi three months later – was sent to England on a children's transport. It was December 1938 and as it was during the school holidays, the children were temporarily housed at St Felix, a girls' boarding-school near Southwold. Peter was carrying his violin when he arrived and had the good fortune to be spotted by Stephanie Hess, the sister of one of the music staff and herself a violinist. She happened to know one of the masters at Blundell's, a boys' public school in Tiverton in Devon, and this led to Peter being given a scholar-ship to go to there. His stay was short-lived. When war broke out, Tiverton was declared a 'protected' area and as Peter was Austrian he had to leave. He came to London to live with the Hess family and tried to go to the Royal Academy of Music but he was unable to get a scholarship to make it possible. He was interned in August 1940, along with other 'friendly enemy aliens'.

The tragedy of Peter's life was that both his parents were killed by the Nazis. As soon as the war was over, Sigi found out through various inter-national organizations that they had been gassed in Belsen and he had to tell Peter that his parents were no more. 'I think, all his life, right up to the end,' Sigi said, 'he always remembered with horror what had happened, and over the years the pain of thinking about it finally led to it being suppressed so deeply that he could no longer feel what his parents were like.' Sigi went on to say that Peter remembered his parents secretly burying whatever money they had in the garden in the village where they lived, and this sense of insecurity that he experienced under the Nazis never left Peter. Where would the next penny come from? He was always a little worried about money even when the Quartet was earning extremely well and he had saved money. 'Some-times,' Sigi continued, 'he would get deeply depressed and I had to assure him that he was sitting on great assets in the form of musical instruments, particularly the world famous Strad on which he played.'

In 1952 Peter married Margit Ullgren. It had been love at first sight. When Peter and his friend, Herbert Lewin, were on holiday in Denmark in 1951, they started chatting up a group of Scandinavian girls. One of them was Margit and Peter made a date. He invited her to come to England for a visit and a year later they were married in Stockholm, where Margit had been born. She must have been very much in love because, from that first visit in the middle of the winter over Christmas and the New Year, one of her most vivid memories is how bitterly cold the house was. In those days central-heating was rare in this country. Moreover the house – in which Sigi also lived – was full of people trying to give her useful advice. During the two weeks they were together, however, she and Peter had already begun house-hunting and, in May 1952, after their wedding, they moved into their own house in Mill Hill. It was a typically suburban area on the fringe of London, without the deep woods and spacious countryside she was used to, and the people seemed suspicious and unfriendly. For her with her limited English and a husband who was often away from home, it must have been traumatic.

Margit has a ready wit and sense of humour. She had three older sisters and one younger brother and, as she once explained, 'If you grow up with three such sisters, all trying to put you down, you soon learn to sharpen your wits and stand up for yourself.' When she was about twenty she went to the Welanson Art School in Stockholm. Unfortunately her parents were soon to divorce. The children remained with their mother but she was forced to sell their house and move to a flat. Margit had to leave the art school and find a job. With determination she gradually made her way into the kind of work she wanted and finally joined a magazine where she designed materials and fashions. When she met Peter in 1951, she was a well-paid freelancer with her own flat and an independent life. Her artistic background helped her to understand Peter and his need to be alone sometimes. She did not continue to work after marrying him but instead brought all her talent and Swedish sense of style to enriching their home in Mill Hill and to bringing up their daughter, Anmarie, who was born in 1956. She did not play a musical in-strument, nor did Anmarie once she had left school.

Martin Lovett was born in 1927. He was the odd man out in the Quartet. He was five or six years younger than the others and he was the only member to have been born in England. His grandparents had left Russia in the 1890s and settled in London in Stoke Newington. Martin's father, Sam Lovett, was a professional cellist but he did not encourage his son to follow a musical career despite the fact that he had an excellent ear and clearly loved music. However, when he was eleven, Martin saw an advertisement in a paper for a cello for £5 and persuaded his father to go and see it with him. Martin offered £2.10s and settled at £3.10s. His father then gave him his early lessons. By this time the Lovetts were living in Leeds where Sam Lovett had a job in a trio playing light music in a hotel. A little while later, he moved to Man-chester to join the Hallé Orchestra whose conductor was John Barbirolli.* At the tender age of fifteen, Martin won a scholarship to the Royal College of Music where he studied with Ivor James, and lived with an aunt in London.

* Later Sir John Barbirolli.

This formal training as a musician and his profound knowledge of musical literature enabled him to bring a studied approach to his playing.

Two weeks after he started at the Royal College, the impressionable Martin met a young Hungarian called Suzanne Rozsa who was there studying the violin. 'She was strikingly attractive and my fate was sealed,' he said. 'When Susi said I was too young, I said I would wait.' He did, and in 1950 he and Susi were married. They settled in Hendon and their two children, Sonia and Peter, were born in 1951 and 1955. Unlike the other children of members of the Amadeus Quartet, Sonia was both sufficiently gifted and interested in music to study it at the University of Sussex. She has gone on to have a successful career as a 'vision mixer' and director for musical programmes on television.

Suzanne Rozsa was born in Budapest into a Jewish family who loved music. When she was six her older brother gave her a small violin and she had lessons with a local teacher. At the age of ten she won a scholarship to the State Academy of Vienna to study with Ernst Morawec and when she was fourteen she won the coveted Kreisler prize. This brought with it a solo performance at an Academy Concert. However, it was not to be. When Hitler marched into Austria in March 1938, Susi was expelled from the Academy. Her teacher, who was himself in difficulties because of his Jewish wife, strongly advised her to leave the country while it was still possible and recommended her to go to London to study with Carl Flesch. Susi's enterprising mother managed to get visas for them for three months and, in July 1938, she and her daughter arrived in England with hand-baggage and a violin. Flesch was sufficiently impressed by the young violinist to reduce his fee. Susi's mother set to work as a dressmaker to keep the two of them and, like Katinka, they were also helped by Bloomsbury House.

Susi won a scholarship to the Royal College of Music to study with Isolde Menges in 1941. She went on to pursue a very successful career both before and after her marriage to Martin. In 1965, along with the cellist Vivian Joseph and the pianist Liza Fuchsova, she formed the Dumka Trio which came to an end in 1980 when Liza Fuchsova died. As well as performing she has been much sought after as a teacher. Her experience of the profession and all that it entails helped her to sympathize with her fellow professionals and to understand what marrying Martin would involve. Susi's resourceful personality and imagination, combined with her determination and vigour, make her someone to be listened to and reckoned with. Although she can sometimes be aggressive and difficult, she is a warm-hearted person and often extremely generous, particularly to her students. The Lovetts' collection of rare instruments and other objects are largely the result of Susi's initiative. She admits that from time to time she has been 'a compulsive shopper, buyer and spender' but points out that most of the things she bought turned out to be 'good buys'. Martin often disapproved and she confesses that sometimes, when she bought things, 'if they were small enough, I would hide them for months until someone who knew about antiques came to the house and then I would produce them, hoping he would say I had bought well!'

Siegmund Nissel was born in 1922, the only child of parents who originally came from Vienna. Before the First World War they had moved to Munich when his father, who had trained as a silversmith, became managing director of a cutlery firm. His mother was a tailor and it was she who probably earned the bulk of the family income. They named their son Siegmund Walter, an indication of the wish then shared by many Jews to give their children Aryan names as a sign of assimilation. When his wife died in 1931 and his son was nine, Sigi's father returned to Vienna and settled in Hutteldorf on the outskirts of the city. He bought a couple of blocks of flats in Vienna and the income he derived from them meant that he no longer had to work but could devote his life to bringing up his son. He was musical and, when he was a young man, he used to sing occasionally as a Natursinger, or untrained singer, in the Vienna cafés and taverns.

Sigi's first violin lessons began in Munich when he was seven. He learnt with a nun who lived a few houses away and taught every kind of musical instrument, both string and wind. When his parents finally realized that their son was unusually gifted they arranged for him to have lessons with Stuhlfaut, the leader of the Bavarian State Orchestra. After the family moved to Vienna, he studied with Max Weissgaerber who had a string quartet and also played with the opera orchestra. Thus from an early age Sigi was introduced to both chamber music and opera.

On 10th November 1938, following the Kristallnacht (so called because of the widespread smashing of glass in Jewish shop windows) in Vienna, Sigi's father was removed to a Nazi concentration camp in Dachau. Sigi was away from the flat at the time, at the Jewish school which Norbert had left some months before, and was told that his father had been arrested and their flat sealed. He was taken to his father's sister who, fearful herself, found a neighbour to shelter him. Sigi's father and his four brothers had all served in the Austrian army in the First World War, so Sigi got in touch with the club of Jewish ex-service people to which his father belonged. Through a German general, they managed to get him out of Dachau on condition that he emigrated. He came home on Sigi's seventeenth birthday, 3rd January 1939, thinner and looking much older, but with his spirit unbroken and his Jewish humour bursting through. On seeing his son's distress, he explained how the Nazis were so concerned about the health of Jews, who tended to put on too much weight, that they rounded them up in this camp and forced them to diet and take exercise. 'They even guarded us with barbed-wire and dogs and machine-guns,' he said, 'and, do you know, I still managed to get in there!'

Many years later, in 1982, the Quartet gave a concert in Dachau, which is today an attractive town with a renowned school of painting. It was a traumatic occasion. Sigi remembers looking down over the town from the castle where they were playing and visualizing the horrors that had been experienced there when it housed the notorious concentration camp.

On 15th March 1939, Sigi came to England on one of the last children's transports to leave Austria. The first months were extremely difficult. He found that, through a misunderstanding, the family in Richmond who had taken him in had not really expected him to stay more than a few weeks. However, he was reluctantly allowed to remain, helping in the house along with his old school friend, Freddie Fleischer, who was living there too and who had been trying so hard to get him to England. He was also very worried about his father, who was still in Vienna. Eventually, by trudging from door to door, he managed to find someone – a Mr Farrer, an ex-mayor of Twickenham – to vouch for his father, and in August 1939, just before the outbreak of war, he too managed to escape to England. Both he and Sigi then stayed with the Farrers.

Isidor Nissel's escape was made possible, not only because of Sigi's persistence in searching for someone in England to vouch for him, but also because of his earlier initiative in persuading a rich American factory owner, Mr Palmer of Kingsport, Tennessee, to vouch for him in the United States, thus guaranteeing to the British authorities that his arrival in Britain was no more than a temporary stop on the way to another country. Whilst on holiday in Austria, Mr Palmer had befriended one of Sigi's uncles and had signed an affidavit guaranteeing his immigration to the United States. Tragically, the uncle had later committed suicide in the Nissels' flat. Sigi had then written pleading for the affidavit to be re-issued in the name of his father.

Well after the war started, two large trunks addressed to Isidor Nissel arrived at the Nine Elms goods-yard in London, having been packed by one of Sigi's uncles and sent from Austria through Germany and Holland. They were full of personal belongings wrapped in Nazi newspapers describing recent events during the war in Austria. Among the precious possessions they contained were silver candlesticks and liqueur goblets made by Sigi's father, much treasured by the present Nissel family.

Sigi was allowed to join the local Air Raid Precaution unit shortly after the outbreak of war and he began having coaching for the matriculation exam of the University of London. This he passed with flying colours in June 1940. The pass list is a poignant reminder of the numerous people like Sigi who were determined to rebuild their shattered education by studying as best they could in England: out of the 500 names it includes no less than 100 which seem to be of foreign origin. In August 1940 Sigi was interned, along with his father, first in Hampden Park near Eastbourne and then in Huyton near Liverpool. He was later transferred to the Isle of Man and it was there that his life-long friendship with Peter began.

I myself was born in London of Welsh and English stock. My father, Evan Griffiths, was a middle-grade civil servant. We lived in the country on the outskirts of London and, with the help of a scholarship I went to Queenswood, a girls' public school. Since I had no brothers or sisters, my parents hoped that as a boarder I would find the companionship I lacked at home. The music director was that great inspirer of young people, Ernest Read,* and it was there that I came to love music and to sing. There was little money to spare and my parents could not afford music lessons, and so my piano playing was largely self-taught. When I was sixteen, however, I had a year's violin teaching which was just sufficient to enable me to play in the school orchestra and, later, in one of the civil service orchestras. It also helped me to understand something of the difficulties involved in playing a stringed instrument. More than fifty years later, whilst at the Music Summer School at Dartington, I listened to a brilliant lecture on 'Jung and Music' by Molly Kemp. She had had a distinguished career as a music teacher, encouraging children and young adults with her innovative ideas. When I congratulated her on the lecture, we realized that she was the teacher, raw from the Royal Academy of Music, who had given me my never-to-be-forgotten one year's study on the violin.

When Sigi came to England in March 1939, I was still at school, not unaware of the political events in Germany but oblivious to the reality of the suffering of the Jews. Indeed, I was not very clear what a Jew was other than someone who pursued a different religion from myself as a Christian. It was not until much later during the war, when my father one day commented on the preponderance of Jews among my university friends and on his evident disquiet, that I began to reflect on what if anything made them different.

I went to St Hugh's College, Oxford, to read PPE – philosophy, politics and economics – in 1939, just after the outbreak of war. Despite the austerity of the war years, the tutorial system, under which one or two students are taught individually, was retained and I owe an everlasting debt to Professor Agnes Headlam-Morley, my 'moral tutor' and Dr Frank Burchardt who taught me economics and statistics. But Oxford was changing. Gradually teachers as well as students were being drafted into the forces or into other war work, and the university welcomed among its academic staff other 'friendly enemy aliens' who had earlier been interned in the same way as Sigi, Norbert and Peter had. Frank had fled from Germany and, like Sigi and Peter, had been interned on the Isle of Man. After my narrow upbringing, Oxford opened up a whole new world, and I leapt at the opportunity to take part in politics, music and sport and to make new friends. I was an active member of the Democratic Socialist Club, sang in the Bach Choir under Sir Thomas Armstrong and joined David Cox's madrigal group. As a diver in the uni-

* Later Sir Ernest Read.

The Amadeus Quartet

Siegmund Nissel

Peter Schidlof

Norbert Brainin

Martin Lovett

The Amadeus Quartet as young men: Norbert Brainin (*top left*), Siegmund Nissel (*top right*), Peter Schidlof (*bottom left*) and Martin Lovett (*bottom right*)

The Amadeus: at the beginning of their career, and in later life

Max Rostal

Imogen Holst

Sir William Glock

Leonard and Dorothy Elmhirst

versity swimming team, I was awarded my 'half-blue' after our match against Cambridge.

Those who went up to the women's colleges in Oxford in 1939 were the last to be allowed to complete a full three-year degree course before being drafted into war work. In 1942, I joined the Ministry of Fuel and Power as a temporary civil servant and worked initially as a statistician under the twenty-six-year old Harold Wilson. I then became a historian, writing the war history of coal and oil – a sufficiently back-room job to enable me to carry on my political activities and to stand as a Labour candidate in Soho for the local elections in Westminster in 1945. I narrowly failed to win.

My first marriage, to a South African engineer who had been living a semi-bohemian existence in Chelsea, was a break with my parents and my middle-class background. The ensuing tensions led to our separating and eventually divorcing. Divorce laws at that time were much stricter, and it was not until 1953 that the 'decree nisi' was granted. Social attitudes towards marriage were very different from what they are today: there was still something faintly shocking about divorce. I can still sense the cloud that hung over me during those years when I woke each morning to remember that I was separated from my husband, and that I was hoping for a divorce, but was unable to do anything about it unless he took action.

At the end of the war I would have liked a career in the civil service, but I was ineligible. Married women were not entitled to join the permanent staff. It was not until the 'marriage bar' was removed in October 1946 that I was able to take the examination that enabled me to do this. I became a statistician, first in the Ministry of Fuel and Power and later in the Central Statistical Office, and then at the Treasury. As a permanent civil servant, political activities were closed to me but I continued to enjoy music and sport. I played squash for the Civil Service and sang with the Treasury Singers. Robert Armstrong's* madrigal group introduced me to those inimitable Byrd four- and five-part masses.

Sigi and I were married in 1957 and our two children, Claire and Daniel, were born in 1958 and 1962. They are both musical and played the piano when they were young. But their gifts were not substantial enough to dispel the ever-present shadow of their father. I too was intimidated and, apart from nursery rhymes and Christmas carols, stopped playing the piano. I became an expert listener, or 'armchair musician'. My main musical entertainments had been opera and symphony concerts and only gradually had they given way to chamber music. I was not at the first Amadeus concert in the Wigmore Hall, but a diary entry shows that I did go shortly afterwards to the complete Beethoven series given by the Busch Quartet at Chelsea Town Hall.

---

* Later Lord Armstrong.

CHAPTER THREE

# Marrying
# the Quartet

_____

Although I had not been at the first Amadeus concert, I subsequently went
to many of their performances, and I often met them backstage in the Green
Room. It was not until the summer of 1953, nearly four years before I married
Sigi, that I attended the Music Summer School at Dartington where they were
performing and came to know them more as individuals and appreciate their
sense of fun. Later that year, in December 1953, I joined them for a meal in
London in the Dorice restaurant in Swiss Cottage. They had played a concert
in the Royal Festival Hall and afterwards they foregathered in their usual
haunt, their Stammlokal. They were all living in north London and it was
a convenient and friendly place to unwind.

I sat next to Norbert. 'Have you heard the story of the two prostitutes chatting about business in the early hours of the morning? One said to the other,
"I've been up them stairs twenty-five times already." "Oh, your poor feet." '

Did I or did I not hear correctly?

As this was the first time I had sat down with them socially, I was a little
nervous and anxious to impress, excited to be sitting next to such a distinguished violinist. His joke caught me wrong-footed. What took me aback
was not the story itself but the fact that, in the still rather prim atmosphere
of the 1950s, he told it to me at all, since I was a comparative stranger. My
very English background told me that, mild though it was, this was not the
kind of story you shared with a 'lady' you scarcely knew.

I was quick to learn that jokes were part of the Quartet's culture and they all
had this gift of story-telling. Each had a proprietary interest in his own particular stories and Sigi later told me that the joke about the prostitutes was
part of his repertory and that Norbert had no business to poach it from him.

As I sat at the table, I tried to piece together who everybody was. It was
not until the end of the meal, when it was time to settle the bill, that I realized
that Norbert's wife was the good-looking dark-haired woman at the far end.
At a sign from Norbert she opened her handbag and produced some money.
The gesture summed up their relationship: without her support and help with
the chores of everyday life, he would be lost.

At my end of the table were Sigi, Kristin Berge and my friend Herbert Lewin, whom I had originally met many years before at Oxford. It was Kristin, a striking woman with blonde hair, and her husband Hans (more familiarly known as Dickie) who had invited Peter and Sigi to share their flat when they came out of internment. Subsequently they had all bought a house together in Mill Hill. Peter had moved out when he married. Herbert Lewin, with his receding chin and friendly, smiling eyes, was an admirer of the Quartet. Although he did not play or sing himself, he had a profound musical understanding and, when he presumed to criticize, he was someone to whom the Quartet would listen. He had met them at the Music Summer School started by William Glock in Bryanston in 1948, and Sigi soon became a special friend. It was at Herbert's suggestion that, earlier in the year, I had been to the summer school – which was to move from Bryanston to Dartington in 1953.

Sigi had driven Kristin, Herbert and me to the restaurant, and shortly afterwards the Schidlofs arrived. Peter Schidlof, tall and aristocratic-looking, sat down opposite us with his wife, Margit. She was small and dainty and, as I already knew she was Swedish, it was not difficult to pick her out with her blonde colouring and snub nose, quiet and smiling. No sooner had Peter sat down than he got up again quickly and, looking worried, asked if anyone had picked up his music from the platform. In the hubbub that followed the other players assured him that he had taken it himself and that it was probably in his satchel. Then they saw the twinkle in his eyes and burst out laughing. Once again Peter was pulling their leg for he knew very well that it was not lost. At Dartington that summer I had already seen enough of the Quartet, or the 'Wolf Gang' as they were aptly named, to know that it was Peter who was the practical joker among them; so much so that you often did not know whether or not to take him seriously.

The Lovetts were the last to arrive. In 1953 both the Brainins and the Lovetts had young daughters, and Martin had stopped to phone home to make sure Sonia, aged two, was all right. With him was his violinist wife, Susi, small, dark and vivacious, and also her mother, looking not unlike a leaner version of Golda Meir.

Ordering the meal was an important matter. If an army marches on its stomach, the Quartet certainly played on its stomach. The Lovetts argued over the menu. Susi's mother had decided views about what she wanted and she was not going to be told what to eat by her daughter and son-in-law. Martin, detecting my amusement at this earnest dispute over the merits of the various dishes, raised his dark, curly head from scrutinizing the menu and peered at me through his thick-rimmed glasses. 'Do you know what is wrong with eating?' he asked: 'it spoils your appetite!'

The Dorice specialized in the central European food most of them had been brought up on, and after concerts they were hungry and thirsty. The Lovetts finally decided on chopped liver followed by Kalbsgulyas mit Nockerl. We all agreed on the chopped liver and I turned to Norbert for expert advice on the main dish. He took the menu with his strong stubby fingers, nails gnawed at the tips, and pointed to Zwiebelrostbraten. 'What about it? It is onions quickly fried with thin b-b-b-bits of steak,' he stuttered. It sounded good and I said yes. Sigi was the last to make up his mind; but the others all knew that after tooth-combing the menu he was sure to order something with chicken in it, for his nickname was 'Chicken Charlie'. In due course he decided on paprika chicken. We finished the meal with Apfelstrudel. When it came to paying, Sigi, the accountant in the Quartet, did some rapid back of envelope calculations and the bill was shared out.

What did we talk about, apart from telling jokes? Not the concert: the post-mortem would come later in rehearsals. Much of the conversation was about old friends who had come to the Green Room and the latest news or gossip. Our chat was interspersed with comments in German, of which I understood hardly a word, although I was at that time going to evening classes at Morley College and studying from a book entitled *Heute Abend*, which, off-puttingly, had been printed in the old German script. Martin Lovett, had learnt German in self-defence and was by this time speaking it fluently, even if with a Cockney accent.

My conversation with Norbert that evening probably ranged over a wide selection of topics – food, literature, philosophy, religion. What he had to say was full of surprises, imaginative and intuitive rather than closely reasoned, triggering off new lines of thought. He was both stimulating and irritating in that he had a good mind that had never been disciplined by the need to be rational; and he would often escape into a fantasy world from which it was impossible to pull him back to earth. But he never talked down to you. Behind that slightly forbidding thick-set exterior with his mop of hair and heavy glasses, there was a humility that is the hallmark of greatness. He was at the same time very full of himself and of his own ideas, and bombastic, already resembling and often behaving outrageously like Mr Toad.* Although he was short and stout and hardly good-looking, women were nonetheless attracted to him. He was admired and respected, and somehow needed the support this adulation gave him.

Though less intellectual than his colleagues, Peter Schidlof was also a good conversationalist, particularly when talking about music and musicians. To sit near him at a meal, as I did on that occasion, was a pleasure because his natural sensitivity and good humour immediately put you at ease. He was

---

* Mr Toad is a character in *The Wind in the Willows*, a children's book by Kenneth Grahame. He is portrayed as being very full of himself, but he was befriended and well liked by the other animal characters in the book.

interested in you, in what you were wearing and what you had to say, and he too was always popular with women. Later, when I came to know him better, I found out what a delight it was to be with him in a foreign city. He could swiftly and instinctively nose out the best restaurants and shops. He loved window-shopping and, always well dressed himself, was an expert guide to fashion for both men and women. Going to a concert or an opera with him was less of a pleasure because his high standards meant that you had to suffer a running commentary on the shortcomings of the performance. Everyone had a soft spot for Peter and the word most commonly used to describe him was 'lovable'.

Martin has sometimes been described as the philosopher of the Quartet and his inquiring mind and wide intellectual grasp made him a person well worth talking to. He was tall and good-looking and just as attractive to women. 'When on tour, I go to the pictures and read a lot,' he said, and Sigi told me that they would often while away the hours together playing chess, occasionally being joined by Norbert who was also a good player. If you wanted to know what films or plays to see, or what books to read, Martin was the person to ask. Both I and the Lovetts had recently been to see Laurence Olivier and Vivien Leigh in *Antony and Cleopatra*. I had been strangely unmoved by the performance and over our meal we tried to discover why.

Anyone meeting Martin for the first time in his later years might be forgiven for not immediately recognizing him as a musician. As his hair whitened and he lost his youthful figure, he came to have a more authoritative presence. This, combined with his direct approach, might suggest he is a successful businessman rather than someone with the fantasy and imagination to be a cellist in a quartet. But the appearance belies the man.

I knew from my brief encounter with Sigi at the summer school and the many stories Herbert told me about him that he had a lively wit and sense of humour. Short and already showing signs that in later years he might become well rounded, he had an appealing square face and kindly eyes. Earlier in the year I had spent a month as an *au pair* with a family of four children at Hallein near Salzburg. They were ardent music-lovers and managed to get me some festival tickets. I went to *Jedermann* and heard Lisa della Casa as Octavian in *Der Rosenkavalier* and Elisabeth Schwarzkopf as Donna Elvira in *Don Giovanni*. When I proudly told Sigi that I had been to Salzburg and that I had visited Mozart's house, he replied, 'Oh yes, but did you visit the delicatessen opposite?' Many years later we were to do just that.

Had Sigi been able to pursue his education without interruption in Austria he might have followed a profession other than that of a musician. He has an excellent mind and says he would like to have been a scientist; but he is also a gifted linguist and competent in many other fields. He once called himself a frustrated footballer. The cellist William Pleeth, with whom the

Amadeus Quartet frequently played, summed up his relationship with Sigi in these words: 'I feel I can talk to Sigi all day and all night. When you have an affection for someone, then you are contentedly alive with that person, there are no reservations spiritually, humanity-wise and intellectually, and you play ping-pong non-stop.' These were true words which I have come to understand during the years of our marriage.

The meal at the Dorice was the first of many. From then onwards, Sigi was a frequent visitor to my flat and he often talks about the time when I cooked him pancakes for tea, a forbidden treat later on when his already chubby figure began to grow chubbier. Norbert too came from time to time and I soon discovered his voracious appetite. One evening, after we had devoured a whole chicken, he asked me if there were still any bits left on the carcase in the kitchen!

However, it was not until the summer of 1956, after we had had several holidays together, along with our mutual friend Herbert, that Sigi and I decided to get married. In those intervening years I had had plenty of time to ponder what family life with a quartet might be like, and how my own life would be changed if I married into one. I joined Sigi briefly for the Edinburgh Festival in the autumn of 1956 and gossips in the music profession began asking, 'Who is Sigi's blonde?' He was the last of the Quartet to take the plunge. Norbert had married in 1948, Martin in 1950 and Peter in 1952. We were married on 5th April 1957, when Sigi was thirty-five. I was almost a year older.

Our 'honeymoon' was really in March 1957 when we spent a week together in Zermatt. I had hoped that Sigi might ski with me but, although he had often done it as a child, a few hours on skis told us that it was a pleasure we would have to forego. For a violinist it was too dangerous: damaging an arm or a finger, or indeed any limb, could seriously interfere with quartet life. Peter often went cross-country or *langlauf* skiing, which is safer, but Sigi found it a strain on his arms and hands. To me it seemed just hard work and not nearly as much fun as downhill skiing. Even tennis was unwise because of the unaccustomed use of the hand muscles. Some well-known artists were exceptions: the violinist Jascha Heifitz and the Guarneri Quartet were all keen tennis players. Table tennis, at which Sigi excelled, was permissible and so of course was swimming.

We were married at the registry office in Burnt Oak. Thirty-five years later our son Daniel was to be married in the selfsame office. It was a brilliantly sunny day and the reception in Sigi's and Kristin's house in Mill Hill spilt over into the garden. It began at three o'clock in the afternoon, mainly with musicians, many of whom had concerts later in the day, and carried on into the evening when our office-worker friends were able to join us. We finally left for a brief few days in the Chilterns at the Rose and Crown on Bledlow Ridge.

At the time of our marriage the Amadeus had been together for nearly ten years. Each of the four players knew that his life was dedicated to the Quartet. The early years are a testing time for a quartet and many may find that as people they do not like each other very much or that musically they are not on quite the same wavelength. One member may discover that he or she is not as committed as earlier on and the ensemble may then collapse. Other careers may beckon – as soloists or composers, or in different ensembles. The early years are lean ones taken up with rehearsing, learning new works and hoping something will happen. Family life, if it is possible to embark on it at all, is continually disrupted by constant travelling.

A long-established quartet with reasonable financial success may find that the pull of material gain keeps them together. In 1957 the Amadeus were earning well enough but their income was not princely and had one of them wanted to break away, other equally well-paid careers would have been possible. But there was no question that the Amadeus Quartet was the only way of life for each of them. I understood what that was going to mean for me. I was earning as much as Sigi and, as we wished to have children and I wanted to give up paid work to look after them myself, at least in their early years, it would involve a cut in our standard of living.

I had been living in Regent's Park Road in a house overlooking Primrose Hill near the Zoo, where I could hear the lions roar at night. It was a lovely flat and I left it reluctantly for life in suburbia. When I moved to Mill Hill, Kristin's husband had recently died but she remained in the house with her eleven-year-old daughter, Belinda. We also had with us a German housekeeper, Christl, so that I was able to continue working without having to spend time on household chores. It was the very house that Margit had found so uninviting when she visited Peter during the Christmas before she married him. In 1957–8, the first winter of our marriage, there was heavy snow and the roof leaked. In the kitchen there was an antiquated Ideal coal-fired boiler similar to the one my parents had had in my childhood. In one of my letters to Sigi in February when he was in the USA, I bluntly wrote saying that I detested the thing: 'It is a monster and either eats fuel ad nauseam or refuses to burn at all and eats the gas poker instead!' Although we finally decided on a more efficient coal-fired boiler, we installed only partial central-heating, for money was short and we had to decide our priorities. A few years earlier the Berges had sold the grand piano in the sitting room to pay for a new carpet. Since Sigi had spurned the old piano I had in my flat, we were without one. We had considered borrowing or renting one, but, when writing to him in the USA, I even went so far as to suggest that perhaps we might buy a piano, even if it meant delaying the heating installation. Such were our priorities.

When I married, I resigned my permanent post in the civil service and was taken back in a temporary capacity. In those days anyone leaving the service before retirement age lost all their pension rights unless there were exceptional circumstances. However, by retiring on marriage I became entitled to a marriage gratuity. It was nothing substantial, but it was a small compensation.

At that time I was working in the Overseas Finance Division of the Treasury and as soon as I arrived in my office each day it was my responsibility to phone the Bank of England to find out the state of the gold and dollar reserves and prepare a note for the Chancellor. There were continual problems with the balance of payments during these years and, as Sigi put it so nicely, it was not until I left the Treasury that the gold reserves began to pick up. He was keenly interested in economics and even read J. R. Hicks's admirable little book on the national income.*

In the summer of 1957, I joined the Quartet at the Aldeburgh Festival and soon afterwards Sigi and I went on holiday to Italy. We had arranged with Kristin Berge that we would bring Belinda with us – she was then a boarder at the Arts Educational School in Tring – so that she could join her mother who was on holiday in Marina Marittima on the Adriatic. When we were on the car-ferry Belinda said quietly, 'Auntie Muriel, I have spots.' By the time we reached Switzerland, she definitely had a fine array of spots. We took her to a doctor who diagnosed chicken-pox, and so we bundled her back into the car and delivered her as fast as we could to her mother. Sigi and I went on to Pisa and thence to what was at that time the unspoilt island of Elba. I too began to develop spots and as I hadn't had chicken-pox we suspected this might be the explanation. We spoke little or no Italian and our efforts to explain the situation to the doctor led him to think in horror that we were saying Belinda had developed small-pox. But he assured us that there was nothing seriously wrong with me and suggested it might be something to do with too much sun.

It was during this holiday that I became pregnant and the news was soon confirmed by my doctor when I returned to England. Shortly afterwards, when I was three months into the pregnancy, I went to the Middlesex Hospital for a check-up. There was a shadow on my chest X-ray. Cancer? Tuberculosis? Much suspense waiting to find out. Further tests established that it was TB and this was the explanation for my spots a month or so earlier. Fortunately the illness was not far enough advanced for me to be infectious. In 1957, however, it was still a killer disease in Britain although it was beginning to be conquered with the new sulphonamide drugs. I was told to stop working immediately, go home and stay in bed indefinitely. Treatment – a daily injection by the local butcher of a district nurse.

* J. R. Hicks, *The Social Framework*, Oxford University Press, London, 1942.

I went back to my office, cancelled my visit to the OECD in Paris where I was due in a day or so, and began to pack up and make essential arrangements for someone else to take over my work. I rang Sigi and asked him to come and fetch me. 'But I and the others in the Quartet are meeting someone from Deutsche Grammophon to discuss a recording contract.' A chill ran down my spine. I could of course take a taxi but at this crisis in my life I needed him. Perhaps his reaction was no different from that of any other professionally involved husband, but it emphasized the fact that I and the child I was carrying were competing with the Quartet. Of course he changed his mind, and within the hour he was at my office in Whitehall to take me home.

# CHAPTER FOUR

# Touring
# the World

After I heard that I had tuberculosis, I spent the next two months in bed, but I was well on the way to recovery before the Quartet left for a world tour lasting seven months. From the middle of January up to the end of August 1958 the Quartet visited eight different countries and played well over a hundred concerts. For the Quartet itself the tour was a test of stamina and endurance as well as musicianship. For me it was my first experience of what it really meant to be a quartet wife. This present chapter and the one that follows are based largely on correspondence between Sigi and me. He is a wonderfully descriptive writer and the many quotations give a feel not only for the excitement and satisfaction of quartet life but also for the hardships which had to be endured both by the Quartet themselves and by their families at home in London.

The tour had originally been planned to start in North America, to continue in Japan, Australia and New Zealand and to finish in Indonesia. In the meantime revolution in Indonesia, in what was formerly known as the Netherlands East Indies, forced a change of course. It was intended that the high cost of the fares for the Quartet would be shared by the various concert promoters, and when the tour of Indonesia, which was being promoted by the Dutch Arts Circle, dropped out, the whole tour was no longer viable. There was a possibility of arranging concerts in Bombay and Calcutta, but something had to be done quickly and pressure was put on the Quartet to replace Indonesia with a visit to South Africa. Reluctantly they agreed. In his inimitable way, the pianist Denis Matthews, who was renowned for his phenomenal knowledge of music and his sharp-witted punning, quipped, 'Your touring will be "done easier".'

The Quartet were due to leave for New York on 15th January. We tearfully said goodbye, only to find that we had to do it all over again twelve hours later because fog prevented them from going that night. The delay meant that there was little opportunity to adjust to the five hours' time difference between London and New York. The concerts immediately crowded in on them one after the other. They arrived at midnight on the 16th and played their first concert on the 17th in the Metropolitan Museum of Art. The same programme – Mozart K387, Schubert Opus 29 and Beethoven Opus 18, no.1 – was repeated the next evening in one of the People's Symphony Concerts in downtown New York. On the 19th they played in the Frick Museum. On the 20th they travelled to Baltimore, and on the 21st to Cincinnati. The 23rd found them almost a thousand miles away in Canada in Montreal and on 26th January they were back in the USA in Boston.

Sigi wrote to me from his hotel in Boston where, to save money, he was sharing a room with Norbert. 'I did my laundry. It was a sight to delight our four eyes. Pants, socks, shirts, ties, dripping all over the place whilst Norbert snored. Darling, I do so feel for you, although Norbert says he never snores [this was a reference to the difficulty I was having with Sigi's snoring] ... We are having fun with a portable sewing-machine Martin bought this afternoon. Actually my new pyjamas tore from top to bottom the first time I wore them and Peter and Martin are having a lovely time trying to repair them. Have just been called to see the first result: it looks like this: ^~^~~^~~. We all roared with laughter. Martin is lying under the bed, helpless ...'

At the end of the month Sigi and Martin briefly escaped from hotel life to stay with the local organizer in Durham in North Carolina. He was a widowed professor at the university and a good friend from previous visits. For them it was a splendid change to be able to cook their own breakfasts and be thoroughly domestic. 'Standing in the kitchen and making breakfast is so like home. I am enjoying it.'

One of the difficulties artists face is the timing of meals. Musicians cannot perform satisfactorily after a large meal and, as most concerts take place in the evenings, this poses problems. Lunch becomes particularly important but it is often interfered with by travelling. What is needed is some kind of nourishing but not too heavy food after a concert. Many small towns are more dead than alive at 10.30 at night so that the Quartet had to rely on arrangements made by the concert organizers. Most of them have the understanding and foresight to lay on a meal, but there is always an occasion when this does not happen. For example, a few days after the Durham concert when they were at Winter Park in Florida, Sigi wrote: 'There was a reception after the concert by the committee, punch and cookies! I was starving, so I asked whether we could have a sandwich. This was not possible but my question was overheard by a girl in the local symphony orchestra, so we were invited to her place to be fed on bacon and eggs, and a very nice party was the result. It was so nice because it was unplanned.' He goes on to describe how they were driven there in her car, and how when they reached the garage she pressed a button and the door swung open. At the time this kind of gadget was almost unheard of in Britain and he comments about 'the things a member of a very unimportant orchestra can have,' making 'the honourable second violin of a not unknown quartet touring the globe look very provincial indeed.'

After their performance in Montreal on 23rd January, they flew up from Florida to be there again on 6th February. The next few days are described by Sigi: 'Since arriving in Montreal on the 5th we have had one mad rush. We left at 10 p.m. after the concert on the 6th and arrived in Hamilton, Ontario, at 2 a.m. We had a concert that same evening on the 7th. On the 8th we travelled from 10 in the morning until 10 at night. On top of it I caught a very bad cold, so stayed in bed the next day until the concert on the 9th in Athens (Ohio). Then yesterday (the 10th) we travelled fourteen and a half hours and arrived here in Galesburg at 2 in the morning. We have a concert tonight. So it was wonderful to get your letters nos. 4 and 5. At the same time I had heaps of business letters as well, so I will be busy until the concert to-night in Knox College (Illinois).'

In the same letter he then went on to discuss business matters. In London I had taken charge of the Nissels' private affairs and the settling of Quartet bills as well as the paying out of money to the other Quartet wives. Our letters thus often included detailed information about our finances, and on this occasion he wrote to me: 'Yes, please settle Martin's cello debt with his part of the £600 when it comes in. Peter tells me that you have suggested to Margit to bank the £150 in our deposit account and pay him the interest. We have talked it over; please pay Margit the £150 and tell her that Peter wants her to buy with it Savings Certificates (I believe the 10th Issue), the same as we have got. She should buy it in her own name.'

At that point the Quartet's secretary, Mrs Wendy Harthan, looked after the general correspondence; but Sigi himself dealt with the accounts and, in consultation with the other members of the Quartet, the planning of concert engagements and recording schedules. Ibbs and Tillett represented the Quartet in Great Britain and the rest of Europe; but elsewhere Sigi himself negotiated directly with individual agents in each country where they played. These plans involved detailed hotel and travel arrangements and contacts with the various concert organizers. In London much of it could have been done over the phone with Wendy Harthan but on tour, before the days of the fax, E-mail and cheap international telephone calls, this meant an enormous volume of correspondence and an endless flow of letters between him and Wendy as well as with other business contacts. By June 1958 she commented that he had written almost a book to her. Detailed planning of 1959 was well under way when they left for North America in January 1958; and in one of my letters at the beginning of March I told Sigi that Katinka was already muttering 'that it didn't seem necessary to go round the world to be away from home all the time if 1959 was going to be any guide, at the present rate of making engagements!'

After concerts in Cleveland (Ohio) and snowbound Philadelphia – 'I have never seen anything like it – cars completely buried in snow, but all the same I enjoyed it' – the Quartet had a few days to spare in the middle of February before going back to Canada and then over to the West Coast. They used them to go to New York and discuss future plans with their agents, Colbert la Berge Concert Management. The outcome was not satisfactory.

When the Quartet first came to North America in 1953 they had had indifferent reviews after their first concert in New York because of an unfortunate series of mishaps. Their début was to have been at the City Hall, traditional haunt of those vampires, the critics. Critics in the United States, where there is no nationwide broadcasting system or other means of publicizing the arts, are in an unusually powerful position and can make or mar an artist's career throughout that vast country. Many a performer has gone to the celebration party after a first concert and awaited with trepidation the arrival of the morning newspapers that may settle their fate for years to come. Through no fault of the Quartet's their concert at the City Hall was cancelled and their début in the city was an all-Mozart programme way up-town at Columbia University. Some critics are not too keen on Mozart programmes and even less keen on traipsing up to Columbia. The Quartet had to travel overnight by train from Cincinnati and, while hunting for something in his suitcase, Norbert cut his finger. A doctor put plastic skin over the cut, but shortly before the concert, Norbert tore it off because he had no sensitivity in his finger. In the panic of leaving for the concert, the music was left in a taxi. A cousin of Peter's managed to produce a set of parts, heavily scribbled over on an out-of-date edition. Inevitably this handicapped their playing. The critics were not damning but they were unenthusiastic, saying that the Amadeus recordings had led them to expect more.

The lukewarm reception put them into the second rank of string quartets on offer and blighted their immediate prospects with music clubs throughout the States. They were used by their agent as the 'cheap' quartet in package deals (or 'cabbage' deals as Sigi preferred to call them) with music societies. At that time Colbert la Berge had a virtual monopoly of all the world's leading string quartets so that they could offer their artists to music societies for a whole season's series for a fixed sum which was then apportioned between their various artists. The Quartetto Italiano was their number one quartet and the Amadeus were very much amongst the 'also rans'.

The Quartet had to wait for their next tour of America before they got the rave reviews from the New York critics they could have had on their first visit. This second American tour in 1954 was a resounding success. Virgil Thomson, the composer and leading music critic in the USA, wrote in the *New York Herald Tribune*: 'The Amadeus Quartet, playing yesterday in Town Hall, made some of the loveliest string music that this devotee has ever heard ... The delight they offered was not merely that of utterly convincing tempos and of that subtle lilt of rhythm that are the mark of those who under-stand and love Vienna. There were also the beauty of sound and the clean execution, the true pitches and ever just balances of those who love playing string quartets and have skill to do it right. Their tone was mat, and the four instruments were ever matched for color of sound and for size of the sound ...' The tour was sold out and many people began to ask why they came to the USA for such ridiculously low sums.

The stranglehold on chamber music by the Colbert la Berge Concert Management was only part of the problem. The lack of records from the Quartet had also been a handicap in America. In the early years, in 1951, they had made a number of 'title' contracts for both Decca and His Master's Voice (HMV), and they had started a series of recordings for an American company, Westminster, which was at that time run by an Englishman, Jimmy Grayson. The recordings were very successful, and it was because of them that the Amadeus was first invited to come to the USA. However, in sub-sequent years they ran into problems, particularly over the distribution of records (which is described in detail in chapter 9). In 1958, during the Quartet's world tour, Sigi wrote: 'Basically it's the lack of gramophone records which is holding us back and our so-called new company, Angel, has been swallowed up by Capitol and they are operating from Los Angeles. A most unsatisfactory state of affairs. I will continue the fight in Los Angeles.' By the time Sigi again reached Los Angeles later in the year he was more hopeful. He had had further talks with Angel and reported that the company had promised about seven long-playing records a year for the next three years and that 'this would help a lot in the future.'

Meanwhile the Quartet's tour had been going extremely well on the West Coast. They had 'absolutely wonderful press notices in all four major papers' after their San Francisco concerts and they 'hit another patch of top form' in Pasadena and Los Angeles. Before leaving the United States at the end of March, Sigi wrote: 'It is a funny country here, one must fight in every town, and then one day one finds oneself being "the hit".' They made about £1,000 each during this part of the tour which he thought 'not too bad but should have been much more.' It was only feasible because of the round trip which had saved so substantially on fares. Nonetheless, he hints that, with their growing families and the need to make enough money to live comfortably, they might soon have to consider settling down to an appointment in a country outside Britain such as Switzerland, or even the USA or Canada: 'We are keeping our eyes and ears open.'

After North America, there followed a few days' well-earned holiday in Honolulu with only one concert. They were able to use a private beach at the famous Waikiki resort with 'perfect sand, surf-bathing and all luxury laid on – fresh pineapple by the pound, ice-cooled pineapple juice, papaya fruit and bananas, the like of which I have never tasted. And the fish; we had a Hawaiian speciality called Mahimaki, grilled with lemon butter and salad. Life is nearly perfect.' Their hostess, Mrs Florence McIntyre, or 'Auntie Flauncy' as they endearingly called her, was a seventy-five-year old lady who hardly stopped talking. She made them comfortable in her house and they became such friends that she wrote to all the wives saying how much she had enjoyed meeting them. She later even sent a present for our baby.

At the beginning of April they arrived in Japan. Here, where the Deutsche Grammophon Company (DGG) represented them and had successfully marketed their records, their reception was rapturous. 'For the first time in our lives we felt like filmstars. Press photographers were round us before we had left the plane properly and we did not believe our eyes; the gramophone companies selling our records in Japan had put up big posters with a welcome to us, little girls handed us armloads of flowers, and then a press conference. Really it was wonderful and we were very tickled.' A few days later there was a press conference at the Imperial Hotel where they were staying: 'I have never seen anything like it, about fifty photographers and reporters and they all fired most intelligent questions at us; we are really getting quite ex-perienced old hands at that sort of thing.'

They had lunch with Dr L. R. Phillips, the British Council representative. 'It turned out to be a jolly good and lively party: what a breath of fresh air to be with cultured English people. It's incredible how natural they are and they have a sense of humour. So we much enjoyed ourselves.' Next day they went sightseeing with 'a very Scottish official' of the British Council called Bill McAlpine. He first took them to a beer hall for a 'good booze, a place that only Japanese frequent, so it had wonderful atmosphere. You see the Japanese are brought up never to show feeling or emotion but when they drink they are off very quickly and drop all their reserve and outer mask and become very jolly and human and full of fun.' Bill then took them to his Japanese house and finally they finished with a 'ravishing meal – your hubby, being "Chicken Charlie", had boiled chicken …' They also visited the Kabuki theatre, and Sigi describes in some detail a play about a girl who had fallen in love with a divinity student who tries to escape from her by taking refuge in a monastery and hiding in a bell. The play lasted about one-and-a-half hours and portrayed only the approach of the girl (played by a man) across the whole of the stage towards the bell. A second play, lasting about two hours, had a lot of dialogue, so they left and had a meal in a Japanese restaurant with a Japanese lady from the concert society. 'We had *sukiyaki*, a kind of boiled beef dish with lots of vegetables, all cooked in front of one. I had quite some difficulty sitting on the floor cross-legged before a very low table.'

They arrived in Tokyo on a Friday and their first concert was the following Monday. 'We had to be in the hall by 5.30 for the press. To cut a long story short the audience numbered 2,600 people and we are repeating this concert four times and all concerts are sold out. Just apply it for a moment to a sold out Festival Hall in London with the same programme. And what an audience. Of course I don't know at what level they listen and indeed whether they get any more out of it than we do by seeing and hearing Kabuki. But I have ... never heard such a silence and such concentration. And the same again in tonight's concert. The enthusiasm is tremendous and yet at the end of the concert, after our encore, another two rounds of applause and they leave you alone and are satisfied. Well, the atmosphere of an occasion begins right in the artists' room. Big and lofty and comfortable, attendants there to hang up your coats, hot towels for refreshment as you come in and between each quartet, and tea always handy.'

Sigi was impressed by the widespread interest in classical music. Even little coffee shops advertised classical music: 'All day long they play good records and you go in and drink coffee to a Mozart symphony and they are always full with a lot of young people who listen intently.'

After Tokyo, the Quartet went to Osaka where they were again tremendously successful. The Leningrad Symphony Orchestra and the renowned cellist Mstislav Rostropovich were there at the same time and they went to each other's concerts. Sigi was thrilled with the orchestra and thought them very good and thorough. He was also impressed by the way the tour was organized. It was done in style, the orchestra being flown into Tokyo in the latest jet planes, thus stealing the headlines for a couple of days.

When he returned to his hotel after dining out, Sigi describes how he had a long chat with Rostropovich and someone from the USSR Ministry of Culture. This marvellous instrumentalist was in the forefront of music life in Russia but he was also a big star and money-earner in the West. He was a regular visitor to the Aldeburgh Festival and Benjamin Britten wrote a cello sonata for him. He greeted you with the bear hug, a testimony to some kind of warm relationship which Russians display to other people. There is a story about him on his birthday when he was staying in a hotel in Rome. The manager said that when Rostropovich rang the bell for his breakfast, he wanted to take it in himself. He had prepared a birthday cake which he wanted to bring into the dark room with the candles burning. When the bell rang, the manager walked in with this big cake, with its candles lit. Rostropovich, realizing what it was all about, jumped out of bed and gave the manager a big bear hug crushing the cake with the cream between the two of them! Apocryphal though the story may be, it is typical of the kind of enthusiasm the man has.

When Sigi got back to his room in the early hours of the morning and started packing, he heard a beautiful sound from an oboe-like instrument being played by a man who was pushing a little movable eating-stall on the bridge over the river: it was the traditional call for announcing his presence, rather like the chimes from an ice-cream man.

On 16th April the Quartet arrived in Hong Kong. The house where they stayed was palatial and comfortable. But Sigi found he could not quite enjoy it: 'I can't really swallow the feudal system with the servants being ordered around in a tone which I would not use for a dog. And it's quite accepted here. I saw the same thing at the house of some very rich English people where we gave a private concert for thirty people last night. What a world of difference from the "Old Boy" by which we were addressed as equals and the No.1, No.2, No.3 boy bringing in refreshments.'

In between their two Hong Kong concerts they played in Macao which was 'very strenuous because it was frightfully hot and humid there. During our stay in Hong Kong we didn't seem to get more than four or five hours sleep per night, if that. So we are a bit worn out now, and I will try to sleep as much as I can on the long plane journeys.' Back in Hong Kong, Sigi went shopping and sent brocades and silks to me and my mother.

But the main thought preying on his mind was the expected arrival of our first child, who was due in the middle of April. Waiting for news was intolerable. He was afraid that the great event might take place while he was in mid-Pacific on the way to New Zealand, and in London we asked Wendy Harthan to arrange for British Airways to transmit messages. 'I am so pleased that BOAC are obliging by passing on the news when I am in transit from Hong Kong to Auckland, a great relief to know that.' Their last concert in Hong Kong was on 19th April and they had already been some days in New Zealand by the time our daughter arrived.

# CHAPTER FIVE

# Our Daughter
# Is Born

When Sigi left for the world tour in the middle of January 1958, I was already six months pregnant and had recovered sufficiently from TB to begin to lead a normal life. In February I was fit enough to return to work on a part-time basis. So once again I began the daily journey from Mill Hill to Whitehall, hoping to find a seat in one of the two carriages London Underground then reserved for non-smokers.

Originally I had intended to stay at the Treasury until the birth of our child and they generously agreed to take me back on three-quarters pay. I spent the next couple of months writing a paper on the problems associated with the sterling currency reserves held by various countries throughout the world. It was suggested that this might be done in association with the Bank of England, but the Bank took one look at me, seven months pregnant as I was, and decided that it would be inappropriate. I was hardly surprised for at that time I had already been something of a problem to them when I went there to discuss the Treasury's regular six-monthly balance of payments forecast. I had not been allowed in the all-male dining-room. We either had to go out for lunch or else the head of the typing pool would take me to the free meal which was patronizingly provided for the female staff. I finished the article without the Bank's direct help and it appeared in the May issue of a new monthly journal, *Economic Trends*, published by the Central Statistical Office. I left the Treasury on 21st March. My five years among colleagues in what might at that time have been thought of as an exclusive club had been immensely enjoyable and I was now venturing into an unknown world.

During those last weeks before the baby was born, my time was spent putting the house in order and dealing with the builders who were installing the central heating. In March, Kristin Berge moved out to stay with the Brainins. She had found a flat in Notting Hill Gate, and Sigi and I discussed in our letters how we might find the money to take over her half share in the house so that she could buy the flat. It was an enormous relief to me when she left as I had never warmed to her, and my mother, who had arranged to be with me at the time of the birth, disliked her. At the end of March I thus had the house to myself and wrote to Sigi saying, 'This fortnight is highly prized as it is perhaps the only time I shall ever really be alone again until the family grows up.'

Our daughter, Claire, was born in the Middlesex Hospital on 26th April. The confinement was traumatic. My mother drove me to the hospital and I took with me the stuffed lion cub given by Sigi to protect me. Earlier I had written describing his 'two ears ... sticking out of my suitcase ready to be flattened with the lid'. However, the matron took one look at him and said he was unhygienic and too big (sixteen inches long) and must go. By this time my mother had already left the hospital and when the matron said my husband could take it back that evening, I explained that he was not around. The birth was a difficult one and I was three days in labour before I finally had a Caesarean. I was terrified that, if I were given a tranquillizing injection or taken from the ward, my mother might visit during that time and be persuaded to take the lion. That is exactly what happened. I am pleased to say that to this day the cub still has blood on his jaws where he bit the matron as he was wrenched away.

Both mother and daughter survived the ordeal and in a fortnight we were back home. After the birth of our child we had arranged for a nanny and old friend, Naddle, to come to us for a while. Despite her seventy years she had huge energy and she was most kind. My mother was now also staying in the house. She was a remarkable woman, full of common sense, even-tempered and caring, and still attractive in her old age. My father had died at the end of 1948 and a few years later she had moved to a bungalow at Barton-on-Sea in Hampshire. With her own car and her garden, she was very independent. She loved walking and strolled daily along the cliffs by the sea with her golden cocker-spaniel. It was here that she met the person who was always referred to as 'my friend'. We never learnt his name or exactly where he lived, but he must have been relatively wealthy. He spent part of his time abroad and one day my mother told me that his chauffeur had turned up at the bungalow to show her a pet lion cub in the car which was on its way to a zoo. On another occasion, when Sigi was flying off from Heathrow, we thought my mother might be interested to join us for the ride. When we arrived it became obvious that she already knew the airport and had in fact stayed at one of the nearby hotels!

During this time I also had the help and support of the wives of the other members of the Quartet. I once wrote to Sigi saying, 'The nice thing about the wives, and indeed the Quartet itself, is that every one is so different in a very positive kind of way so that one day you can say I like so and so best and the next day, as the mood takes you, you say, no, I like so and so best.' They all lived nearby. The Schidlofs were in Mill Hill itself, the Brainins in Edgware and the Lovetts in Hendon. Margit Schidlof was particularly pleased about Claire for her daughter, Anmarie, had been born not so long before in December 1956. Throughout this long world tour we shared news and companionship. I would take over to Susi the vivid letters Sigi wrote from Japan and she would then show me the films sent back by Martin. 'He always made sure he himself was in the film so the children could keep contact with him that way,' Susi said; 'we saw him getting a little bit fatter and at one time he grew a beard!' We too had bought a ciné camera, a second-hand Swiss Bolex, and I took it with me to hospital so that Sigi could later see something of our baby from her very first day. Susi thought her 'a ravishingly beautiful baby – like a doll'.

Sigi was just about as far away as he could be when Claire was born. The suspense and the distance between us were unbearable, particularly for Sigi. On 24th April, he wrote to me from Tauranga in New Zealand saying that he had wanted to phone me, but as he could only do so at a time when I was likely to be asleep in the early hours of the morning, he had decided not to. However, Martin phoned Susi and heard that I had gone into hospital. 'I am afraid I was not a hero at that moment. The news, though of course long expected, hit me in the stomach and I just made the basin to be sick in. Yesterday, Friday was ANZAC day with restricted telegram service so I could not stand it any longer and phoned home. I heard from Mummy [my mother] that the baby was expected during the night ... Darling, please feel me as I surround you with my thoughts and love.' He asked my mother to let him know as soon as she had news, but the long-awaited telegram did not arrive until the 28th when the Quartet was in Rotorua. 'It was with indescribable joy and relief that I at last had the N E W S in my hands this morning at about 10.30 a.m. local time. The strain of waiting and knowing that you were already in hospital was tremendous. I am so happy now that all has gone well, and am so looking forward to hearing your voice in a few hours.' There is a note in his diary saying that he spent £3 on a telephone call to me in hospital. His voice sounded extremely distant – more like the mud gurgling in the nearby geysers in Rotorua than my husband.

Of course he wanted to be home, and he described life in New Zealand as being at a low ebb after the impact of the Far East. 'The country is very beautiful indeed and varied but the weekends are deadly. Absolutely nothing is going on, even on Saturday. All the shops are closed; just a few cinemas and I seem to have seen all the flicks, and they are so bad I cannot face going in even to while away the time.' He also complained about the hotels: 'Whether you like it or not they bring you tea at 7 a.m. and there is nothing you can do to keep the maids out of the room at this god-forsaken hour.' Often there was no heating despite the cold and sleety weather. The audience used to bring hot water bottles to keep their hands and feet warm. From time to time his humour burst through: 'One amusing incident: walking in the street a man shouted at me, "Get on the other side of the pavement". Explanation – they have a white line in the pavement and one is expected to stay on the left side. Really a very sensible idea. So I am trying hard to give the slow-down sign, but am thinking of fixing myself up with a rear light and side mirrors!'

What was extraordinary about the tour was that in the space of five weeks the Quartet were to play twenty-four concerts in a country of no more than two million people. This remarkable situation had come about because of the efforts of the New Zealand Confederation of Music Societies. Quite a number of European refugees had settled in Australia and New Zealand where, although there were good orchestras and a country-wide broadcasting system, there was virtually no chamber music. People like Fred Turnovski wanted to continue something in the European tradition and they formed the Confederation to encourage small music societies all over the country. They joined forces with a similar organization in Australia called Musica Viva. This had been started by Richard Goldner and Robert Pickler, two ex-European musicians who had fled to Australia before the war, and it then continued to flourish under the vision and leadership of Charles Berg and Ken Tribe. The two societies in Australia and New Zealand became powerful enough to engage the world's leading chamber ensembles, such as the Pascal String Trio, the Smetana and the Cleveland Quartets and the Deller Consort, as well as famous soloists like Yehudi Menuhin and Isaac Stern. In these early days they were working on a shoe-string budget and, although there were no agents involved with the Amadeus Quartet, the fee was extremely low. They did, however, pay all expenses including food at the hotel where the Quartet were staying.

By the time he reached Australia, Sigi had already had the first photographs of Claire and he was more cheerful. He had been shopping – fruit, delicatessen for a cheap picnic lunch in the hotel room, paper handkerchiefs, aspirin, airmail letters. 'Sydney is much better, in spite of my cold which does not seem to improve. I am feeling very much more alive here. To start with it's incredibly beautiful weather, have not seen a cloud yet, temperature is round about seventy degrees and nice and dry. People are really much more alive here. We arrived rather late at night, and it was made worse by two hours' time difference with New Zealand, and went straight to bed. We live in the Hampstead/Golders Green district of Sydney so there are heaps of Espresso Bar places and "Dorices", which is a most welcome change. Then we went to a concert of the Alma Trio (their last here before going to New Zealand) whom we had met in Los Angeles and San Francisco, a very good concert. After that a combined "au revoir" and "welcome" party at the Wenkarts, a Hungarian family on the committee of Musica Viva. It turned out to be a huge affair as we were joined by all the leading Sydney musicians and the New

York Ballet musicians we had met in Osaka. Absolutely wonderful food. It's really extraordinary. Seventy-five per cent of the audience and committee come from Austria or Hungary originally. Heard some very good new jokes ... "Doctor, closing up his consulting rooms, nurse gone off, all alone, drinks a glass of sherry, a ring at the door – a woman – must see you doctor – impossible, no one here any more, nurse gone, all alone – but must see you doctor – all right, sit down, have a drink with me, nice conversation, getting on fine, doctor looks out of the window and suddenly shouts to the woman – come on, quick, undress and lie on the bed, my wife is coming!" '

Their first concert in Australia, on 2nd June, was in Canberra, and the next in Killara, a suburb of Sydney. There they hit the headlines in a most embarrassing way. 'The first half of the concert, which consisted of Haydn and Dvořák, had gone very well. In the second half we played *Death and the Maiden*. There was already some most objectionable coughing, but in the slow movement just one person kept up a barrage, without the slightest attempt to minimize the noise. Well, Norbert, bless his heart, lost his temper and stopped playing and whined in Puppi's [the Brainins' daughter] complaining voice, "I can't play like that", and then, scowling into the audience, shouted "I don't want any more coughing." And so, amidst perfect, but somewhat embarrassed, silence the concert came to an unnatural end. Of course one should never display temper, but I did so feel for Norbert who, after all, has to play the most intricate embroidery work in the slow movement, requiring the utmost concentration. This morning, on the front page of *The Herald*, it said, "Coughing stopped concert – never anything like it in Sydney – Schnabel only scowled and grunted at coughing etc." The critic gave us one on the head, saying that we really only stopped because we were not playing our London best, but after all why should he (the critic) criticize us when even so we gave a dazzling display etc. etc. By 9 a.m. four newspapers came with reporters and photographers because we were really in the news. It's all very embarrassing and we have certainly started in Sydney with a bang, if slightly on the wrong foot. But never mind, I have your letters and I love you. I am so happy, so don't you go and worry; we are so rich for we have each other and a lovely healthy Claire ...'

On 11th June the Quartet gave their first concert in Sydney itself. It went extremely well and they had excellent write-ups. Sigi thought it one of their best concerts, 'So we have, I think, wiped out our first incident.'

Although Australia was more lively than New Zealand, its hotels were often no better. Their agent was trying to save money by booking them into the cheapest hotels. In Melbourne they were booked into 'a lousy hole, dark, damp and dirty'. So they went on strike and changed to a modern hotel with private bathroom and central heating. In Bendigo there was no heating in the hotel or the hall and the temperature was well below freezing. In Armadale, a small university town, Sigi wrote, 'They really are not normal here, they just ignore heating altogether (it was twenty-seven degrees last night) because admittedly most of the year it's very hot. They had two electric bars in a hall larger than the Wigmore Hall and, just fancy, a big hole over the stage which serves as a ventilation system. There was an icy wind blowing on our backs all the time and playing havoc with our strings. No sooner had we played two minutes and the A string would be practically B flat.'

Back in Sydney there were friends around. The Russian violinist David Oistrakh was also touring Australia and they went to each other's concerts. On 8th July they were at the airport together and Sigi sadly saw him fly off to London. In Canberra there were Bert and Bid Woodrow, friends of mine whom Sigi had met whilst Bert was working at the Australian High Commission in London. They took him for a drive into the bush, 'a most incredible countryside,' and he then 'spent a lovely afternoon with them in a real home, with good conversation, tea and crumpets and everything that makes life pleasant.'

When they returned to Sydney there were complicated business negotiations with Musica Viva over the respective shares of the Australian and New Zealand societies for the 'Round the World' ticket, but on 22nd July they finally left for two concerts in Adelaide and then the long flight to Perth, the last town of their tour before they left for South Africa.

In Perth the Australian Broadcasting Corporation and the Western Australia Chamber Music Society gave a joint reception for the Quartet and the conductor Raphael Kubelik. Kubelik's father had been a well-known violinist in Czechoslovakia, but he himself had emigrated to London. The next day they were joined by the American pianist Gary Graffman, described by Sigi as 'cherubic, kind and intelligent'. The last of their three concerts in Perth was on 30th July and they then had to wait around for a week before the next available flight to Johannesburg. A note on their agent's itinerary reminds them to have yellow fever injections! Fortunately there were many pleasant ways of whiling away the time. 'We met so many nice people and saw good films, heard good concerts and played a lot of poker. We also made friends with the owner of a first-class Italian restaurant called Rudi, where we ate almost every day. Rudi is very musical too, goes to all the concerts in town.' The actor Emlyn Williams was there and they went to hear him. 'It's amazing,' wrote Sigi: 'the constant flow of artists from all over the world.' Once again he was astonished by the attendances at chamber-music concerts and mentioned that they had had to fit in a hurriedly arranged extra lunchtime concert at the university attended by some 700 people.

After an excellent lunch with good wine in an Italian restaurant to celebrate the start of Kubelik's tour and the end of theirs, Sigi played two games of chess with the conductor. 'Each won one game, very satisfactory. He is such a nice and genuine man. Then a cup of tea with the Graffmans who have the room next door and we share a balcony. We may go to the flicks whilst Kubelik and Graffman rehearse this evening and then we will follow it with a poker party. Both Kubelik and Graffman love the game, so we four will be their guinea pigs. Well, maybe beginner's luck? Would be nice to get a cut on soloist and conductor's fees!' A few days later he wrote, 'We are playing a lot of poker. Your hubby is about £4 to the good.' Sigi then goes on to relate how, laughingly, Kubelik promised to speed up the last item in the orchestra's programme so that he would be back in time for some good games.

They were due to leave Perth on 6th August but were delayed a whole day. After a twenty-four hour flight with stop-overs in the Cocos Islands and in Mauritius, they arrived in Johannesburg. The tour in South Africa was greatly helped by their agent, Peta Fisher. Sigi describes her as 'a delightful person, every bit as upset about the political set-up in South Africa as we were, and we became good friends.' From Johannesburg he wrote, 'Only one ticket left in the "Round the World" ticket – Jo'burg/London.' But in the next letter he mentioned some slightly disturbing news: '...I had a touch of nerves three days ago in the Verdi Quartet. I have to start off the last movement with a fugal theme, all spiccato and my bloody bow just would not jump from nerves. I must hold out for the last six concerts still before us, but I will also see a doctor, possibly Russell Brain (?), about my right and left shoulder. I have not written about it before but I am sure it's nothing that a little rest and lots of wifely attention and love won't cure.' A week later in Cape Town, in his last letter of the tour he wrote that he was feeling much better and that it was probably the altitude in Johannesburg which had bothered him. On 27th August the Quartet flew home and they arrived at Heathrow the next morning.

My letters meanwhile had been full of news about our baby. Initially she had not been at all docile: she had a strong will of her own and screamed and screamed till she got her way, but she was beginning to settle down. In May, not long after she was born, I wrote to Sigi, 'I don't feel any different now we have Claire. No more and no less "fulfilled" than before; just me still. If anything I miss you more. I don't think Claire cares a damn about you just yet as she is only interested in *grub* and clean nappies. But she feels it indirectly because it is Mum who needs you now, not she.' Shortly before I married I had given up smoking and in one of my final letters before he returned I warned him that he would not be allowed to smoke in her room: 'I wish you wouldn't smoke. It was so nice last night not having to clear up a nasty smelly room after my guests had left!'

Our letters were quite different in character. Not only were Sigi's beautifully descriptive of the events of the tour but they were always warm and loving. I once wrote saying that I was 'just not capable of writing your sort of letter however much I love you – something of the English ingrained restraint I suppose. But often and often I wish I could.' If from time to time I was depressed at Sigi's long absences, it rarely shows in my letters and in many ways I was surprisingly content. 'I used to think once that I might terribly miss my gay social life but for the time being anyway I am perfectly happy without it. You needn't worry that I shall turn into cabbage, though. Given good health I have far too much vitality for that. But for a while I just want to sit back and get a fresh view of life. There is nothing like a quiet retreat for a time to freshen and refurbish one's ideas. Something usually germinates quietly.' Philosophically I looked back over the past eighteen months, 'wonderfully filled with joy and sorrow for me and excitement of a different kind for you'. One way and another I had had quite a bit to cope with emotionally and physically since our engagement in January 1957 – marriage, sharing a house with someone I didn't much like, the Quartet's long world tour, TB, childbirth and, not least, giving up a job after sixteen years. 'But it is all shaking itself out and I have peace of mind once again and the devil no longer lurks round the corner.'

I had only recently mastered the idiosyncrasies of our Morris Oxford car and Margit Schidlof nobly offered to come with me, along with four-months-old Claire, to meet our husbands at Heathrow airport. Claire was very friendly and gave her father a smile – possibly a wry one for she was soon to understand that from now on she was going to have to share me with someone else who was as important to me as herself. Reporters were there and she had her first photograph taken in the company of her father. Thus the world tour ended, and our family was united.

CHAPTER SIX

# On Tour
# with the Quartet

In our letters we had discussed holiday plans after the world tour. I was keen for us to get away to make sure that Sigi did not spend his well-earned rest sorting through a mass of business papers. But at the same time I was anxious not to do anything to upset Claire, particularly with long car journeys.

On 11th September, a couple of weeks after the Quartet returned home, we set out for Vienna. Proudly taking our daughter between us in her carry-cot, we strode across the tarmac at Heathrow together with another Austrian refugee, the composer and musicologist Egon Wellesz, whose fourth string quartet had been given its first performance in England by the Amadeus some years earlier. In Vienna we stayed in a top-floor flat in Vogelweidplatz belonging to Sigi's cousin Helly Brand. There was no lift and, when we reached the street, Claire – now nearly five months old and a hefty thirteen pounder – had to be carried. It was still the days of heavy prams and solid pushchairs, long before manufacturers tumbled to the need for some really lightweight way of taking babies around. The visit was to bring home the reality that my daughter was still very much part of me and that wherever I went she had to go too, however much I wanted to be alone with Sigi on this our second honeymoon. She was well able to assert herself and grumbled a good deal, partly perhaps because all the excitement had diminished my milk supply and she was being weaned onto a bottle.

Helly had remained in Vienna throughout the war with her mother, who was not Jewish. Her father, one of Sigi's uncles, had been killed fighting for the Austrians during the First World War. Helly's mother then married Adolf Nissel, a younger brother of her first husband. Aghast at what was happening in Austria, he committed suicide in 1938, as already mentioned. When we visited Vienna, Helly and her husband were living in a villa in Linzerstrasse which had originally belonged to Sigi's father, although it had never been occupied by him. He sold it in 1938 to a German to enable him to pay the 'Jew tax' and 'fleeing tax' imposed by the government at a rate of forty-five per cent of all assets. After the war Austrian refugees were entitled to buy back property sold in this way at the price they had received for it. Sigi's father arranged with the Brand family to put up the necessary money for the repurchase, and then for them to buy back the villa from him at the prevailing market price. This left him with sufficient funds to re-purchase the two small blocks of flats he had bought in Vienna when he left Munich, which he had also had to sell when he fled to London. These now needed attention. They were old and in a poor state of repair but, as in Britain, there was rigid rent control and little money available to look after them properly.

Before we left London, Sigi had made an appointment to see a leading neurologist in Vienna, Dr Hoff. He was still worried that at the end of the world tour he had found it difficult to play the quick spiccato passages in the Verdi quartet. Similar problems had already occurred earlier when the Quartet was in Honolulu. There was something wrong somewhere. Dr Hoff detected calcium deposits at the back of his neck and recommended electrical treatment which was acutely unpleasant.

When we returned to London after a few days in the Semmering, concert life began again in earnest. That Sigi wasn't really well was now clear. But he soldiered on. In October the other members of the Quartet recorded Schubert's *Trout* quintet for HMV with Hephzibah Menuhin on the piano and James Merrett on the double bass. Then the whole quartet came together again for seventeen concerts, mainly in Scotland and the north of England, immediately followed by an extensive tour of Germany and ending with a radio engagement in Cologne on 19th December. 1959 started with concerts in England, Holland and Germany. After a few days at home, Sigi left at the beginning of February for a tour in Scandinavia, Switzerland and Italy.

At the end of March we had planned to leave Claire, now nearly a year old, with my mother and have a fortnight's holiday in Sicily followed by Easter in Rome. 'I remember buying a rail ticket from Stockholm to Taormina,' Sigi said. 'You can't have done,' was my reply, 'because you were already on tour in Italy when we met at the railway station in Rome.' Then we realized that he had indeed bought that ticket in Stockholm to cover three months' touring, including our holiday, finishing at the end of April with a series of concerts in Germany and a recording of *Death and the Maiden* in Hanover.

There were clouds in our married life. Sigi was no longer fun in his old carefree way, and I reflected ruefully on this during our holiday in Sicily. Some of our friends may well have begun wondering whether our marriage was going through a bad patch and I was conscious of the unspoken criticism that perhaps I was part of the trouble. Sigi was now seeing neurologists in London, initially Sir Russell Brain at the London Hospital and then Michael Kremer at the Middlesex who was finally to diagnose the cause of the illness.

The worry of not knowing what was wrong, and the fact that he was one of four players who all had families to keep added further tensions to the constant strain of concert-giving. It was not surprising we thought part of his trouble might be psychological. So he now consulted psychiatrists, and in particular Eva Rosenfeld, a most perceptive and highly cultivated woman. She came from Vienna and had been a close friend of Anna and Siegmund Freud. In 1936 she and her husband had moved to London and she was appointed secretary of the Rehabilitation Fund which was concerned with bringing analysts out of Austria.* Not only did she help Sigi to sort out some of his problems, but she also helped me to understand more about the kind of person I had married and about the make-up of our two personalities which could lead to tensions. I have always been more aggressive than Sigi, ready to give as good as I get, reflecting perhaps my Celtic background. I speak out and people soon know where they stand with me. Sigi wielded the guilt-machine, rather like an amiable dog who, oblivious of the sticks and stones hurled at it, just puts on a doleful expression, hoping that its tormentor will feel ashamed.

Nevertheless our summer together in 1959 was a real joy. We had cousin Helly's two teenage daughters to stay with us in London, and we then left by car with Claire for a brief holiday at Villefranche in the south of France. This was followed by a gathering of the whole Quartet in Zermatt, where they played a Brahms programme at the Casals Summer School. My mother, who had never been abroad before, joined us there. During the few days' holiday we took after the concert we thus had for the first time the marvellous experience of being a happy family relaxing together.

At the Summer School I listened with excitement to Pablo Casals playing and teaching the cello and to Mieczyslaw Horszowski playing the piano. Both musicians were great mountaineers and had been made honorary Swiss mountain guides. Casals could be very sarcastic. Once when a strapping young man was playing, he lost his temper, strode up to him, took the cello himself and started to play. 'Look,' he shouted, 'you are a big man and I am only a small chap but I've got twice your strength ... that's how it goes!' There is also a story about Casals at a masterclass where he was listening to a student playing Schubert's *Arpeggione* sonata. His performance was absolutely terrible and everyone was wondering when the maestro would explode. But he let him play the piece through without comment and when he had finished he said, 'Thank you; would you play it again, please.' If anything it was worse than the first time but again the student was dismissed without comment. People who had been listening asked him, 'Why didn't you say anything, and why did you let him play it a second time?' Casals replied, 'It was so bad that Schubert must have turned in his grave. I had to

* Lisa Appignanesi and John Forrester, *Freud's Women*, Weidenfeld and Nicolson, London, 1992.

let him play it a second time so that Schubert could lie the right way round.'

Shortly after we returned from our summer together, I had my first taste of touring with the Quartet when I joined them for their concerts in the Hague and Brussels in October 1959. 'You must do a lot of travelling with your husband?' This question, with variations, was a common opening from fellow guests at parties after concerts. Unless I was in a particularly good mood, the answer was a chilly 'no'. It usually put me on the defensive, depending of course on the way it was asked and the person who was asking it.

So why was I irritated? It was the unconscious assumption that wives are just appendages of their husbands. Another variant of the question is, 'Do you have children?' It makes you feel you are being put down and do not have a life of your own. Above all, such a question shows a lack of imagination. If you have children, who looks after them when both parents are away? The Victorian age, when nannies and governesses were cheap and reliable and a mother could confidently leave her family to be looked after by someone else, is behind us. What is more, although it was still rare in the 1960s, most women with children today also have jobs and cannot easily leave them to go off with their husbands.

Moreover, while I was on tour with the Quartet, what was I to do other than darn my husband's socks? Giving concerts is a continual strain and when performers arrive in a town they do not want to go sightseeing or be sociable. Some towns are a pleasure to visit but many, particularly in industrial areas, have little to offer the lone visitor. Concert tours were always tightly scheduled. For the most part there were different hotels each night, short snatched naps on arrival, hastily eaten snacks before performances and, if they were lucky, a proper meal after the concert.

As a professional musician herself, Martin's wife Susi well understood the problems facing the Quartet while on tour: 'You have to travel, and you have to put up with the inconvenience of aeroplanes and cancelled flights and long taxi drives – to arrive in a hotel which has forgotten to book you or has an impossible room on the fourth floor; you have to carry your luggage upstairs, and then you get ready to play.' Sigi delights in telling the story of the moment he arrived at a hotel desk to hear Martin's voice at the other end of the manager's telephone. The town was Wuppertal and immediately outside Martin's room there was an overhead railway carrying the city's tramcar network. 'I asked for a quiet room and this is impossibly noisy.' 'Sir, the room is quiet, the noise is outside!'

I was not alone amongst the wives in mostly remaining at home. We all had children to look after and none too much money to spend on hotels. Katinka, who had a cousin in Hamburg, would sometimes go with them to Germany, particularly when their daughter was away at boarding school. Margit and Susi would occasionally go to Holland or Belgium or Germany, specially if the Quartet was touring by car. Susi not only had two young children but she also had a job playing with both the English Chamber Orchestra and the English Opera Group. This itself involved a fair amount of touring and if she was to be away from home she felt it should only be for her work. If it was just a holiday with the Quartet, she would feel guilty about it. The Lovetts relied on *au pairs* and Susi's mother to look after their children when they were away. Without Mama, Susi could not have managed. She tells how some of the *au pairs* were marvellous but some were not: 'One of them beat Peter – terrible, horrendous – and another was a kleptomaniac.'

All the same I did tour with the Quartet on a number of occasions. In the early years, when Claire was our only child, she cheerfully stayed with my mother in her bungalow at Barton-on-Sea. In the spring of 1961, just before Claire's third birthday, I left with Sigi for the Quartet's tour of Germany. I have always enjoyed going away with Sigi in our car, just the two of us setting off to explore together, and this occasion was no exception. The atmosphere of expectancy and contentment was enhanced by Claire's farewell: 'It's been nice seeing you,' she said, using that oft repeated phrase as she waved goodbye from Granny's arms. It was at about the same age when she attempted a career as a back-seat driver. 'Put the girlie down,' and 'Stop the tinkie,' were two of her more felicitous expressions: we interpreted them as referring to the gear lever and the trafficator, which used to make a pinging sound. She had a gift for the apt phrase which she has carried through into the fluent writing of her later years.

During our two weeks in Germany we went first to Hamburg where we stayed at that lovely hotel, the Atlantic. From there we went to Witten, Bielefeld, Cologne, Bonn, Mannheim, Frankfurt, Würzburg and Munich and then, after Karlsruhe, back along the *Romantische Strasse* in time for me to be home for Claire's birthday on 26th April. I had never been to Germany before and it was a new experience. I would have got more out of it had I been able to speak the language, but my efforts to learn German were brought to an abrupt halt when I married Sigi. What was the point of struggling with those awkward sounds, and grappling with that difficult grammar, when I had someone beside me to translate? A few people we met spoke English, but as soon as the conversation over the dinner table began to flow, they invariably lapsed into German and I was left gloomily to study the wallpaper. It was perhaps as difficult for them as it was for me. Moreover, as I observed their family lives, it was evident that the *hausfrau* role for wives was still dominant: it was another generation before attitudes changed. All this made me uncomfortable, and probably influenced me against going on future tours in Germany.

In Hamburg we visited the Essbergers, a ship-owning family the Quartet had come to know through Deutsche Grammophon Gesellschaft. DGG, in their quest for improving recording techniques, used the private studio of Professor Tienhaus, who was an expert in acoustics. He lived and had his studio in the Essbergers' house and in June 1955 the Quartet recorded two Mozart quartets there, K499 in D major and K589 in B flat major.

The Essberger family not only frequently entertained the Quartet but also held private concerts for them in their grand house overlooking the Elbe estuary. At one of these gatherings, Sigi found himself sitting next to Dr Hjalmar Schacht, whose brilliant financial advice to Hitler helped to make the German war effort possible. Such moments inevitably bring a deep sense of shock. Many people have asked how the three refugees in the Amadeus Quartet felt about their visits to Germany, particularly as the people who ran the music clubs were often industrialists who could only have survived through being well connected with the Nazis. In the 1950s, in their early days, they had mixed feelings. Their first tour, a brief one, had been organized by the British Council and they agreed to go. The time had come, they felt, to make a fresh start, and if music was needed in a reconstructed Europe, who were they to refuse it? Also, there was at the back of their minds the not unpleasing thought that here they were in a country which had thrown them out and where people now flocked to hear them play. So soon, through the efforts of their agent, Ernst Erhardt, whom they found most sympathetic, they were making extensive tours of Germany.

During these years of our marriage before our second child was born, I too joined the Quartet for a number of short visits to France, Holland and Belgium. There was also a brief but unforgettable visit to Prague in October 1961, followed by a short stay in Budapest. Prague I remember as a beautiful city with its historic buildings well preserved, but otherwise depressingly grimy and dirty. We visited the overcrowded Jewish cemetery, where graves are crammed one on top of the other and where, on the Wall of Remembrance for those who lost their lives under Nazi persecution, we saw with grim eyes the family name of Nissel, including one person with the name of Siegmund. Sigi's family had originally come from Nikolsburg just within the Czech border.

In Prague the Quartet had the temerity to play Dvořák – the *American* quartet, Opus 96 – to the Czechs. One evening after a concert we sat over a meal with the Smetana Quartet, who played all their repertoire from memory. The Amadeus argued that the effort put into playing a work from memory is much better spent on the performance and interpretation of the music. It so happened that at the concert that evening a member of the Amadeus had had a lapse of concentration for a second or so and had left out one or two notes. Members of the Smetana Quartet had been at the concert, so they could come back with the perfect answer, 'You can make mistakes even with the music in front of you!'

We went by train from Prague to Budapest, going through many towns and villages that brought back childhood memories for Sigi. His mother had had a brother and sister who lived in Budapest, but we could find no trace of them.

When we reached Budapest we were fêted. Not only did the Quartet play Bartók but also the fine string quartet no.3 by Matyas Seiber, a Hungarian living in London. Annie Fischer, the world-famous pianist with whom the Quartet had often performed, came to the two concerts and afterwards she and her husband entertained us lavishly with rich Hungarian food. Budapest was very lively. The acute business sense of the Hungarians and their determination to succeed within their communist state was in marked contrast to the more negative attitude of the Czechs in Prague. After the war the wave of Hungarian emigrants to Australia injected some of this vitality into Sydney, so much so that Australians say that today Budapest is no longer called Budapest but simply 'Buda', the 'Pest' having come to Sydney.

In March 1963, I spent two weeks with the Quartet in Moscow and Leningrad. The tour was organized by the British Council and the USSR Ministry of Culture, the Minister at that time being the long-surviving Mrs Furtseva. The concert party consisted of Benjamin Britten and Peter Pears, Norman Del Mar, Barry Tuckwell, George Malcolm and the Amadeus Quartet. Norman's wife, Pauline, was with us and also Marion, then Countess of Harewood, who was a close friend of Benjamin Britten and Peter Pears. The concerts focussed on British music and the Amadeus programmes included Britten's string quartet no.2 and Matyas Seiber's quartet no.3. In Moscow and Leningrad, Mstislav Rostropovich played Schubert's *Arpeggione* sonata and Britten's sonata for cello with Britten himself at the piano.

Whereas the rest of the party apart from George Malcolm went by air, Sigi and I decided to go by train on the Trans-Siberian Express. We set off by going from Harwich to the Hook of Holland and then on to Berlin, where we spent a night with friends. In the morning we rejoined the train, which this time was carrying George Malcolm with his harpsichord. We had the memorable experience of chuffing across the snowy plains of Poland, with the samovar steaming at the end of the corridor and the attendant playing chess with Sigi, accompanied by the Polish railway-guards in their handsome grey fur hats and greatcoats. At Brest-Litovsk at midnight, we had to get out while the wheels were adjusted for the different-width rail-gauge in the USSR. We went into the vast waiting-room with its ceiling-to-floor red chenille curtains, and to our disappointment were offered champagne, not vodka.

On reaching Moscow we soon ran into problems. Although the Quartet had been promised roubles, they were not forthcoming. But, said the Russians, if the Quartet agreed to do a television broadcast they could earn some roubles; and this is how we managed to have enough money to eat during

The Quartet and their wives:
the Brainins, the Nissels, the
Lovetts and the Schidlofs

Muriel Nissel

*Above:* Muriel and Siegmund Nissel

*Right:* Claire and Daniel Nissel with Anmarie Schidlof (*top*)

Margit and Peter Schidlof

Katinka and Norbert Brainin

Susi Lovett

Martin Lovett and their daughter Sonia

Mrs Griffiths, Muriel Nissel's mother

Jean Hubbard and Daniel

The Nissels' cottage in Tuscany

Nissel and Brainin
with Henrietta
Polak-Schwarz

The Quartet: early
days in Bryanston
(*top*), and a little
later in Dartington
(*bottom*)

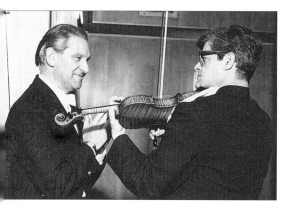

William Pleeth with Brainin

Cecil Aronowitz

Szigetti with Muriel
Nissel and her son
Daniel

Clifford Curzon

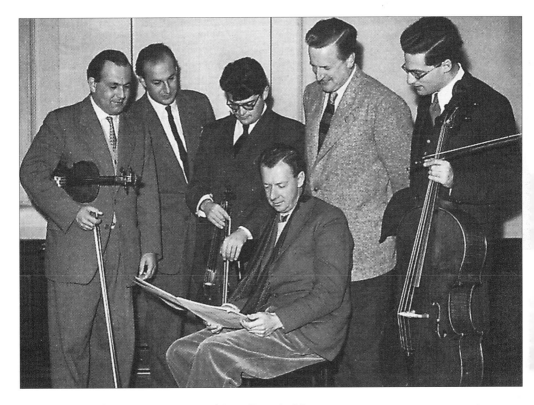

The Quartet with Benjamin Britten and Peter Pears in Moscow

Michael Tippett with John Amis at Dartington

Schloss Elmau

The Quartet at Baalbek
and at Honolulu (*below*)

our first days in Moscow. It was February and very cold, but we were still not able to buy fur hats. Norbert did have one, though, so I playfully snatched it from him and put it on. It suited me well and we started to fool around pretending to bargain, whereupon a burly Russian asked us in Yiddish, 'Bist du a Yid?' – or 'Are you a Jew?' We knew Marion had a good heart, so we asked if she could lend us some money. Like the other 'soloists', she had been issued with roubles and had some to spare. She gave us a hundred-rouble note, which we found difficult to change. Since the Quartet was treated as a 'single soloist', Sigi and I each had a one-eighth share.

In Moscow we met Shostakovich. We also went to David Oistrakh's violin class and were tremendously impressed by its high standard. The Quartet had already met him in London and Sydney and there were bear hugs all round. Once when in London he had phoned to say that he had unfortunately missed the Amadeus concert: would they be prepared to play to him at his hotel? They agreed but, on second thoughts, phoned back to ask if he would be willing to come to one of their homes with his violin so that they could all make music together. This he did, and after the Quartet had played to him, he inquired if they had another viola in the house so that he might join them to play Mozart's C major quintet.

Our hotel in Moscow was comfortable enough and we did not need the spare plugs we had brought for the washbasins. Guarding the long corridor outside our room was the ever-vigilant attendant. Although the service was impossibly slow, the food was good and each day I ate caviar for breakfast whilst Sigi devoured a plateful of sprats.

Again we were fêted and the receptions were endless. As I was the only wife accompanying the Quartet, I was usually served first at dinner. I well remember the occasion when, with the British ambassador on my right and the French ambassador on my left, I had to make the first cut into a large sturgeon on a silver platter with the begloved waiter trying to tell me in sign language which was the best end to break into. On another occasion we were entertained at the Austrian Embassy where we were shown an alcove in the drawing-room where special visitors were seated. Private conversations, even whispered ones, could be heard quite clearly on the opposite side of the room. We also visited the Italian Embassy which the Russians had just returned to its owners. It had long lain derelict and was in the process of being refurbished. The vast entrance hall contained just one piece of furniture – a grand piano – which had been installed for the wife of the ambassador, Signora Straneo, an English lady whom the Quartet had met during their visits to the Darting-ton Summer School of Music.

As Marion, Pauline and I had time on our hands, we set off each day in the palatial Moscow underground to explore the city. Since there was at this point a slight thaw in attitudes to modern art, we were able to visit an exhibition of paintings by Fernand Léger who, being a communist, was one of the first such artists to be shown in public. We visited GUM, the city's big department store, and stared with amused eyes at the windows where dust had accumulated on displays of old-fashioned underwear. We saw the steam rising from the heated open-air pools where people were swimming in sub-zero air temperatures. Accompanying us there was usually the Quartet's interpreter, Masha Greenberg, who was a postgraduate student studying Australian literature. We struck up a friendship and, when I was back in London, I sent her various books and she in turn sent me a set of Haydn piano sonatas. One day, when the Leningrad Philharmonic first came to play at the Proms, there was a ring at our front door in Mill Hill and a young man announced himself as 'Ashkenazy, pianist'. He was in London with the orchestra and had brought with him a present from Masha to the Quartet – eight little pots of caviar!

On one occasion I went on my own to dine with Eddie Bolland, an old colleague from Oxford days, who was a First Secretary at the British Embassy in Moscow. Sigi had an engagement elsewhere and it was not long before he was asked where his wife was. There were telephone calls to my colleague's flat in the diplomatic compound: he explained to me that the Russians would be keeping track of my movements.

After a week in Moscow we went on by train to Leningrad, an unforgettable journey in a luxurious sleeper reminiscent of Victorian England, with its red velvet curtains and shaded lamps. We attended the Kirov Ballet where the beauty of the dancing was marred by the uninspiring choreography of a 'modern' ballet. The high point of our visit was the Hermitage. It is one of the great museums of the world and contains amongst its buildings the Winter Palace, the former residence of the Russian Emperors, which was stormed by the revolutionaries in November 1917. The buildings themselves are a remarkable memorial to the wealth and power of the Tsars; and the breath-taking collection of art treasures they contain makes it easier to understand the resentment such a concentration of riches must have provoked amongst the common people.

At the end of our visit we had plenty of roubles left and nothing much to spend them on. We did, however, come home with a magnificent collec-tion of records, not just Tchaikovsky, Rachmaninov and Scriabin, but also Mozart's *Sinfonia Concertante* played by David Oistrakh and Rudolf Barshai. The records were not of high quality, but they were cheap and certainly good enough to add to our small collection at home. Non-negotiable credit is a common problem for artists who venture to play in countries with blocked currencies and who are not paid until they have finished their concerts. Years later, when I was at a conference in Sofia in Bulgaria, I strug-gled home with a rug under my arm bought with a small part of the currency which the Amadeus had earned earlier and which had been similarly blocked.

Sigi and I wanted to visit Warsaw on our return journey. Trying to get visas was a nightmare. We were finally defeated because our fares back to London were being met by the Russians and the Poles would only grant visas to people who paid in hard currency. The fact that, once in Warsaw, we would have used sterling travellers' cheques was irrelevant. So, having a few days to spare, we again broke our journey in West Berlin and we were unexpectedly enchanted by the vulgarity and bright lights of capitalist advertisements in that city.

My next tour with the Quartet was in 1965. In the summer of that year the whole Quartet and their families – all fourteen of us – went to the USA for three months. Most of our time was spent at a summer school in Aspen, Colorado (see chapter 10). In 1967 I went with the Quartet to Japan. Shortly afterwards I returned to the civil service and, with two young children at home, I no longer had any time for touring, apart from joining the Quartet for brief visits, often to stay with friends, or combined with business visits of my own.

'Well, it's either another unscheduled stop in Cuba, or that's the Amadeus String Quartet!' A sly Jak cartoon, *Evening Standard*, London, 9th September 1969

# CHAPTER SEVEN

# What Happens
# When You Are Ill?

What happens in a string quartet if you are ill and can't play? I was to find out early in our married life, for in the summer of 1960 Sigi was operated on for a tumour on his brain.

If you are in an orchestra and fall ill, you can find a substitute: if you are a soloist, you just don't play. But with only four players life is different, particularly if you have been together for many years. It is scarcely practicable to call in another player, and for any serious quartet that would anyhow be out of the question. The repertory for string trios is limited – and indeed virtually non-existent if there is no cellist. If a violin is missing, particularly if it is the second fiddle, it is possible to team up with other instruments such as the piano or woodwind. But life becomes difficult.

In the 1950s, when the work and fees of the Quartet were on the increase, they considered how they might insure themselves against prolonged illness and sought the advice of Carl Flesch, an insurance-broker who was the son of the famous violinist. The policy they took out for a comparatively modest premium insured a percentage of the fee for each concert in the coming season, the percentage varying from country to country and in accordance with the nature of the engagement and the expenses that were involved. This insurance cover greatly helped the Quartet and their families during major illnesses that involved large-scale cancellations or replacements of concerts. The weakness of the arrangement was that, if an illness occurred towards the end of the insurance period, the next season could not be covered. At Sigi's suggestion the solution was to take out two policies running at half-yearly intervals, entailing two medical examinations a year, so that the Quartet was insured for at least six months ahead.

Only rarely did the various minor illnesses lead to the cancellation of concerts, although possibly they were often played when they should not have been. One of the worst Quartet experiences arising from injury was the ill-starred opening concert given in 1953 during their first tour of North America. Amongst other misfortunes that occurred, Norbert had to play with a cut finger (see chapter 4). On another occasion Sigi broke his little finger after slipping during a rehearsal and coming down heavily on a table. It turned out to be a hair-line fracture. Despite the pain, he continued with the rehearsal and played in a concert next morning at the Pebble Mill studios in Birmingham. All four players had illnesses and operations that interfered only indirectly or briefly with Quartet life. Coughs and colds, even flu, had to be stoically borne and many a concert was given with one or more of them registering temperatures way above normal. You never actually cough during a performance: the inhibitions are too strong. At worst your nose runs onto the fiddle and you hope it does no damage to the varnish. In such circumstances, artists' rooms often do not help. They can be ice-cold after a hot concert hall, or they can be very hot with the adjoining platform subject to jets of chilly air coming from unknown quarters or from the air-conditioning. Sometimes the draught is so strong that it turns over the pages of the music.

The first illness to result in major cancellations of concerts was the tumour on the brain for which Sigi was finally operated on in August 1960. He had already shown symptoms of stress as early as the beginning of 1958 during the world tour, and playing had become increasingly troublesome, and often a nightmare. DGG had planned a complete set of Beethoven records with the Quartet in 1959 and the first group, the three Rasumovsky quartets, Opus 59, was completed in the second half of May. The recordings were clearly taxing for Sigi, particularly the scherzo in the first quartet with its spiccato passages involving quick changes from string to string. But the resulting performances are superb and the peculiar intensity of Opus 59, no.1, is a reminder of the suffering that went into its playing.

The early months of 1960 had seen the Quartet in Hanover recording Brahms's quartet Opus 67 in B flat. This was followed by a ten-week tour of North America and then a further three weeks in Germany. During the end of May and the beginning of June, the Quartet recorded the last two Beethoven quartets composed during the middle period of his life, Opus 95 and Opus 74 (sometimes known as *The Harp*). Thereafter concerts became more and more of an ordeal. Each morning I would hear Sigi retching with anxiety in the bathroom. The sound revolted me and I hated myself for not being able to give him the sympathy he needed. At the end of May, in Birmingham, he could not face leaving the hotel room and going onto the platform so that the Quartet had to drive back without playing the concert. The next day, at Claydon House in Buckinghamshire, the home of the Verney family, he managed to play once again. We had supper with the family afterwards and, as I went downstairs to the dining room, I passed a tiny pair of shoes outside a bedroom door and wondered what the future held for us and our baby daughter.

After recording Opus 95 and Opus 74, the Quartet went straight to the Festival at Aldeburgh where they were due to play with both Clifford Curzon and Gervase de Peyer. We set off by car with Claire. Half-way there, Sigi stopped and asked me to drive, something I never normally did when he was around. During the Festival we went to the first performance of Benjamin Britten's *A Midsummer Night's Dream*. We had to leave in the middle because Sigi was feeling ill. I drove through the Suffolk lanes in the dark back to Alderton, my first experience of night driving. We were staying with Tom and Ann Eustace, friends whom we had met a few years earlier at the 1957 Festival. Tom was a doctor and the next day he told me that my husband was seriously ill. He probably had an idea what the trouble was.

At this stage of his illness Sigi was taken into the Middlesex Hospital for tests. I, together with Claire, went to stay with my mother in her bungalow in Barton-on-Sea and worriedly made hasty visits to Sigi and the house in Mill Hill. I was three months pregnant and, not surprisingly, I miscarried.

A tumour was found in the front of Sigi's brain. The cause of the illness, which had taken over two years to diagnose, was almost a relief in that he knew at last that it was something physical that was behind his troubles and not some nebulous mental illness. He came home for the weekend before he was operated on, on 28th August, by Valentine Logue at the antiquated old Hospital for Nervous Diseases in Maida Vale. The operation had to take place there because the theatre at the Middlesex was temporarily out of use. Our much loved violinist friend, Vera Kantrovitch, visited him the night before the operation. I hadn't the courage to do it myself. There are times in life when the self splits in two. One half, coolly and seemingly oblivious of events, carries on with everyday tasks while the other half perceives a terrifying yawning gulf between one conscious moment and the next. In these times of crisis the support of friends is a tremendous help and comfort. One such friend was Imogen Holst who asked a straightforward question. Were we all right financially?

Even if the tumour proved to be benign and Sigi's operation was successful, there was the lurking fear that playing the violin might no longer be possible. As the tumour was in the front of the brain, in the middle, it was possible for the surgeon to cut the skull either to the left or to the right. Sigi chose the right because he considered his bow arm, which is controlled mainly from that side of the brain, to be the more important. Under the bright lights of the concert platform you can still see over his right brow the now slightly shrunken triangle cut out during the operation. Not only did the tumour turn out to be benign but there was no damage to the tissue of the brain. We knew almost at once that he would still be able to play. How well was a matter of doubt.

When Sigi was in the recovery ward, Norbert and Peter were due to play Mozart's *Sinfonia Concertante* at the Proms. I knew how much Sigi would have liked to hear it, so, tucked beneath my coat, I took with me to the hospital a little transistor radio, specially bought for the purpose: they were a novelty at the time. Imagine my surprise when I arrived to find that he already had just such a radio beside him. The young houseman who was looking after him had sensed that it would give Sigi pleasure to listen to the concert and had decided to find one for him. He was Gerald Stern, now a famous neurologist; and we have remained friends ever since.

Shortly afterwards Sigi was moved back to the Middlesex Hospital and he remained there throughout September. In those days children were not allowed to visit patients in the hospital, and his only sight of Claire was on the pavement below his ward window on the fourth floor. She is quite sure, however, that she did once visit her father. Whatever the truth of the matter, the trauma of the whole episode made a lasting impression on this small two-year-old.

Sigi was his old self once more, and in October the three of us went to Spain in search of the sun. We stayed for just over two weeks near what was at that time the small port of Marbella. We then rented a car and did a tour of Cordoba, Seville, Jerez and Malaga. Our daughter was a model of forbearance, both on the long, bumpy car journeys and when faced with ever-changing hotels and baby-sitters. She took with her Ferdinand the Bull, a toy which, once wound-up, charged around with frantic energy. He helped her to while away those long waits before meals were served.

During Sigi's illness, Norbert, Martin and Peter had whenever possible played trios and also piano quartets with Denis Matthews. All four members of the Quartet began playing together again at a concert in Canterbury on 11th November, more than four months after their previous concert. A week later they gave a concert in Ipswich and we had the pleasure of staying with Tom and Ann Eustace once again knowing that everything was going to be all right.

This was the first time a member of the Quartet had had a serious illness. The next crisis was in 1964 when Martin had a nervous breakdown, triggered off by an attack of paratyphoid (a type of typhoid fever) which he had contracted a little while earlier. The causes of mental illness are complex and all but impossible to identify. But it is hardly surprising that musicians are affected by the enormous pressures under which they play. That there are likely to be tensions between members of a quartet is obvious, but those between certain of them can be more hurtful than others. This was how matters stood at that point between Martin and Norbert. Martin was particularly sensitive to criticism from Norbert and, however wild his criticisms might sometimes be, respect for Norbert's sheer genius meant that they had to be listened to.

During rehearsals, tensions and rows often reached a high pitch. One such incident occurred in the early months of 1964 in Amsterdam before a concert that included one of the three Prussian quartets, a set of late works by Mozart. The King of Prussia, for whom the quartets were written, was himself a fine cellist and all three of them frequently have a melodic line with the leading voice in the high register of the cello. Whilst they were rehearsing in Amsterdam, Martin was getting increasingly tense and he finally exploded when Norbert continued to make derogatory remarks. The major row that ensued led to each threatening never to play another note with the other again. However – as had happened in the past – peace was made and both Amsterdam concerts were duly performed.

A few days later, when the Quartet went to Hanover to record Mozart's A major quartet, K464, it became increasingly clear that Martin was beginning to suffer a nervous breakdown. The atmosphere at the recording sessions was fraught with the other members of the Quartet hardly daring to do anything but follow Martin in the finer shades of interpretation, such as tempi and the subtleties of rubato. The DGG team in charge was not aware of the situation and the sessions were completed without serious incident. The recording is very good.

When he returned to London, Martin was persuaded to see a doctor and a few days later Sigi and I drove him with Susi to the Halliwick Hospital in Friern Barnet. This was one of the most daunting experiences of my life and I was not a little scared. There, in the back of our car, was this strange character, unrecognizable as the cellist of the renowned Amadeus Quartet. He became a patient of Dr Benaim who treated him with drugs in combination with therapy sessions. He began to paint and produced some remarkable work which brought out the artistic talent he has subsequently continued to nurture. After some weeks he was discharged from hospital and a few months later he was able to start playing again. He has never had a relapse.

After Sigi's operation to remove the brain tumour and Martin's breakdown, the Quartet was free from serious illness throughout the rest of the 1960s and the whole of the 1970s. In 1981, however, it struck again. Sigi had a heart attack followed by open heart surgery in 1983. The impact of this on the Quartet is described in chapter 17.

There were a number of more minor illnesses, some of which entailed cancelling concerts. In April 1963 Peter had an emergency operation for appendicitis. As it was the Easter holiday period, the Quartet missed only a few concerts in Germany. Some years later, in January 1966, Norbert went into Edgware General Hospital for observation. Fortunately it was a false alarm, but once again it led to cancellation of concerts, as happened on another occasion when he had an attack of flu. It was a more serious matter when he broke the sinew holding the top joint of his thumb in the spring of 1975. He was driving to the airport after spending Easter at his house in Barga in Tuscany when he put his hand beneath him to straighten out his coat and accidentally sat on it. His not inconsiderable weight gave him a 'hammer' thumb and all concerts had to be cancelled until the end of June. By co-incidence, the rest of the Quartet found out what had happened before Norbert himself told them. Martin's son, Peter, had been working on a temporary basis with a firm of insurance agents who chanced to insure the work of both Norbert and the other members of the Quartet. Norbert rang them immediately to find out what the position was and Peter picked up the message.

Sigi had minor illnesses as well as major ones. He once had a boil which forced him to play the whole of a Beethoven quartet series in Paris, in March 1977, sitting on a rubber cushion. As soon as he returned to London, he went into the Royal Free Hospital to have it cut out. He was troubled by diverticulitis throughout 1976 and suffered bouts of discomfort and high temperature, which led to his having yet another operation in 1977.

At the beginning of July in 1985, just before we were due to go off on holiday to Italy, Sigi broke his leg while walking in the park behind our house with our Dalmatian, Ceri, who a few years earlier had given us much joy by producing nine beautiful liver-and-white-spotted pups. We decided not to cancel our holiday plans but, instead of driving from London, to fly to Pisa and hire a car there. A month later Sigi flew to Zurich, with his leg still in plaster, and played a concert with the Quartet in Baden to celebrate the eightieth birthday of their old teacher Max Rostal. He went on to teach at a summer school in Kirkrade in Holland, and later in August he both taught and played a couple of concerts at a summer school in Città di Castello in Umbria, in Italy. He vividly remembers playing quartet arrangements of Bach fugues with his leg stuck out in front of him. First-class therapy in the clinic at the local spa soon helped put him back on his feet.

Whenever illness struck, the Quartet made great efforts to ensure that their audiences were not disappointed and that the Quartet's good name was not tarnished by any hint of unreliability. Such an attitude must always prevail in a group like a string quartet with professional pride and a reputation to maintain.

CHAPTER EIGHT

# Do You Play
# on a Strad?

---

When the Quartet made its début at the Wigmore Hall in January 1948, Norbert was playing on a Peter Guarnerius violin, Sigi on a Grancino, Peter on a Testore viola and Martin on a Peter Guarnerius cello. They were reasonably good instruments but not outstanding. At their final concert in Cheltenham in June 1987, they were all playing on Stradivarius instruments. They also had Tourte bows. Other bows, Norbert once said – even Villaumes and Peccates – 'are all walking-sticks.'

For young musicians without money the problem of obtaining a satisfactory musical instrument is formidable. There are always competing claims. They have to live, insure their instruments, perhaps pay for lessons and, particularly if they have families, pay rent and mortgages. The Amadeus were no exception and each member has a story to tell about the anxiety and sacrifices that lay behind the acquisition of the instruments they played on in that first concert. Their experiences also demonstrate how, if you are already well known, there are more opportunities to play on good instruments. People take pleasure in lending or even giving you an instrument, and sometimes also in letting it be known that they have done so.

When he came to England, Sigi brought with him a violin his father had bought in Vienna. It turned out to be a dud. This early experience gave him an aversion to violin dealers. 'Who knows whether the instrument I brought from Vienna really was no good? Maybe the dealer suggested it in order to get hold of what might have been quite a reasonable instrument; I simply don't know. Young people are always at the mercy of dealers who are much older and much more experienced.' Whereas Norbert has always found pleasure in buying and selling instruments, not only to play on but also as a collector, the effect of this early experience on Sigi was that he came to dislike dealers so much that he never bothered to take an interest in instruments. 'If you really want to get to know about them, you have to handle a lot of them, and try them out and get to know their sound. Consequently I personally know very little about instruments or their value. I do, however, know what is a good instrument as soon as I take it in my hands and play it, and I can more or less with certainty distinguish between Strads, del Gesùs, Guadagninis, Tononis, etc.'

Norbert also brought a violin with him when he left Vienna at the age of fifteen. When the Brainin family moved to London in March 1938, two consignments of furniture and other personal belongings were despatched to England. Only one of them arrived and in it was Norbert's violin, the first full-sized one he ever had. When Norbert took lessons from Carl Flesch, his teacher decided that the violin was not good enough for such a gifted player. Flesch's son then lent him an old Viennese fiddle made by Martin Stoss. Norbert tells the story of how he once broke off a small fragment of the violin with the nut of his bow and was terrified that Flesch might take it away from him. 'I didn't know what to do, so I took an envelope – the glue was real glue in those days – and I moistened it with a bit of water and a bit of spit and I rubbed it into the place where the piece broke off, and also into the piece itself, and put it on. Next day I went to the lesson and the knob was all right and it didn't come off. Immediately afterwards – it was during the school holidays – I hot-footed it to Hill's in Bond Street. There was an old man there: his name was Mr Wilson. He was over eighty and he had completely white hair and a very red face. I told him what had happened and asked him if he could make a proper job of it. A few days later when I came back, he brought in the fiddle and announced in a loud voice, because he was slightly deaf, "You did a very good job; we couldn't get it off!" All they had done was fine it down and polish it up. Maybe the piece is still in place today.'

Some years later, during the war, Norbert bought a Vuillaume for £140 with the help of his uncles. It was with this violin that he won first prize in the Carl Flesch Competition in 1946. He sold it back to Hill's when he went to live with Martin because, 'although I made a few guinea here and there by teaching and playing in concerts – illegally of course – it was the only means I had of paying for my keep.' Norbert and Sigi have never quite mastered some phrases in the English language and he used to refer to earning 'a few guinea' in much the same way as Sigi still talks about his 'pyjama'.

In the summer of 1947, soon after Norbert, Sigi, Peter and Martin seriously began rehearsing together as a quartet, they were asked by Imogen Holst, who was in charge of music in the Arts Department at Dartington Hall, to give a concert in the Banqueting Hall. The concert (already referred to in chapter 1) was a resounding success and one of the consequences was that, at Imogen's instigation, Dorothy and Leonard Elmhirst – who were themselves great music-lovers – offered to buy Norbert a violin worthy of the leader of this gifted group. He chose a Peter Guarnerius of Venice, for which the Elmhirsts paid £1,250. Norbert was to play on this instrument when the Amadeus Quartet made its début.

Ink and wash sketch of the Amadeus by Milein Cosman

After Sigi had come out of internment and begun lessons with Max Rostal, it soon became clear that he needed a better violin. When Norbert bought the Vuillaume and was no longer playing on the Viennese Martin Stoss that Carl Flesch's son had lent him, Sigi borrowed it for a while. Later he somehow managed to put enough money together to buy a Grancino, the instrument he was playing on at the Quartet's first concert. He bought it from Hill's for £150. W. E. Hill and Sons were the major authority on instruments. If they said a particular instrument was made by so-and-so, their certificate was law. Theirs was the place where young students like Sigi went begging: 'Please could I have a look at the instruments?' They would size you up as you walked through the door and would have a good idea of what it was worthwhile showing you.

Instruments in a quartet must to some degree match each other. If one has a tone that is much superior to the others, the balance can fall apart. When Norbert acquired the Peter Guarnerius from the Elmhirsts, this posed just such a problem for Sigi. The Grancino he had recently managed to buy did not complement Norbert's new instrument. By dint of much scraping and saving, and with a loan from Elias Broder, the boss for whom he had worked in the foundry in Hackney during the war, Sigi also bought a Peter Guarnerius from Hill's for £1,500. Both his and Norbert's were fine violins. They were well matched and helped establish the Quartet in its early career.

The next major change came towards the end of the 1950s. Dolf Polak, an old friend who was a doctor and also a good amateur musician, had always had the ambition to own a Strad. According to Sigi, 'he did not feel justified in playing it himself but, if Norbert would choose one for him, he would like to lend it to the Amadeus Quartet.' So that is how Norbert first came to play on a Strad.

A further change came soon afterwards. Norbert describes how 'we went to Dundee and were invited to the house of Dr Emerson who had a big house in the middle of nowhere. Over dinner he told me about a Guarnerius del Gesù in very bad condition. Before her recent death, it had been the property of a lady named Lisa Honeyman, and was now with her sister in Esher, near London. Hill's had bid £3,000 for it but there was a stipulation by Mrs Honeyman that it should be sold in Scotland to a British violinist. I didn't have the money, so I asked Martin Cahn [a well-to-do German refugee]* if he would guarantee an overdraft, which he did. I then made an offer of £3,100 to the solicitor who was an executor of the will. It was accepted. The violin was a ruin, so I took it to Hill's and asked them to restore it. Mr Desmond Hill was astonished when he saw it and wondered how on earth I had managed to get hold of it!' It took about ten months to repair. Although Sigi described it as 'a bit of a rough diamond', it once again became a wonderful fiddle with a distinctive and powerful tone, and Norbert played on it for many years.

When Norbert bought the Guarnerius del Gesù Sigi took over the Strad that had been lent to the Quartet by Dolf Polak and he has played on it ever since. Many years later, when the Quartet had been playing in New York, he found that it had a name – the Payne Strad of 1731. Keen musicians and dealers often come to the artists' room after a concert and ask to look at their instruments. Someone thought he had identified it, and the next day he produced Herbert Goodkind's *Iconography of Antonio Stradivarius* and showed Sigi the photograph of it in the book.†

We were eventually able to buy the Strad. A musician playing on a borrowed instrument always runs the risk that the owner may suddenly take it back. Often, too, it may have become so much a part of a player's life that ownership becomes doubly desirable. Partly through money from the sale of Sigi's father's flats in Vienna and various small sums which we both inherited from our families, we were, by the end of the 1960s, in the fortunate position of having sufficient capital to buy the instrument outright. We were thus not saddled with the bank loans that so often dog musicians struggling to make a living for themselves and their families.

* Martin Cahn was an amateur viola player whose home was in London.
† Herbert K. Goodkind, *Violin Iconography of Antonio Stradivarius, 1644–1737*, published by the author, 780 pages, New York, 1972, page 227.

Meanwhile, our friend Dolf Polak played for many years on Sigi's Peter Guarnerius. When he returned it, we then lent it first to the Chilingirian Quartet, who were at one time students of Sigi's, until they themselves were able to buy their own instruments; and then to the Auryn Quartet, who later bought it from us.

Peter's story, too, is one of being lent successive instruments which he then bought. When he started playing the viola, he borrowed a Testore belonging to Martin Cahn, who had already helped Norbert. It was on this instrument that Peter was playing in the Wigmore Hall concert. He was later lent a very good Bergonzi viola by Major Gubbins, a friend of Stephanie Hess who had looked after Peter when he first came to England. He kept it on loan for many years and eventually bought it.

He then had the good fortune to be lent the famous Macdonald viola made by Stradivarius in 1701. This instrument came onto the market in the USA and was bought for him by Sylvio Samama in 1963. Peter subsequently persuaded Sylvio to sell it to him and he continued to play on it until his death.

Sylvio Samama was the son-in-law of Henrietta Polak-Schwarz, who lived in Holland, and had supported the Quartet in many ways. The story of how he met Henrietta's daughter, Ans, is a strange and happy one. He had been a soldier in the French Army during the war and, soon after it ended, he became a student in Paris studying psychology. During his vacation in 1946, he went to help at a camp funded by a Jewish-American organization to aid people who had survived concentration camps. The first priority was to restore them to health, and Sylvio went there to help cook. The woman in charge of one of the groups at the rehabilitation camp was a nurse from Holland who was herself a Jewish survivor. She and Sylvio fell in love and they married.

Martin had certain advantages in that his father, Sam Lovett, was a professional cellist. After his schoolboy purchase of a cello (already described in chapter 2) he acquired a Grancino cello and then a Montagnano, a fine instrument. At the Quartet's début he was playing on a Peter Guarnerius. Then, on his wife's initiative, he approached Henrietta Polak-Schwarz. Susi had heard that one of the finest Strad cellos in the world was coming up for sale, the Vaslin cello of 1725, known as Belle Blonde because of its light colour. Henrietta Polak-Schwarz bought the cello for Martin and she later sold it to him.

Unlike Sigi and Peter, Norbert has owned and played on a number of different instruments over the years. In 1969 he bought another Guarnerius del Gesù, known as the Rode, made in 1734. It was a marvellous violin and less rough than the earlier del Gesù which he had had restored. 'It had a beautiful tone, but I had to play it in a certain way. It liked to be played in a very smooth loving kind of way and I wanted to make other sounds, particularly when we played the late Beethoven quartets. I wanted to play differently, and I couldn't do it on that violin. And I noticed that Stradivarii always have a much more objective kind of sound. In fact they sound exactly as you play them.' Thus Norbert set out to acquire a Strad, the Chaconne of 1725. It was at first loaned to him and then, in 1981, he bought it. It was the instrument on which he was playing at the Quartet's last concert.

After Peter's death, Norbert had the chance to play on yet another Strad, the Gibson-Huberman of 1713. It is an unusual story. In 1936, this violin was stolen from the Carnegie Hall in New York during a concert at which Huberman was playing. Huberman habitually had two violins with him – this Strad and a Guarnerius del Gesù – and he was playing on the latter when the Strad disappeared. It was missing for fifty years and only came to light when a lady started hawking around a dirty-looking instrument to various dealers in New York, who barely took one glance at it before expressing their disdain. The lady with the fiddle was the widow of a man who had been imprisoned for child molesting and had died of cancer in a prison hospital. He had been playing in a kind of 'Palm Court' orchestra for many years and knew that his violin was a fine one. As he lay dying, he told his wife that she should do something about it after his death.

According to his widow, her husband had bought the violin for $100 many years before, just after it was stolen. Indeed, some newspaper clippings about the theft were still inside the fiddle case. Eventually she showed it to Rachel Goodkind, the daughter of Herbert Goodkind, the compiler of the Stradivarius iconography. She immediately rang up the London violin-dealer, Charles Beare, who in turn got hold of photographs of it and copies of certificates and letters authenticating it from Hill's. He identified the fiddle as the one stolen from Huberman before the war and informed the insurance company concerned. Beares did a first-class clean up of the instrument and it was displayed at an exhibition in Cremona in 1987 to mark the 250th anniversary of Stradivarius's death.*

That was where Norbert first set eyes on it. 'I saw it was beautiful although it did not sound very good at that time.' In the autumn of 1987, Charles Beare showed it to Norbert again and rated it the best-sounding Stradivarius of them all. It was eventually acquired for Norbert. 'It is so beautiful, in fact underneath all the dirt the varnish was so well preserved – glorious red varnish – and it sounds absolutely marvellous. I always play on it now; it is better than the Chaconne, which I have sold.'

During the forty years they were together, the Quartet had the good fortune never to lose or damage an instrument. Problems they certainly had. Sharp

* Herbert Goodkind lists the Gibson-Huberman violin among Stradivarius instruments that had been lost or stolen. 'Most,' he says, 'have been recovered.' Ibid, page 40.

changes in temperature and humidity could affect the glue holding the instruments together and they might open up whilst on tour. Strings would break in the middle of concerts. Sigi tells how he once had trouble with his pegs. 'I took them to Hill's and had them re-coned but they were still not entirely satisfactory. We went to Paris during a very cold winter and played in the Salle Gaveau. The organizers had lit an open fire in the artists' room, which was boiling hot, but the hall remained ice-cold. Because of the danger of slipping pegs, I pushed them in very hard before going onto the platform, and they lasted satisfactorily through the opening Haydn. We started the second item, Beethoven's Opus 135, where the main theme is broken up into short little phrases between the instruments and, at exactly the moment when it was my turn to carry the musical thought – a downward leap on the A string from F to B natural – my peg slipped, whirled down, and we came to an embarrassed standstill. It being near the beginning of the work, we began again and I pushed my peg in as hard as I could but, on that Saturday afternoon, the gremlins were around. At exactly the same spot on the repeat, the A string peg slipped once more; terrible looks from my colleagues. We started once more, but in the slow movement and again in the last movement it slipped and interrupted the performance. Never have twenty-seven minutes seemed so long in my life. When we finally came back to the artists' room Peter went for me: "You bloody fool, you don't even know how to look after your instrument." He took hold of the fiddle and said, "There's nothing wrong with your peg;" then Norbert piped up: "That's my fiddle." So he then got hold of my instrument. Peter had very, very strong hands and handed the fiddle back to me saying, "That won't slip now." I handed it back to him and said, "You tune it then." Whereupon he took hold of the peg, tried to tune it and broke it clean off. What to do? Paris, Saturday afternoon, no violin repairer available, audience waiting, organizers getting impatient. So we hunted the depths of the Salle Gaveau for the caretaker. When we found him, he produced a pair of pliers with which Peter managed to tune the stump to somewhere near an A. We walked onto the platform with the pliers in the pocket of Peter's tails. There were no more interruptions. But for the rest of the concert my A was the Quartet A!'

There were other near disasters. One Saturday afternoon following a successful concert, also in Paris, the Quartet was in a relaxed mood and went to a café on the Champs Elysées near the Rond Point. As is usual after a concert, a lot of people sat down with them, and amongst them there was an Australian student who had a car. On her way home she was going near their hotel, so Martin asked if he and his cello could have a lift with her. The rest of the Quartet then chimed in, 'Would you please take our instruments too as we are going on to dinner elsewhere.' They stayed in the café chatting and after a while a waiter called Sigi aside and gave him a somewhat garbled message from Martin. The gist of it was that he should go outside into the Champs Elysées and look for Peter's viola on a nearby bench. As he was going through the door he collided with Martin who triumphantly held Peter's viola. Apparently when Martin and the Australian student loaded up the car, they had left Peter's instrument sitting on the bench, each thinking the other had checked everything.

On another occasion, when we were on holiday, we were taking our car with us by motor-rail from Boulogne to Milan. We and the children had already boarded the train but, as there was a little time to spare before it left, Sigi and I decided that we would have a coffee. He took his violin with him as he would normally do. We had our coffee and went back to the train. The guard blew the whistle and Sigi suddenly gasped, 'Where's my fiddle?' He opened the door and raced down the platform to the guard. In unfamiliarly fluent French he persuaded him to hold up the train and ran with him to retrieve the fiddle from the café. They made it. Sigi boarded the last coach and the train started. These were anxious moments for the rest of us as we did not know whether Sigi had been left behind.

Probably most performers can tell similar stories. Maria Lidka once left her violin in a taxi. By a remarkable coincidence the next person to take the taxi was the wife of Robert Masters, who played the violin in a piano quartet. When she opened the case, she recognized Maria Lidka's name and immediately phoned her.

Being part of a quartet meant that the players could help each other whilst travelling. It was always a challenge to smuggle the cumbersome cello onto a plane without paying for it. They would start by buying a ticket for the cello, but they would try not to use it. At the check-in desk, Peter would present all the tickets except the one for the cello. Martin, Norbert and Sigi would then close up, hiding the cello behind them, and Sigi would ask a series of questions to divert attention, like 'Do you serve Kosher meals on the plane?', 'Are we leaving on time?', or 'Is there a danger we may miss our connection?' More often than not – before the present tight security arrangements – this might work. The next hurdle was gaining entry into the plane. Efficient stewards at the top of the gangway would ask if they had a ticket for the cello, to which they of course replied, 'Yes, we have.' Only once did a super-efficient steward go on to say, 'Have you actually checked it in?' Once on the plane the cello would go into one of the many places the Quartet had managed to discover on each type of aircraft where it could be stowed without being seen or causing an obstruction. Looking back over the forty years of the Quartet's existence, Susi said she thought that the strain on Martin had been not merely the physical effort of carrying a heavy cello and loading it into cars and taxis, but anxiety at the prospect of having to do so.

At various times it seemed as if they might also have to smuggle on the fiddles as well. At the end of their North American tour in December 1967, Sigi wrote to Mariedi Anders, the Quartet's agent in the USA, saying, 'We nearly could not fly home on the Pan Am flight! They would not allow the two violins and Peter's viola into the cabin. Apparently, under a new safety rule, our fiddle cases are an inch longer than what is allowed. They would not even let us demonstrate that they fit perfectly under the seat.' Occasionally, when Martin had been compelled to put his cello in the hold, he had supervised the loading and strapping. But how can you strap down a violin case safely? Who would be responsible for any damage to these superb instruments, which could never be replaced if anything happened to them? Sigi tried to argue that if he tied the fiddle case to his body, he would only be so many inches fatter, and that there were plenty of people on board who were fatter than he was together with the case. 'There were ugly scenes at the gate. We threatened to go home by boat (heaven forbid!) and eventually some top brass turned up who allowed us to take them into the cabin. He happened to play the guitar and admitted that he himself would never allow it to go into the hold.' This was the second time the problem had occurred in the States, and if the rule had continued in force it could have made it difficult for the Quartet to tour there. Fortunately it was relaxed, and on their later visits there was no further trouble.

Cherished instruments become an integral part of a performer's way of life. They have to be guarded and cared for like children, and never left unattended, even in a car. Should they be lost or damaged, the trauma is profound.

# CHAPTER NINE

# Making
# Records

As the years went by, recording became increasingly important to the Amadeus. At the beginning of their career, concerts and radio broadcasts had predominated and it was not until the end of the 1950s that income from recording became significant. Whereas in 1950 they spent only eight days recording, in 1959 it was as many as twenty-four and, throughout the next decade, an average of sixteen days a year. Moreover, these recordings began to take place in Germany rather than in London.

In the early days the Quartet ran into many difficulties over contracts and distribution. The complexities and ramifications of the arrangements with gramophone companies are a mystery to the outside world and, as the Amadeus were soon to find out, very often to the musicians as well. But records and the publicity they generate are critical to the success of a group. Tours by the Amadeus in North America in particular suffered because their records were not widely available there. They had started with a few 'title' contracts for Decca and His Master's Voice (HMV) in 1949 and 1950, and in January 1951 they made a series of recordings for the American Westminster company. It was because of the high quality of these recordings that the Quartet was invited to come to the USA for the first time in 1953. Soon afterwards, however, this company ran into difficulties and folded up. Then, again in 1953, HMV – whose partner in the USA was RCA Victor – approached the Quartet to enter into an 'exclusive' contract with them. No sooner had they come to a verbal understanding than DGG also asked them to make an exclusive contract. Some hard bargaining took place between the gramophone companies. HMV did not release the Amadeus from their verbal agreement, but they did agree to improve their royalties and advance payments to bring them into line with the offer from DGG.

Following the talks between HMV and DGG, the Amadeus proposed an HMV/DGG joint contract. But although the two companies were in principle willing to make one, such an arrangement was at first found to be impossible because of their separate international links. The problem was that HMV had a contractual commitment to pass on any recordings they did both to

RCA Victor in the USA and to Columbia in Germany. Similarly, although in Europe and Japan DGG distributed under its own yellow label, in America they were obliged to pass on their recordings to the American Decca company. Accordingly, both in America and Germany competitors would have had access to the same tapes and plans for future activities.

The two companies found a solution, however, by drawing up a special joint contract that altered their legal obligations towards their international partners. Such a contract was signed on 1st May 1953. HMV retained distribution rights in the UK and the Commonwealth, and DGG took over the rest of Europe and Japan: RCA, being the partner of HMV, became the Amadeus's distributor in America. It seemed an ideal arrangement. The Quartet would record either for DGG in Germany or for HMV in Britain, and each company would then simply use the same tapes.

Soon afterwards, unfortunately for the Quartet the connection between HMV (EMI) and RCA was broken because of the US anti-trust laws. In order to have an outlet in the USA, HMV then bought the Angel company based in Los Angeles. This company, which already had the Hollywood Quartet under contract, was slow in publishing and lukewarm in promoting the Amadeus. Then Angel was bought by Capitol who persuaded HMV to cut back on its less profitable business in chamber music. HMV therefore asked to be released from their joint contract with DGG who consequently became the sole and exclusive company for the Amadeus Quartet in 1959.

Initially DGG had weak sales in the USA, partly because some Americans still did not readily buy from a company with a German name. DGG were aware of this and started distributing under the name of Polydor. Even so, the distribution of Amadeus recordings in America, unlike in Japan, was never satisfactory. They were at a disadvantage compared with the Juilliard who, after the break-up between HMV and RCA in America, had become the house quartet for RCA and with the Guarneri who were the house quartet for Columbia.

The Amadeus continued to have an exclusive contract with DGG for the next twenty years. During this time, and during the earlier period when there was the joint contract with HMV, they recorded (and sometimes re-recorded) all the string quartets by Beethoven and Mozart, around thirty by Haydn, the three by Brahms, and nearly all the quartets by Schubert. They also re-corded quartets by Dvořák, Mendelssohn, Smetana, Tchaikovsky and Verdi. However, the recordings of Benjamin Britten's quartets nos. 2 and 3 were done for Decca because Britten was exclusively an artist for Decca and special arrangements had to be made between the companies to make it possible. Likewise a dispensation had to be granted when the Amadeus made a re-cording of a work by the Canadian composer, Ernest MacMillan, for CBS in 1967. A full list of the Quartet's recordings is given in Appendix 4.

The recordings they made in conjunction with other artists were of great importance. The cellist William Pleeth and the viola player Cecil Aronowitz regularly joined them to record quintets and sextets. The Mozart wind quartets brought them together with various members of the Berlin Philharmonic Orchestra – the flautist Andreas Blau, the oboist Lothar Koch and the horn players Gerd Seifert and Manfred Klier. The Brahms clarinet quintet was recorded with Karl Leister, also a member of the Berlin Philharmonic. However, they recorded the Mozart clarinet quintet with Gervase de Peyer. They were joined by various pianists to record the Beethoven, Brahms and Mozart piano quartets – Emil Gilels, Murray Perahia and Walter Klien. They played Schubert's *Trout* quintet in 1958 with Hephzibah Menuhin and James Merrett, and again in 1975 with Emil Gilels and Rainer Zepperitz.

A major disappointment was that it was impossible for them to record with Clifford Curzon, with whom they regularly gave many concerts. He was exclusively an artist for Decca, who would not release him, and in just the same way DGG would not release the Amadeus. The only record they made together was of the two Mozart piano quartets in 1952, well before the Amadeus became exclusive artists for HMV.* Apart from the Brahms piano quintet, in which they were joined by Christopher Eschenbach, the Amadeus did not record any of the important and popular piano quintets such as those by Dvořák, César Franck, Brahms and Schumann, which they habitually played in concerts with Clifford Curzon. The Quartet had a tremendous admiration for Clifford. He was the pianist with the best tone they had ever come across and he could make the piano sing in such a way that you would forget that it was a percussion instrument. Moreover, he knew how to blend with them to produce real chamber music. Tremendous nervous energy went into his playing. With his small head and Jewish nose he would pick at things, birdlike, until he was satisfied. Musically he was a perfectionist: never content with the good, it had to be the best. Although he could be kind and thoughtful, he was never an easy person. Sigi used to turn the pages for him in the *Trout* quintet (there being no part for the second fiddle), but he regarded it as a worse strain than performing himself. After a second's delay in the page-turning, Clifford might say, 'You can't read music,' to which Sigi would reply, 'You can't even play two bars from memory.' Rosamund Strode, who was Benjamin Britten's amanuensis, recalls that Clifford would never have a woman as a page-turner, although on one occasion she was allowed to turn pages during a recording. 'I believe that was unique,' she said.

The Quartet had a long and fruitful association with Cecil Aronowitz.

* The BBC, however, are now planning to issue some of the recordings they have in their archives of Clifford Curzon playing with the Amadeus.

They recorded all the Mozart viola quintets with him, starting as far back as 1951, when they recorded Mozart's G minor quintet, K516, for the Westminster company. Bruckner, Beethoven and Brahms followed in the 1960s. Cecil's collaboration with the Amadeus took him all over the world with them. They loved him and admired his vitality, his musicianship and his ability to make music out of what they regarded as 'an old cigar box' of a viola. Laughingly, Norbert once said that Cecil's great pride was that his viola case was more expensive than his viola. During one concert, the 'box' came unstuck and he had to borrow an Amati, an excellent viola. He didn't like it nearly as much. Cecil's pianist widow, Nicola, has written of Cecil's tremendous respect for the 'boys', as the Amadeus Quartet were sometimes known. 'What he loved best about playing with them,' she writes, 'was that every concert and every recording was an event; there was never any sense of routine or of boredom.'

In 1978, while playing the Mozart C major quintet with another group at the Maltings in Suffolk, Cecil suddenly collapsed with a stroke and died soon afterwards. He fell on top of his much loved instrument, smashing it. It was painstakingly and lovingly repaired by Charles Beare. A few years later, an ex-pupil, Eric Rycroft, bought it from Nicola and coaxed it back to life. He now plays it in Cecil's native South Africa both as a soloist and in the Endler Trio, and also as principal viola in the Cape Philharmonic Orchestra.

Throughout his playing career Cecil was also a teacher. Towards the end of his life, he became head of strings first of all at the Royal Northern College in Manchester and then at the new School for Advanced Musical Studies at the Maltings in Snape. Sir Peter Pears said of him at his memorial concert, 'to watch him at work was to be aware that he was a great teacher, immensely gentle and tirelessly persistent.'

He was always kind and generous, and his flat was a gathering place for many people. When talking about his eccentricities, Nobert has told how Cecil liked to put jam on everthing he ate. One day when he was in a restaurant and had asked for fish and chips, he said to the waiter, 'Have you any jam?' 'Sorry sir, but we do have some marmalade.' Who has ever heard of marmalade and fish! Cecil loved children and, although he and Nicola were later to have a son and a daughter, during the time when the Quartet children were young he did not have any of his own. Claire, Anmarie, Sonia and Peter will all certainly remember the white-bearded Father Christmas in a red gown who came through the big window of his Holland Park flat carrying a sack with presents for the many children at his Christmas parties.

After Cecil died, the Amadeus rarely played viola quintets. He had been so much a part of their ensemble that a satisfactory replacement was scarcely possible. For a while, when they were at the Cologne Conservatoire, they played with a fellow teacher, Rainer Moog. Then occasionally they were joined by Kenneth Essex, with whom they had played at the outset of their career.

The only other person with whom they developed such a close relationship was William Pleeth, more familiarly known as 'Bill'. As with Cecil Aronowitz, the Quartet's association with him began early. In 1952, they recorded the Schubert cello quintet, D956 in C major, with him at the EMI studios in London. Then in 1965 they re-recorded it for DGG. In the same period they also recorded the two Brahms sextets, Opus 18 in B flat major and Opus 36 in G major, with both William Pleeth and Cecil Aronowitz.

Before the Quartet was formed, Norbert had played in a successful piano trio with Pleeth and Edmund Rubbra, and Bill was upset when Norbert finally decided that the Quartet was to be a full-time commitment. Bill's playing was fiery and full of temperament, and he had a remarkable tone quality ranging from a finely spun sensitive tone to the gruff grittiness that is sometimes called for. His sense of colour and his musical understanding were qualities the Quartet itself could often learn from. Like Cecil, he quite naturally became what might be called a 'fifth member'. He was also an excellent teacher. His outstanding pupil was Jacqueline du Pré whom he nursed all the way from a child into a fully mature artist – 'my cello daddy,' as she used to call him. He was always reliable and fun to be with, both during rehearsals and after concerts.

On one occasion during the mid-1960s, when the Quartet was scheduled to do a succession of recordings with other artists, DGG had arranged for them to record with Cecil Aronowitz at their studio in West Berlin. The recording was to begin on Easter Monday. When Sigi went to the safe to get his passport, he realized with horror that he had lodged it with our bank. With difficulty he managed to get hold of the manager, who was prepared to come and open the bank's safe; but unfortunately this needed the collaboration of a second person who was on a sailing holiday over the weekend. The Passport Office was unhelpful. However, this was long before airlines could insist on examining your passport before agreeing to carry you as a passenger and there was nothing to prevent Sigi leaving the country without a valid passport. So, anxiously, he left for London airport carrying his out-of-date passport. When the Quartet arrived at Frankfurt, they and Cecil were to catch the onward flight to West Berlin, which was still encircled by East Germany. To his relief Sigi found that the German airport authorities were accustomed to such problems and he was able immediately to obtain a temporary document entitling him to enter Germany and thus fly on to Berlin. All was well on that occasion, but it is an example of the problems that add to the tensions of a performer's life.

Relations with DGG were to become strained when the Amadeus wanted to re-record all the Beethoven quartets. Their original recordings had been made between 1959 and 1963. In the meantime the Quartet had played many Beethoven programmes and complete cycles throughout the world, and they wished to document the steady development of their interpretation during this long period. They had also, in 1974, made a television recording of five Beethoven quartets for Polyphon who produced television tapes for commercial sale. DGG argued that the early Amadeus recordings were still selling well and the Quartet would merely create their own competition if they attempted to re-record. However, DGG did agree to re-record the late Beethoven quartets, starting with Opus 133 and Opus 135, in June 1977. The set was completed with Opus 131 in July 1981, but only this final recording was made using the new digital techniques, so that the set was already out of date technically when it appeared.

From 1981 onwards the Amadeus recordings dwindled to little more than a trickle. They merely re-recorded some of the more popular quartets, such as Mozart's *Hunt*, Haydn's *Emperor* and Schubert's *Death and the Maiden*; and in March 1986 they made their last record with DGG, the Schubert cello quintet, with Robert Cohen on the cello.

At the beginning of 1987 – surprisingly, because it had now been bought by DGG's parent company – the Amadeus came to an agreement with Decca to record all the Beethoven quartets. The first part of the set, Opus 59, no.3, and Opus 74, was completed in July 1987. Sadly, their dream of re-recording the complete set could never be realized because of Peter's tragic death a month later.

The association with DGG, which came to an end in 1986, had been long and close. In 1973, the Quartet's twenty-fifth anniversary, they had been given DGG's most prestigious award, the Golden Gramophone. The break with the company was distressing and the sudden coldness upsetting, for many of the people who had worked with the Quartet had come to be regarded as friends. Moreover, they heard only indirectly through Michael MacLeod, their administrator, that they were to be quietly dropped. No word of explanation for the change in policy. No recognition of nearly thirty years' collaboration with the company. There was of course a change of generation at DGG and some of the original staff who had been so supportive earlier in their career, like Frau Professor Schiller and Dr Steinhausen, the technical director in Hanover, were no longer with the company. Some of the newer people in DGG were increasingly critical of their style of playing and anxious to replace them with younger quartets.

While the Amadeus had been DGG artists, they had had many a good time together. They fondly remember one such occasion. One day, when they had worked very hard and the producer had decided 'they had it in the bag,' they all began to fool around to relieve the tension that builds up during an intensive session. Sigi has described what happened: 'We had been recording

Beethoven Opus 18, no.5, and what we did was each of us play someone else's instrument. Norbert played the cello, Peter played the first fiddle, I played the viola and Martin played the second fiddle holding my violin between his knees. We started the variation movement, and the recording technicians thought this was a tremendous thing, and kept the microphones on without telling us. Then next Christmas a parcel arrived, a present from DGG to us, and in it were tiny little seven-inch records for each of us with a properly printed label on each side. A very nice letter was included wishing us a happy Christmas and asking whether we would be so kind as to compare the test record of the Gottlieb Quartet on one side with the same movement played on the other side by the Amadeus. The names of the players in the Gottlieb Quartet were given as Peter Schidel, Martin Lovnin, Siegmund Nisslof and Norbert Brainett.' Maybe with tongue in cheek, Sigi added, 'The awful thing is that some of the things in the foolish record were not much worse than those which had been unsatisfactory in the real recording session!'

Another time, to celebrate the silver jubilee of one of the DGG directors, the company decided to produce a special record. On one side there were classical artists producing 'pop' numbers and on the other pop artists trying to produce some classical music. Fischer-Dieskau and the Amadeus were rather better in the pop field than the pop artists were in the classical world.

The Quartet never liked recording bits and pieces. They felt that if they went for a whole movement, or at least large parts of one, they would get closer to a public performance. So they always went for the big take. In some cases, which were rare, they managed to do whole movements without any editing. For instance, in the Schubert G major quartet recorded in 1951, some of the long movements were done in this way. Sigi felt particularly happy about the Beethoven Opus 18s because they were recorded all in one go in Hanover in September 1961. 'I immediately felt we had done a very, very good job.'

The way they worked was influenced by the recording techniques of the time. When they first recorded the Mozart G major quartet in 1950, EMI was using the prevailing method of recording on wax. This matrix was then used to prepare the master print from which the records were made in the factory. The process meant that it was not possible to listen back to what had just been recorded because putting a needle on the wax would have destroyed the grooves. The only way of working was to make a number of test records for the Quartet to choose from.

An additional problem was that records were limited to four minutes per side so that suitable breaks in the music had to be carefully selected. Consequently on many occasions a side was rounded off at a place where a break would never have occurred in a concert. It might also happen that if there was a tight squeeze before a suitable break, a movement might have to be played faster than would ever have seemed possible. Old recordings of quartets, such as the Busch or Flonzaley, for example, are much influenced by such technical limitations.

The next major development in recording techniques was the invention of the variable groove. Loud passages need a wider groove than soft ones. When a means was found of varying the width accordingly, it was possible to get much more onto a record than previously, say, some eight or nine minutes instead of four. The Schubert G major was recorded by the Quartet in this way. These records were still 78 rpm, and the variable grooves can be seen shimmering on the surface of the record.

The first long-playing records, with a speed of $33\frac{1}{3}$ rpm, came on the market soon after the Amadeus started recording. Initially these were mono recordings: stereo was not introduced until rather later in the 1950s. Another substantial advance was the introduction of tapes. It meant that whatever was played was recorded on tape at the same time and could immediately be listened to afterwards. There was no need to wait for a test record to decide what was to be selected. This not only gave the Quartet a much greater chance to improve on what they had just been playing in the studio but made it possible to splice sections of recordings, combining a very good recording of the first half of a movement from take 1 with a good second half from take 2.

Originally the Quartet would sit down with the producer, listen back to the various tapes and prepare an editing plan. Later, when they had more experience of working with a particular team led by a producer whose musical judgement they could trust, they would discuss the recording session with the team and leave the producer to decide on the final editing. The disadvantage was that not being 'in' on the final detailed work of editing took away something of the feeling that they themselves had made the record.*

The process of recording invariably helps to improve the playing itself. When players listen back, they can criticize themselves and get suggestions from the producer. It is rather like playing in front of a mirror. The replay shows up whether, for example, the playing was together and whether somebody was too loud or too soft: there could be no argument about it. The concentration that results from this continuous process of criticizing and being criticized is something that is not achieved to quite the same degree in rehearsals for public concerts. As Sigi says, 'When you have gone again and again through a learning process, hopefully the results in the next concert make it quite apparent that you have gone deeper into the music. It might

* In his book, *The Amadeus Quartet* (Robson Books, London, 1981), Daniel Snowman gives a most revealing description of the way the Quartet worked during their recording of the Verdi quartet, in October 1979, in Munich (pages 84–94).

even be said that you don't really know a piece until you have recorded it and played it in public.'

However, the way the Amadeus played works after recording sessions rarely changed dramatically. Any changes were of a subtle nature, such as slight variations in tempi within a movement. The experience they had gained both from playing in public and from recordings helped to explain why they felt so deeply that they should re-record the Beethoven quartets. In their later years, they thought they played with much greater freedom and projection than early on when they were more concerned to make sure that everything was neat, together and in tune. Their playing may have become rougher but it was more eloquent and the artistic results better.

They tried mainly to record works they had already played in public. But there were exceptions. They learnt some of the early Mozart quartets and divertimenti specifically for recording. Mozart was so much part of their life that it is hardly surprising that the results were amazingly good. Indeed there is a quality in all their Schubert and Mozart records that corresponds to the talent and gifts natural to them.

All the same, recording can never be the same as playing to a live audience in a concert hall. Being in a recording studio creates a different attitude amongst players. The studio has neither the deadness nor the big echo of certain halls, and there is naturally no audience. A long pause, which might be eloquent in a concert hall, does not work in the same way on a record because little of the special atmosphere comes over. Records cannot replace live concerts since the presence of both artist and audience at the particular moment of a performance affects the psyche of both. That being said, in their records the Amadeus did seek to recapture something of how they played a work in public.

# CHAPTER TEN

# We All Go
## to the United States

───────────

After the operation to remove the tumour on his brain in August 1960, Sigi started playing again in November that year, little more than four months after the Quartet's previous concert. 1961 saw them fully back in action with concerts as far afield as Scandinavia, Austria, Hungary, Czechoslovakia and North America as well as on regular tours of Germany and the UK. In 1962 they had their busiest year ever with no less than 135 concerts, ten radio sessions and two major recording periods doing the late Beethoven quartets for DGG in Berlin.

Despite this full schedule, Sigi managed to be back from concerts in Israel and Cyprus at the beginning of September 1962 in time for the birth of our second child, Daniel, at midnight on 18th September 1962. His father decided his birthday should be Tuesday the 18th rather than Wednesday the 19th, since Tuesday's child is 'full of grace', whereas Wednesday's is 'full of woe'. Claire, who was four and a half, strongly resented this intruder in our family. Her nursery school found that they could no longer handle her and in the middle of the autumn term, much to everyone's relief, we managed to persuade the local infants' school to take her. She loved it and flourished.

There was a further change in our household in the spring of 1963 when Jean Hubbard became our much loved housekeeper. While we had previously relied on lodgers for baby-sitting, we decided that with the arrival of our second child we needed living-in help. Jean worked part-time for us and also studied singing part-time at the Guildhall School of Music and Dance. When she came at the age of sixteen she was a plump country bumpkin, unrecognizable in later years when the horn-rimmed glasses had given way to contact lenses and she had become a slim, sophisticated and much travelled young lady. She had been helping in a nursery school run by a friend of mine, who had been organ scholar at St Hugh's College when we were at Oxford and had been teaching singing to Jean. She had a blunt Yorkshire approach to life, an easy outgoing personality and a firm but kindly way with the children. During the seven years she was with us, she helped give them the stability that is so important in early life. With many regrets, we finally said goodbye to her at the wedding reception in our house in 1970 when she became Mrs Haines. She was never to develop into a professional singer but she has continued to give pleasure to the many people who have heard her in amateur performances.

By the mid-1960s the Quartet had been active for almost twenty years and was well established. It had survived the serious illnesses of two of its members. All four were playing on good instruments, whether bought or borrowed; they were all married with children and their families were living in comfortable houses. Their ambition was to remain established as an internationally famous string quartet. This inevitably entailed extensive touring but, with their growing families and the continual strains of separation from them, they had been considering whether they might find a congenial university which could give them a certain security for at least part of the year.

At that time there were no posts for string quartets at universities in the United Kingdom but there were possibilities in the United States. The Griller String Quartet, who had originally been based in England, had achieved just that at Berkeley in California and, while the Amadeus were touring North America in 1960 and 1963, they were keeping half an ear to the ground. But they were aware of the disadvantages of settling in the USA for a long period. A residency in the USA would tend to isolate them, and they would inevitably lose some of the prestige and stimulus of being a European quartet. They would have less flexibility for touring worldwide, and more time would have to be spent giving concerts in small American towns.

In 1965 the Amadeus were invited to play and teach at the prestigious Summer School at Aspen in Colorado. This was to be followed by an extensive tour of the United States and, as the Quartet would be away for a long time, the families all decided to go too – making a party of eight grown-ups and six children. The visit would give a much needed opportunity for husbands and wives and children to be together. The Brainins and the Nissels went by boat and on 11th June Sigi and I, together with Claire, aged seven, and Daniel, aged two and a half, embarked from Southampton on the *Queen Elizabeth*.

It took five days for us to reach New York. Sigi, Claire and Daniel got up early to watch as we sailed past the Statue of Liberty, only to see it hazily through fog. We stayed for a few days in the Wellington Hotel on 57th Street. It was immensely exciting at long last actually living amongst those towering buildings we had seen so often in photographs: the streets, with numbers but mostly without names, criss-crossing in solid squares, except for a defiant Broadway daring to snake its obtrusive way from one straight line to another. So unlike anything we had known in Europe. 'Jay walking' was prohibited and you were not supposed to cross the road except when the sign flashed 'Walk'. Sirens howled from police cars and ambulances. If anything personifies New York, it is this continual wailing, not just during the day but all night long. The people were bluntly friendly and kind with the children. Everything was extremely expensive and, if we were to enjoy ourselves, we had to close our minds to converting prices from dollars to sterling. We also had to get used to the enormous portions served in restaurants. It was my first visit to New York as well as the children's, so we did the usual tourist things like going to the top of the Empire State Building, then the tallest building in New York, and visiting the World Fair. For Daniel it was a new experience to go around with Dad. The Quartet had hardly been home at all during the 1964–5 season and he had not seen much of his father apart from a holiday in Cornwall and a visit to the Dartington Summer School the previous summer. When Sigi picked him up to take him across the street a look of surprise, almost terror, came into his small boy's face and a couple of arms were thrust beseechingly towards me!

Friends made us feel welcome. Vera Colbert (the daughter of Henry and Ann Colbert who had originally been the Quartet's agents in North America) and her husband, Lucien, drove us on sightseeing tours around New York, as did Sigi's childhood friend from Munich days, Gordon Lindauer, and his wife, Ruth. Gordon – like Sigi – had escaped from Germany and come first to England before going to the USA. In New York, like so many immigrants, he had worked extremely hard. His job was in a meat-packing factory and eventually he managed not only to buy a comfortable apartment in a block opposite the Cloisters, way uptown in Manhattan, but also to send both of his children to university and establish them in successful professional careers.

William Baumol and his wife Hilda also came over to New York from Princeton to see us. I had recently completed my research in Britain for a book on the performing arts which Professor Baumol was writing together with Professor Bowen,* and in the spring I had sent him the last batch of papers. My brief acquaintance with William whilst he was in London at the beginning of the study had told me that he had one of the finest minds I had encountered. A comparison with a computer would be an insult but, when you fed him a problem, you waited for a response which would come through quickly and with logical precision, tempered with human understanding and experience. He was not only a great economist, with chairs at both Princeton and New York University, but also an artist, a gift Princeton recognized by giving him a studio on the campus where he taught sculpture to students.

I was a little apprehensive about the meeting with the Baumols. Although they had met the Quartet after a concert during the Beethoven series at the Fishmongers' Hall in London in 1964, they did not really know Sigi, and

* William J. Baumol and William G. Bowen, *Performing Arts: the Economic Dilemma*, the Twentieth Century Fund, New York, 1966.

I feared that my musical husband and this high-powered academic might not take to each other. But I need not have worried. When they came to New York, we went to see Edward Albee's powerful four-character play, *Who's Afraid of Virginia Woolf?* and over the meal we had afterwards William and Sigi soon found a bond in good food and telling jokes. Warm-hearted Hilda put us at our ease too. Sharp-featured, hunched and less than five feet high, she and William – dome-headed and a tall straight six feet – looked an incongruous pair. We had many common interests. They became dear friends and holidays were often shared together over the rest of our lives.

William's 'Fafufnik' stories were classics and were quickly added to Sigi's already abundant store of jokes. 'Once,' said William imitating a Bronx Jewish accent, 'Fafufnik goes to a very fashionable and expensive tailor – Cohen and Cohen on Park Avenue. He says, "Mr Cohen, I would like to order a soot." "Yes, Mr Fafufnik." "How much would a soot be?" "About $2,000." "That's a lot of money: how come that you are so much more expensive than any other tailor?" "I vwill tell you. Foist of all you get the normal measuring, very skilfully done so that it should rreally fit you properly but, in addition to that, vwe have on our staff a trained psychologist who vwill give you a little analysis so that vwe know vwhat kind of poissonality you are. Vwhen vwe know that, vwe send it by bush telegraph into the midst of Australia vwhere vwe have an agent to collect the right kind of vwool to make the right kind of cloth to suit your poissonality. The vwool is gathered and is vwoven and sent to us. Vwe can then begin to make the soot and you vwill have three to four fittings so that vwe can make a really finished product." "I can now see why you charge $2,000 with all those services, but I have a praablem: I have to go to a Bar-mitzvah in only two days and I need a new suit for that." "Mr Fafufnik, you can have it!" '

When the Baumols heard that we were coming to New York, Hilda had written asking us to stay with them in Princeton, but I had replied saying that the idea of four Nissels in their house on top of all the work they had to do 'is not one which should be entertained and the Nissels in holiday mood would feel themselves an unnecessary interference.' But stay with them we did, and they and their two children, then aged fifteen and thirteen, were marvellously kind and hospitable. It was unusually hot, and every day I took the children to a nearby swimming pool whilst William wrote and Sigi practised Michael Tippett's third string quartet, newly written for the Amadeus, in the Baumols' study, the only air-conditioned room in their rambling old university house with its strange musk-like scent. A huge fan on the top floor drew in air with a loud whirring sound to cool the rest of the house.

At the end of June we flew to Denver in Colorado and rented a car to take us to Aspen. The Festival lasted for nine weeks. Teaching played an important part and provided a wide range of options for the students, with college credits being available in most subjects. The Amadeus gave chamber-music tuition and one of Sigi's students, Tony Rapport, subsequently came to England on a Fulbright scholarship to form a string quartet in London and continue her lessons with him. The Amadeus also took part in many concerts and gave the American première of Tippett's third quartet. The composer himself was at the Summer School and helped with the interpretation of this complicated and difficult work. They had known him for many years and had a great respect for him. One of the stories they tell is how, some years later, they visited him at his house in Wiltshire to get his critical views on their playing of his second string quartet. They had played it so many times that they feared they might have moved away from what he intended. To their surprise he was deeply moved by his own music and, with tears in his eyes, said, 'Damn it, it makes me cry!'

Concerts in Aspen at that time took place in a large marquee. It was all very informal and the children often came for part of a performance. Afterwards, just when it was supper-time followed by bedtime for the children, the cocktail round would begin – nearly always with the same people, and usually with the same food and waiters. Although we had good friends among the many musicians, it was not easy to make satisfactory arrangements for baby-sitting. Travelling abroad with small children is always a problem. Routines are disturbed and familiar toys are not around to comfort a fretful child. Daniel always liked to go to bed sucking an old piece of pyjama. At the beginning of the tour we took the precaution of cutting it in half and hiding this second piece so that it could be produced quickly if the other half was lost. During our three months in the USA, the remaining piece had to be cut in half so many times that it was little more than a tiny rag when we finally came home! Somewhere to play was another problem. We were in a first-floor apartment with no space outside except in the dusty road. However, there were three students in the same block who took pity on Claire and Daniel – Peter Dominic, his friend Paul, and Carris Durrance whose parents were involved in the Chamber Music Society in Denver. One night we came back to find a rocking-horse had mysteriously arrived on our balcony. The students had found it in someone's back garden and had quietly 'borrowed' it. Unfortunately it was missed by its owner and had to go back. But many months later, when we returned to London, a large crate arrived and inside we found a collection of bright yellow wooden pieces which fitted together to make a real, solid rocking-camel! They had made it themselves and sent it to our children with their love. We still have it, and it has given great pleasure to the many children who have ridden it.

After we had been in Aspen for nearly three weeks, the Quartet left for a fortnight on the West Coast where they were to take part in the Stanford

Honorary degrees at the University of York, 1968 (*above*) and Nissel, Schidlof
and Lovett as new recipients of the Order of the British Empire, 1970 (*below*)

Nissel and Brainin with Sir Edward
Heath after the Silver Jubilee concert,
1973

Michael MacLeod, the Quartet's
administrator

The Nissels, Fanny Waterman and the Duchess of Kent admire the silk
programme specially commissioned for the Edward Boyle Memorial
Concert at the Royal Opera House

Nissel teaching the Auer Quartet at the Amadeus Summer Course, 1991

Città di Castello, 1986

Muriel and Siegmund Nissel, 1998

Summer Festival of the Arts, teaching in the music department and giving concerts. Their welcome was tremendous. Robert Commanday, the music critic on the *San Francisco Chronicle*, wrote, 'A sense of adventure always accompanies the first hearing of a visiting string quartet and the discovery of its uniquely complex personality. The Amadeus String Quartet opened its series of six concerts at the Stanford Mozart Festival on Monday and what a remarkable personality it turned out to have. The healthy vitality of their playing is immediately apparent ... it was full-bodied Haydn: they played as though the ink were still drying.' Part of the secret that lay behind this vigour and spontaneity was the large and varied repertoire they managed to put together. Some idea of this repertoire is documented in Appendix 1. Although it relates to a later season, that of 1972–3, the extent and diversity of the programming is clear, even on long tours like those in Japan and Australia. Mariedi Anders, who had recently become their agent in North America, was amazed. 'You wanted a different programme on each day,' she once said; 'that is unique.' The Amadeus found this a way of staying fresh, an element which is sometimes missing from other quartets. Looking back on their career, Sigi thought that one of the reasons for their popularity was that there was always a sense of adventure about their concerts.

When the Quartet went to the West Coast I remained in Aspen. I found the separation from Sigi unbearable and so I decided to join them in Stanford. Katinka drove me and the children to Boulder whence we took a bus to Denver and then flew to San Francisco. For the first few days we stayed on the campus but then Adolf Baller, the pianist of the Alma Trio, and his wife kindly lent us their house in Palo Alto whilst they were away. They had a large dog and a swimming pool, and the children were immensely happy. When we were there, we managed to explore some possible places by the sea for a holiday after the Aspen Summer School was over. We discovered the beautiful little town of Carmel, named after the bay discovered at the beginning of the seventeenth century by a Spanish explorer who had with him a group of Carmelite monks. A natural pool had formed inside the sand dunes and it would be quite safe for the children to bathe. We immediately reserved a chalet attached to a hotel.

The Quartet returned to Aspen after Stanford and played its last concert there on 28th August. We then began our family holiday in the Carmel chalet. This was followed by brief visits to San Francisco and to Disneyland in Los Angeles: then after a tour through Yosemite National Park we drove across the hot Arizona desert to the Grand Canyon.

We had a short stay in San Francisco where I met Mariedi Anders for the first time. The Quartet had never been satisfied with the way they had been treated by their original agents, Henry and Ann Colbert, and in January 1964 they had concluded an agreement with Mariedi Anders Artists Management to represent them in North America. The Colbert agency had a virtual monopoly of chamber music, so they must have been well aware of the prevailing fees, and Sigi was puzzled how they could be so out of touch, or reluctant in the case of the Amadeus, to give them top fees. For the forthcoming tour of North America in 1965 their new agent guaranteed them a tour of thirty concerts at $1,000 per concert compared with the $600–$800 being offered by the Colberts. This new fee was more in line with what quartets such as the Juilliard were receiving.* After the break-up with the Colbert agency, Sigi wrote to Vera Colbert, Henry and Ann's daughter, saying, 'Your mother surely must have known from our correspondence and attitude prior to the last tour that we were dead serious in being dissatisfied with the USA fees, particularly as the profit earned there is now far below the corresponding figure in Europe per concert played ... The firm offer we have now received proves beyond a shadow of doubt that our expectations of what we are worth in USA are based on hard reality.'

Mariedi Anders' first contact with the Amadeus had been in July 1959 when she met Martin and Susi at the Casals Festival in Prades. She vividly remembers the meeting and she has described it in her thick Viennese accent: 'When I was at the Casals Festival in Prades, Lovett was there playing the cello. It was actually my first trip abroad and my husband Ernst bought me a Mercedes, a white convertible with two red leather seats. I got in touch with Lovett and they drove with me from Prades to Molitg-les-Bains where I was staying. There were only two seats and Susi was sitting next to me but, as the top was open, Martin somehow also managed to get in by standing up. That's when he told me about the Amadeus Quartet: I didn't even know he was the cellist of the Quartet. That is how it all started – in my new car.'

Mariedi was a keen music lover and an admirer of the Amadeus Quartet. She asked Martin why the Quartet did not play in San Francisco. He said their agents were no good and suggested she might try and find out what could be done. This prompted her to ferret out the possibilities by contacting agents and concert organizers. She then began to think that she herself might become an agent.

She and Ernst had come to the USA as refugees from Vienna shortly before the war. With some $8 in their pockets they went to Milwaukee, where she found a job as a cigarette girl in a nightclub and Ernst started work as an 'oiler' in a hotel. They also secretly made *liptauer* cheese in their tiny apartment. They did not have a car, so Mariedi took a bus to the outskirts of the city where there were large dairy farms who sold her cottage cheese wholesale.

---

* However, according to the biography written by Nat Brandt, the Budapest Quartet were being offered $1,350 by the Buffalo Music Society in 1964: Nat Brandt, *Con Brio, Four Russians Called the Budapest String Quartet*, Oxford University Press, Oxford and New York, 1993, page 164.

This was then mixed with butter, paprika, caraway seeds, onions, etc. Little did they realize that the pounds and pounds of onions they were cutting up would smell out the whole apartment block. They used to sell the cheese, which they named Eldorado, at the various delicatessen shops in Milwaukee. One day they were greeted by a furious customer who told them that when she opened the jar the *liptauer* had literally exploded in her face and made the most horrible mess in the shop! So that was the end of the *liptauer* business. Along with two friends, Ernst then began to develop a successful business in fluorescent lighting, first in Milwaukee and then in San Francisco.

When the Quartet first began informal discussions with Mariedi, which paved the way for the agreement they eventually reached, they had been worried because she lived in San Francisco whereas most agencies were concentrated in New York around Carnegie Hall. However, according to Sigi, unlike most agents she overcame this handicap by spending money on telephone calls rather than letters, and negotiations with music clubs were usually concluded speedily. By the time the Amadeus Quartet joined it, her concert agency had been going for barely four years, but she already represented a number of well-known groups. Her 1964–5 list included the Borodin, Vegh and La Salle Quartets as well as the Alma Trio and the Deller Consort. She was clearly delighted to include the Quartet among her artists. When she sent them the contract for signature, she wrote, 'What I feel in my heart for you all has nothing to do with business. It is called admiration, affection and friendship and does not need a signature. It will, however, give you assurance that when I talk to clients about the AMADEUS QUARTET, it will be done with great pride and love!' This, of course, was the honeymoon period and there were arguments to come; but over the years the Quartet and Mariedi kept their warm friendship and respect for each other.

At the end of September, after four months together, I and the children had to leave Sigi behind. We flew back to New York from Phoenix where the Quartet was to perform a complete Beethoven cycle at the University of Arizona. Mariedi Anders wrote to them, 'Meine Liebsten, how are you? Heartbroken because the families have gone home? On the other hand recuperating from the long trips in the desert heat? All told, I hope you are in excellent shape and enjoying life.' After that she went on to write about business matters. There were another thirty-five concerts before they could return home. The first was on 18th October at Riverside in California and, as it marked the opening of their North American tours under her management, she sent them a telegram, '...I send each of you a hug and a kiss and a tender thought with best wishes for a huge success.'

Shortly after we were airborne Daniel suddenly realized that his Daddy wasn't there and he let out the most heart-rending howl. He could utter an extraordinarily unearthly wail and we had some while previously nicknamed him 'Hacotel', because of its association with the Wailing Wall in Jerusalem where Jews come to pray. We had to change planes in New York to take the night flight to London and we found ourselves fog-bound. The airport became more and more crowded as the waiting passengers piled in. It was very hot and the children were fretful. Daniel, now just three years old, discovered escalators and could suddenly be seen disappearing up to the next floor. And there were also doors which could be opened automatically by standing in front of them. Claire managed to lose one of her milk teeth and her mouth started to bleed. Then we were joined by a nine-year-old who had been put on a plane in Washington by his parents with instructions to change in New York. He was on his way back to school, a journey he had done many times before, but he was very lonely. About 3 a.m. we were bundled into buses and taken to a nearby hotel where all four of us managed to get a few hours' rest before returning to the airport, now more crowded than ever. Flights were leaving again, but in those days BOAC, unlike BA today, had little thought to spare for mothers with young children. Their attitude was unbelievably callous and uncaring, and so different from the American airlines who made a real attempt to help. It was a free-for-all with people pushing and shoving. I, with luggage and three kids, didn't stand much of a chance. However, we did finally get airborne and a small – and much appreciated – consolation at the end of the journey was the lady who complimented me on the good behaviour of the children.

The Amadeus finally returned to London at the beginning of December 1965. There had been some vague discussions and offers of residencies by universities in the United States but few serious negotiations. The Quartet and their families came back convinced that they should remain in Europe. Maybe they would have a securer life and a higher standard of living if they spent most of their time in North America, but it could be at the cost of the growing reputation they had attained as a world famous quartet in Europe. They had a devoted audience in all its main cities, and the families too felt their roots to be in Europe. A residency in the United States, like that which the Griller Quartet had had at Berkeley, would not have prevented them from continuing to play in Europe, but crossing the Atlantic for such concerts would have had to be organized as part of prolonged tours. Making a short trip across the Channel to play the odd few concerts in Paris or Amsterdam would no longer have been part of their programme.

# CHAPTER ELEVEN

# Festivals and
# Summer Schools

————————

The Aspen Festival was just one of many such events in which the Amadeus Quartet participated. Festivals and summer schools are an important part of the life of any successful quartet and during their career the Amadeus played at most of the world's most famous music festivals. In Europe, to name but a few, they played in Edinburgh, Aldeburgh, Salzburg, Vienna, Menton, Aix-en-Provence, St Jean-de-Luz, Berlin, Schloss Elmau, Bergen, Holland, Flanders and Prague – and in Japan they played in Osaka.

The leading festivals were Edinburgh and Salzburg, and anyone invited to appear there was immediately recognized as being in the top-rank of international artists. Moreover, as most of the concerts in the Edinburgh Festival were widely broadcast, both in Britain and abroad, there was extensive publicity. The Festival had been started in 1947, soon after the end of the war, under the directorship of Rudolf Bing. In its opening year Sigi had played there with the Jacques Orchestra and met up with his violin teacher from Vienna, Max Weissgaerber, who came to Edinburgh with the Vienna Opera. When the opera was in London after the Festival, the four members who were soon to become the Amadeus Quartet played to him. The Amadeus performed at the Edinburgh Festival for the first time in 1951. A few years later, in 1954, they were invited to the Salzburg Festival. I was spending part of my summer holiday in Hallein with the Mittermayer family, with whom I had been *au pair* the previous summer, and as the Quartet and their wives were staying nearby on Lake Fuschl, I cycled over to visit them.

Festivals and specialist music courses mattered to the Nissel family too in that we could often combine them with holidays. There were many French festivals, most of which usually took place during the summer, and we would drive through France with the children. I would look after them while Sigi rehearsed and played concerts, and afterwards we would have a family holiday. There were three events which played a prominent part in our family life. The first was the Aldeburgh Festival, which was usually held in June, the second the British/German music fortnight which regularly took place in January in Schloss Elmau near the Austrian border in Bavaria, and the third the Music Summer School at Dartington in August.

The Aldeburgh Festival, although it did not have as much prestige internationally as Edinburgh or Salzburg, was well known worldwide because of the influence of Benjamin Britten. For the Quartet its significance lay in the association and friendship with both Benjamin Britten and Peter Pears. The Amadeus played at the Festival almost every year from its inception in 1952, often with Ben himself at the piano. We have fond memories of the Red House where they both lived and of Peter watering the roses by syphoning out the bath water after a dry May and hot sunshine in June.

I first went there in 1957 when we stayed in a cottage not far from Aldeburgh which Kristin Berge had recently bought. During this visit I came under the spell of Imogen Holst. That summer she conducted madrigals on the Mere in the twilight and we listened from our punt with Marion, then Countess of Harewood, alongside with her three young boys. Imogen had the unusual gift of being able to combine a keen intellect with spontaneity and enthusiasm. Later I had the good fortune to become a member of the amateur fringe to her professional group, the Purcell Singers, where I sang Bach cantatas with Rosamund Strode, Sue Pears, Maureen Garnham, Walter Todds, Basil Douglas and others. We only met occasionally when Imo was in London, but the enthusiasm she brought to our rehearsals was unforgettable. If we gave a good performance it was a wonderful lift to the heart to hear Imo's inimitable cry, 'Ai-i-i yai-ii- yai-ii,' as she almost danced with excitement.

At the Aldeburgh Festival in the early summer of 1960, Sigi was already very ill suffering symptoms of his brain tumour. The Quartet's last concert, which included the César Franck quintet with Clifford Curzon at the piano, was to be broadcast and it must have been a nightmare. Sigi remembers the BBC balancer, who did not realize he was ill, at one point saying to him, 'Wakey, wakey'. After Aldeburgh, Sigi was to play only one more concert – in Temple Newsam in Yorkshire – before innumerable tests eventually led to the diagnosis of the tumour and the operation to remove it.

In 1964 the Amadeus played the Schubert cello quintet with Rostropovich as second cello. It was an extraordinary performance. In the adagio movement the first fiddle and the cello have a dialogue together around a colourless accompaniment from the inner strings who have long sustained notes like a chorale. Rostropovich insisted on playing the movement at a very slow tempo so that it took on an entirely different character. Four years later, at the Edinburgh Festival in 1968, they played the piece with him again but at the more usually accepted speed.

The Queen opened a fine new concert hall at the Maltings in Snape in 1967. Until this time the Festival events had mainly taken place in the Jubilee

Hall in Aldeburgh, or in churches, such as those in Aldeburgh, Blythburgh and Orford. The Jubilee Hall was both too small and acoustically unsatisfactory and the churches were not right for large-scale secular works. The new hall, which seated around 800, changed all that. It was not only beautiful but acoustically one of the finest in the world. In 1969 the Quartet opened the Festival there with Purcell's *Chacony* in G minor followed by Schubert's *Trout* quintet, with Britten as pianist.

On this occasion we were staying with our friends the Usherwoods at their cottage on the Green in Walberswick. Later in the evening we saw a glow in the sky. It was not until we listened to the news the next morning that we heard that the new concert hall at the Maltings had been totally destroyed by fire. Adrian Beers, who had performed with the Amadeus earlier in the day, had left his fine eighteenth-century double-bass in the building. It too was burnt, along with Britten's Steinway which had been brought over from the Red House specially for the concert. Although the hall was totally gutted, the four walls were left standing and within a year it had been rebuilt. It was an impressive feat and demonstrated the resolve and will-power of Britten himself who, once he had decided to do something, would see it through with determination and vigour.

Not long afterwards, at the end of 1972, Ben became extremely ill and in May 1973 he was operated on for a heart condition. He was desperately anxious to complete the score of his opera, *Death in Venice*, and delayed going into hospital as long as possible. As soon as the opera was finished, he was operated on in the National Heart Hospital in London and he was recuperating when it was first performed in June at the Aldeburgh Festival. It was broadcast live from the Maltings and, against doctor's orders, Ben switched on the radio and listened to part of it. He heard a tape not long afterwards and a special performance was staged for him in September, just before the opera reopened at the Maltings for a short season.*

Ben never really recovered from the operation and was too frail for further surgery. He suffered a kind of stroke which affected his right hand, and it was a terrible blow to him to find that he was only able to play the piano with his left hand. He did no writing for a long time. Initially he did not feel fit enough to start anything new, but in 1974 he made some alterations to an early string quartet which he had written in 1931. He then wrote a piece for Peter Pears and the harpist Osian Ellis, *Canticle V*. This was followed by a suite for orchestra and a number of other compositions and arrangements, mainly for voice.

Although his last work was written in the summer of 1976 for the children of Suffolk for Queen Elizabeth's Silver Jubilee in 1977, his last major com-

* Humphrey Carpenter, *Benjamin Britten: a Biography*, Faber and Faber, London, 1992, part 4, chapters 8 and 9.

position, dating from 1975, was the third string quartet, Opus 94, written for the Amadeus and dedicated to Hans Keller. The Quartet had frequently performed his second string quartet, Opus 36, completed in 1945, and they had been pressing him to write a piece specially for them. When he came to write the third quartet he knew them and their playing so well that, as with many of his compositions, the individual parts fit each performer. A particular example in this last quartet is the high solo part in the middle movement which Norbert plays with such feeling. But Ben had problems getting the last movement right. He had been longing to return to Venice, which he loved, and that year he managed it once again. Whilst he was there he found the answer. Not only is the last movement full of quotations from *Death in Venice*, but it is called *La Serenissima*, the name by which Venice is often known.

The Quartet played the completed work to Ben in the library of the Red House at the end of September 1976. The work was scheduled for performance in December and the Quartet had been urged to learn it quickly so that they could play it to him before they went on tour for some weeks in the autumn. It was a poignant occasion. Rosamund Strode, who made the copy of the score they used ('the most difficult bit of deciphering of his writing I have ever had to do'), remembers that he was still 'very much ticking over' when they came. She went on to say that he went down quickly after that, and within a few weeks he was dead. When the Quartet had finished playing, Ben turned to his friend Donald Mitchell, the musicologist and publisher, saying, 'It works.' In these last years in particular he needed the assurance of performance as confirmation that the ideas he had on paper did actually work. After the rehearsal, which must have been tremendously stressful to both composer and performers, Ben asked for drinks – he was not a great drinker, but on an occasion like this he confessed, 'Yes, thank God, I am allowed to drink.'

We all went to Ben's funeral in Aldeburgh Parish Church on 7th December 1976. Just over a week later, on 19th December, the Amadeus gave the first performance of the third string quartet in the Maltings. They went there early to rehearse and I drove up later bringing with me the artist Milein Cosman, the wife of Hans Keller to whom the work was dedicated, and William and Hilda Baumol who were staying with us. It was one of the most difficult occasions the Quartet have ever experienced.

After Ben's death the Quartet continued to perform at Aldeburgh and Snape, though less regularly. They were there in 1977 and 1978; and, in April 1979 they both played at the Maltings and taught there for two weeks at the newly created Britten-Pears School for Advanced Musical Studies. In October 1981 they performed the Mozart clarinet quintet with Benny Goodman, and in June 1986 the Brahms G minor piano quartet with Murray Perahia.

A festival of a very different kind was the annual German/British music

Ink sketch of Norbert Brainin by Milein Cosman

fortnight which usually took place every January in Schloss Elmau in southern Bavaria. From the musical standpoint it was not particularly significant, other than as a place which promoted English music; but for our own families and for the many Germans who stayed there it was a comfortable 'guest house' in most beautiful surroundings.

We admired the sense of purpose that underlay the activities at the Schloss and we loved and respected Sieglinde Mesirca and her family who owned and ran it. It had been built during the First World War by Sieglinde's father, Johannes Mueller, on an estate where there had originally been a hunting lodge – now a guest house – used by the Bavarian kings. Mueller was a priest who became a kind of spiritual guru, preaching the joy of life and the importance of culture in relaxation. He soon had an influential following, sufficient to enable him to build this substantial 'castle' at a time when resources must have been tight. It became the fashionable centre for a particular type of German who went there for holidays. Mueller must also have been a practical business man in that, instead of having staff to run the courses, he managed to persuade families to send their daughters, known as 'Helferinnen', on a kind of *au pair* basis to work and learn domestic and household management. Indeed, it became a meeting place for the young people who went there.

After Johannes Mueller died, Schloss Elmau continued to be run on similar lines by the Mueller family. Concerts were a regular feature of the programmes and Hans Oppenheim, who had been director of the Dartington Hall Music Group in Devon during the war, was appointed music director. It was probably 'Oppy', as he was familiarly known, who suggested to Sieglinde Mesirca that the Amadeus Quartet, who often played nearby in Munich, should be invited to take part in the British/German music fortnight. Along with Benjamin Britten, Peter Pears, George Malcolm, Graham Johnson, Osian Ellis and many others from Britain, the Quartet were regular visitors.

Elmau is a lovely place in both summer and winter. We spent a number of winter holidays there, and on the many occasions when there was snow it was possible to ski cross-country. There was, however, no downhill ski-ing so, when in later years this was what I and the children preferred, we gradually dropped our visits. Sigi, after playing concerts in Elmau with the Quartet, would come and join us at a ski resort. He would walk in his Russian fur hat along the snow-hardened paths across the slopes and meet up with us for lunch after we had finished our morning's activities.

In summer Elmau is magnificent country for walking. In 1961 all the families and children went there for a summer festival in the first three weeks of August. Sigi and I had already been on holiday in Antibes with three-year-old Claire and when we went to Elmau we arranged for my mother to join us. She, very English and very reserved, travelled out with Susi's mother, very Hungarian and bursting with vitality. They were much the same age but they made a strange pair. Once she had arrived in Elmau my mother was bemused by the cultural emphasis on peace and quiet and classed it an 'old people's place'. The countryside and absence of cars made it ideal for children generally but not for very young children. Rest and silence ruled in the afternoons after lunch. Try keeping a three-year-old quiet for a couple of hours! As cars were not allowed this meant that if we wanted to go anywhere on the estate, such as to swim in the lake a couple of miles away, we had to lump our hefty daughter with us.

There were other problems. All the doors to the rooms looked alike to a toddler who cannot read so we hung a small scarf outside our bedroom. We were politely asked to remove it. Visitors were expected to conform to certain customs that were part of the Elmau tradition. There was afternoon tea in the elegantly furnished salon, poured into china cups and handed round by Sieglinde Mesirca herself. On Sunday mornings the Helferinnen wakened guests by singing hymns and you were expected to leave a small gift outside your door. In the evening there was country dancing. Men had to wear white shirts and you were invited to put on white pumps and go and practise in the morning. There was a daily seating list for meals taken at long tables.

I never felt entirely at home in Elmau, partly because I had been too inhibited to continue my German lessons after I married Sigi. Although I could get the gist of most ordinary conversations, I could not speak the language. Nor did the people there, who were mostly wealthy middle-class Germans with a very bourgeois outlook, stimulate me to make further efforts. We did of course have some real friends like Finny Prager, a doctor and regular visitor to Elmau. In a later chapter, I describe the debt I owe her for being such a help to me when, in January 1981, Sigi suffered a heart attack while the Quartet was paying its customary winter visit and was taken to hospital in Garmisch-Partenkirchen.

The third festival that played a prominent part in Quartet life was the Dartington Summer School of Music. It was started in 1948 with William Glock as its director. William, good-looking with his lion's head and penetrating eyes, had an air of authority and integrity about him. He did not mince words and many were afraid of him. But he was at heart a kind man, and much loved and respected. His wife Ann was French – elegant and beautiful, charm personified. The Summer School, originally held at Bryanston School in Dorset, moved to Dartington Hall in 1953 and rapidly became one of the outstanding centres in Europe for the teaching of composition and performance and for music-making in relaxed and congenial surroundings.

There are many beautiful places in England and none more so than

Dartington Hall, nestling in the Devonshire hills in the valley of the Dart as it flows down from Dartmoor. Its glory lies not just in the natural beauty of the countryside but in its gardens and the skill with which its buildings, old and new, have been blended into the landscape. The earliest reference to the Hall is in a royal charter of AD 833, but the oldest building still standing, probably then a manor house, dates from the thirteenth century. Close by is a barn, now used as a theatre, dating from the fourteenth century. The court-yard and banqueting hall came later in the fourteenth century when Richard II's half-brother, John Holand, made Dartington Hall into a great country house. The service quarters housing the sixty-odd knights and squires who formed his household still survive on one side of the present courtyard. After a succession of tenants, the Manor of Dartington came into the possession of the Champernowne family whose home it was for well over three hundred years.

During the nineteenth century the estate fell into disrepair. When it was bought by Dorothy and Leonard Elmhirst in 1925, the banqueting hall was roofless, and what remained of the surrounding buildings was being used for various purposes, mainly for farming. The Elmhirsts set about restoring the buildings as part of their vision for Dartington Hall as the centre of a venture in rural regeneration. The project, which took more than ten years, included a new roof for the banqueting hall. The original hammer-beam roof, which had been one of the first of its kind, predating the larger and more ornate one of Westminster Hall in London, was faithfully reconstructed. There were also new buildings. In the 1930s the Elmhirsts started a co-educational school, run on 'progressive' principles, with separate buildings for the juniors (Aller Park) and for the seniors (Foxhole). Our children went there to complete their sixth-form education and both remember it as a time of great happiness. The school, alas, no longer exists. In the 1950s a new building was tucked into the hillside opposite the Hall to house the College of Arts (Higher Close). The complex is now used by the Dartington Hall Trust and College of Arts.

The Summer School was particularly important for the Amadeus Quartet, not just because of the influence of William Glock – who made them play works by composers such as Bartók which they would probably not have done at such an early stage in their development – but because its visitors in-cluded many people who were concerned with running music clubs through-out Britain. It was these music clubs that were the bread and butter of the Quartet in the early days. The Summer School was designed to appeal equally to students and young professionals, to teachers and to ordinary concert-goers: 'this symbiosis of professional and amateur was to remain a character-istic feature,' William Glock writes in his autobiography.* Distinguished

* William Glock, *Notes in Advance*, Oxford University Press, Oxford, 1991, chapter 7.

musicians were invited both from this country and from abroad. In the first year they included the composers Paul Hindemith and Priaulx Rainier and the musicologist and teacher, Nadia Boulanger – spinsterish with her long grey hair framing her face, and austere as she peered through her glasses, but immensely lively and brimming over with musical knowledge and advice.

The Amadeus went there during this first year at Bryanston, playing in various combinations, morning, noon and night. In addition to Haydn, Mozart and Beethoven quartets they included a contemporary work by Priaulx Rainier and an early English quartet by Matthew Locke. They played piano quartets with Karl Ulrich Schnabel, piano trios and quartets with William Glock himself and viola quintets with Kenneth Essex. Peter and Norbert played Mozart duos with Peter on the violin and Norbert on the viola; then Norbert played the violin and Peter the viola in Mozart's *Symphonia Concertante*. They also played Purcell fantasias and his *Chacony* in G minor. Imogen Holst, who was at this first Summer School, despaired of the way they played the *Chacony*. At Morley College, during the war years, Michael Tippett had introduced the various members of the Quartet to the contrapuntal features of English composers such as Dowland, Gibbons and Purcell, but for them it was an alien style. There was something about the rhythms and the absence of vibrato in the English seventeenth-century way of playing that eluded them. Sigi remembers how Imogen finally decided that they had better give up playing the *Chacony*. 'Much as I love them,' she said, 'they can't do Purcell.' It would probably have been difficult for anyone at that time to produce the kind of sound Imogen had in her mind because it was a new approach to playing and a forerunner of later developments. More than twenty years later, however, they were invited – no doubt with Imogen's approval – to play it in the Maltings at the opening of the Aldeburgh Festival in 1969 (already referred to earlier in this chapter).

The Amadeus not only had advice from Imogen Holst but from other eminent teachers like Georges Enesco too. In his autobiography, William Glock describes how on one occasion Enesco took the Quartet through the tempi of each movement of the Beethoven quartets. The information, so the story goes, had been passed down to him through Hermuth Berger and his father who had had it directly from Beethoven. 'Little was said,' writes William Glock, 'but from his seat at the piano he managed in a few gestures to communicate not only the tempos but also the essence of each movement. He knew everything from memory.'* Sigi too remembers the staggering knowledge he had of each individual part in the quartets. He remembers the occasion on which Enesco played the Bach *Chaconne* as well: 'On shuffled this very old man with a bent back, his face looking down on the floor with

* Ibid, chapter 6.

the back almost at right angles to the legs. He put the violin under his chin, stood upright and started playing. He played like a young god. The shape of the music flowed from his bow and his violin in an uninterrupted stream of most wonderful phrases. The rhythm was overwhelming and convincing, not rigid.'

When the Summer School moved to Dartington, at the suggestion of my old colleague from Oxford days, Herbert Lewin, I myself went there. I had been to William Glock's series of lectures at the Arts Council and had been impressed by his formidable knowledge of music and his stimulating and imaginative approach. In that year, 1953, the Amadeus played works by Racine Fricker, Matyas Seiber, Haydn, Mozart and Beethoven. At one of their concerts they had played Beethoven's Opus 135, their first attempt at these late quartets, and afterwards a few of us listened to the Busch recording and discussed the two approaches. The culmination of the week was a recital by Dietrich Fischer-Dieskau of Schubert's *Die Winterreise* and Beethoven's *An die Ferne Geliebte* with William Glock at the piano. At that time he was twenty-eight years old, tall, stately and elegant. He could bring out the inner meaning of the words in an incomparable manner and give colour to a song in a way that made you feel you could almost touch it.

But the Summer School was not all music, and I remember cream teas on Dartmoor and a tennis foursome with Herbert Lewin, April Cantelo (who had also been in the Arts Department with Imogen Holst, both as singer and instrumentalist) and Colin Davis, then better known as a gifted clarinettist with a remarkable tone quality rather than as a conductor. At that time Colin and April were married and their small daughter ran around the court pretending she was a ball-boy. And there were those other unforgettable moments such as strolling back to Foxhole late at night singing themes from Mozart's G minor symphony long before it became a pop record.

As other festivals and tours intervened, Amadeus Quartet visits were more intermittent. However, from 1962 until 1973, it was a regular feature in our summer diary, apart from 1965, the year when we all went to the USA. On each visit there were familiar faces and old friends amongst musicians, visitors and staff. Bee Musson, the kindly registrar, beautiful, kind and quietly efficient in her wheel-chair; Florence Burton, the domestic bursar; and of course the Summer School secretary, John Amis, ebullient, humorous, flamboyant, larger than life. Not only did he have a fantastically wide musical knowledge and understanding but he had great organizing gifts and skill in taking decisions. This extraordinary personality was a tremendous force at the Dartington Summer School. He was always ready in a crisis to come up with the appropriate witty remark to calm things down. Then there were the Troglodytes – or 'Trogs' as they were called – the people working backroom to make sure that everything was in the right place at the right time. They were the unpaid stage managers who had free board and lodging in return for a lot of hard work and some opportunities to participate in the School's activities. In later years our children sometimes joined this dutiful band.

In his dealings with the Quartet, John Amis has described himself as 'heavily Christian' in contrast to their being 'heavily Jewish'. Each year when they met in Dartington, they would say, 'Hello, Amis, now this year no Jewish jokes, but – have you heard the one about ...' And so it would go on. They always haggled about fees but it was mostly good tempered. John recollects how William Glock once rang him up to say, 'The Am. Quartet are coming for $^{11}/_{20}$ of their normal fee.' The discussions would break up with their standard joke about the Jewish bloke who found that someone else had been sleeping with his wife. He goes towards him, fingering the lapel of his jacket, and says, 'You absolute bastard, you swine – oh, I say, nice piece of material.'

It was most enjoyable for the families. The Quartet themselves, who had such a marvellous sense of humour, were good fun – they were still sometimes affectionately called 'the boys' and 'the Wolf Gang'. They had that gift of fooling and precise timing in dumb show reminiscent of the old Chaplin films. I remember one incident when Norbert couldn't quite fit their luggage into the boot of the car: Peter went over, kicked it, simulated the closing of the lid, got back into the car and pretended to drive off. I often thought how privileged I was to be with them and how very different holidays would have been without them.

Certain family events in Dartington stand out. In 1964 Daniel, not quite two years old, being taught how to dance on the lawn in the courtyard by Josef Szigeti: our small son so tiny and Szigeti so tall and lanky. Then in 1966 when we took both children with us and our young housekeeper Jean Hubbard. That year Janet Baker was giving concerts and Margaret Ritchie was the singing coach. Jean, who was studying singing with Fabian Smith at the Guildhall School of Music in London, had the most lovely natural voice and she sang in Margaret Ritchie's master class. A few bars after she had started, Margaret Ritchie stopped her and commented on the long hair hiding her face: 'Part the curtains, dear, and begin again.' In 1969 we listened spellbound to Alfred Brendel playing Beethoven's *Diabelli Variations*. Later in the week we joined him and his little daughter Doris for a visit to Dartmoor and cream tea at Ashburton. He smiled as he climbed around the Dartmoor tors, his fingers plastered for protection but his tortured face relaxed and happy.

The Summer School also gave me a chance to take part in some of its activities. I would start the day with a rehearsal in the Great Hall of the choral work for the week which was to be performed by the Summer School choir on the final Friday evening. It was here in 1976 that a very young Simon Rattle conducted the choir in Stravinsky's *Mass*. There was also to be a performance of *The Soldier's Tale*. Daniel, not yet fourteen, had recently been playing timpani in a performance of Verdi's *Requiem* at Highgate School and he boldly asked if he might take part. 'There could be a problem,' said Simon Rattle. 'Do you have a Musicians's Union card?' 'No-o.' 'Well, it is a rule with the orchestra that only those with cards are allowed to play: I am very sorry but I have to say no.' What a gentle way of not putting a boy down!

After the morning choral rehearsal, in addition to the multitude of master classes and chamber music and other rehearsals, there was usually a lecture in the Barn Theatre. In the earlier years at Bryanston and Dartington a distinguished list of speakers had given talks on literature, the theatre, philosophy and the visual arts. In the later Dartington years this type of lecture was less prominent. There were talks, however. One day the subject might be art with Philip James, Art Director at the Arts Council, or the critic David Sylvester as speaker. The next day there might be a talk on a musical topic by Hans Keller, Anthony Hopkins or William Glock; or the musicians themselves might discuss the works to be played.

The list of eminent musicians who came to Dartington is endless. Many were old and famous, like Josef Szigeti, Vlado Perlemuter and Frederick Grinke, but many too were young and as yet unknown. It is with surprise and pleasure that you watch the video, carefully put together by that lovable photographer Charles Davies, and unexpectedly spot some young face, now wrinkled and well known, among those wandering through the Courtyard.

CHAPTER TWELVE

# A Change
# of Life-Style

─────────

When the two children and I came back from the United States at the end of
September 1965, leaving Sigi behind to complete the tour, one of the first
things I did was to take delivery of a new car, a Volvo Estate, a snub-nosed
creature that looked quite horrible after the larger, more streamlined
American variety. But Volvo owners in Britain in those days were a select
group, almost a club, and we flashed our lights at each other as we passed
on the road. The next thing was to start searching for a new house. Although
we had altered our house in Mill Hill to make the most of the space available,
we wanted a larger one. Moreover, my mother, who in 1961 had moved
from Barton-on-Sea to a bungalow near Watford, was seventy-five and we
could foresee the time when she might wish to be even nearer to us. It was
also becoming clear that once both children, now aged three and seven, were
at school I would want a job away from home. This would almost certainly
mean travelling into central London and, as I had discovered when we first
married and I was still working in the Civil Service, it was an awkward and
time-consuming journey from Mill Hill.

For professional musicians, being able to afford a suitable house for a
growing family is as big a problem as acquiring a good instrument on which
to play. We were fortunate. By this time not only was the Quartet earning
well, but we had enough money from other sources to clear the mortgage on
the Mill Hill house and still have something left over.

I began to look for a house in a more convenient neighbourhood and, in
October, I sent Sigi a rough plan of a possible one in Golders Green. It had
been empty for some while and was in a poor state for it had been requi-
sitioned during the war and, after having been turned into seven flatlets, it
had never been re-instated as a single dwelling. Indeed, it had the reputation
of being the red-light house of the neighbourhood. Estimates suggested that
it would need a lot of thought and effort as well as money to turn it into the
kind of home we wanted. But it was the right size and well situated in a quiet
road not far from Golders Green Underground station. It was thus within
easy reach of the rest of the Quartet who were then living in Mill Hill, Edgware

and Hendon. Above all, it had a magnificent outlook as it backed immediately onto Golders Hill Park and Hampstead Heath, something that immediately attracted my mother who decided that, despite the two flights of stairs, she would in due course be happy to live in a flat converted for her on the top floor. The park itself had swings and a small zoo, and it was regularly patrolled by brown-uniformed keepers who helped to keep it safe for children. It also had a beautiful garden which had originally been attached to Ivy House where Anna Pavlova had lived. That had later been incorporated into the park when the Middlesex Polytechnic (later to become the University of Middlesex) took over the building to accommodate the School of Speech and Drama.

Our purchase of the house, which was virtually completed whilst Sigi was still in North America, was one of the best things we ever did and we have never ceased to enjoy living in it. It must have been a difficult time for him because he had left England at the beginning of June and was not due home until early December – a tour not far short of six months. As the Quartet was moving about continuously, it was uncertain whether my letters would reach him and we were still diffident about using the telephone because it was so expensive.

Today, in the 1990s, we would be corresponding by fax or E-mail. At one point on the tour he wrote saying that they had been asked to play Haydn's *Seven Last Words* at a memorial concert for John F. Kennedy in New York on 22nd November, and would I please look in our music cupboard to find the parts on which they had put their own markings. I found them and they reached New York in time – but it would have been much quicker and more reliable if it had been possible to fax them. One day more recently, when the clarinettist Richard Stoltzman was staying with us, he came in flourishing a drawing his young son had just sent him by fax. How satisfying it would have been if Claire could have done the same for her Dad in 1965. She was, however, already exercising her gift for writing and, to his pleasure, started sending him letters. He wrote, 'The spelling is extremely good and the writing too, but above all she told a very nice story and it is a lovely letter.'

When our husbands were away, the wives in the Quartet had to shoulder more or less sole responsibility for dealing with the household chores and the day-to-day problems of bringing up the children. Although we always had the love and support of a real father in the background and the benefit of a comfortable income coming into the household, sometimes when Sigi was absent for a long period, I even went so far as to think of ourselves as a single-parent family. Katinka Brainin neatly described the problems of family life and being married to a quartet: 'If you have young children it is quite difficult because the poor child has only half a parent, most of the time anyhow, and you feel you don't do justice to either the child or your husband.

You are a bit torn because you want to be with your husband, but then you have a bad conscience because if you give him too much time then you are not with the child.'

It was never easy for us wives to adjust to our husbands' comings and goings. Susi said, 'It was difficult when he left, and it was difficult when he came back.' When the Quartet returned from a long tour it was all bustle. Margit described it as being fun when Peter came home but, as he was always on the go, often nervous and tense, she nevertheless welcomed being able to take a breather and get back a sense of balance when he left. Katinka expressed it in a similar way: 'It is not exactly a relaxing life; it is quite a hassle. The advantages are that you sometimes have peace and quiet: the first three or four days when Norbert has gone I can relax.' I felt much the same and the days immediately after Sigi left were times of quiet reflection, finding my own self again. Even in a happily married couple there are still two people whose different interests and personalities occasionally become stifled. There is a longing to get away from it all, to go off and do your own thing, to discover inside your head whether you can still live alone. Irresponsibly to go crazy.

It was perhaps the hardest for Margit who, before she married Peter in 1952, had had a professional life of her own in Sweden. By the time I married Sigi in 1958, she had been in England for six years and had had time to make friends; but life was still lonely for her and she needed Peter's help and support in dealing with Anmarie, their lively and demanding daughter. Although at first, when Peter left to go on tour, she felt she could relax, this soon gave way to unhappiness. She did not mind being alone, and she loved cooking and looking after the house; but there was no one to talk to and she felt very isolated in Mill Hill. It was a little easier when Anmarie went to school because she then made more friends. In those exceptionally busy years in the early 1960s, Margit, like all of us, was often depressed, so much so that she confessed that from time to time when she began a letter to Peter it was so doleful she couldn't send it. Anmarie too must have been upset when her father left. Once on Peter's birthday, when she wanted to visit her friends and her mother remonstrated with her, she replied, 'Why should I be here? He's never here for my birthday.' But looking back on it all, Margit concluded philosophically that she didn't think she would have been happy with a husband who left at eight in the morning and came back at six in the evening. 'I would rather have had my life than a grey nothing.'

Sigi and I always tried to have a long summer holiday with the children and then take a couple of weeks on our own without them, thus giving us a chance to adjust to each other. We also tried to meet, if even for a short while, in the winter when the children and I went ski-ing and Sigi would join us for a few days' walking and 'après ski', as after Elmau. During the brief periods when Sigi was home I wanted to spend as much time as possible with him. This meant less time for the children and they resented it. Then there was the problem of discipline: Sigi wanted to show his affection, but at the same time he did not want to spoil them. They often behaved badly just to attract his attention. Claire would come home and leave her muddy boots in the middle of the sitting-room floor, waiting for her father to react. He usually did, and then the fur would fly. Then later there were the usual teenage rebellions. When in 1973 the Quartet were to celebrate their twenty-fifth anniversary with a concert followed by a party in the Royal Festival Hall at which Sir Edward Heath and other distinguished visitors were guests, Claire boldly proclaimed that she would only come if she could wear jeans. Sigi said 'no'. A compromise was eventually reached whereby she did wear jeans but they were topped by a splendid tunic.

Sigi's last concert of the 1965–6 season, a broadcast in London, was at the end of June and in mid-July 1966 we moved into The Park in Golders Green. We just had time to organize the removal van, transfer our belongings, entertain our friends the Baumols to a first meal, and then leave almost immediately for three concerts in Switzerland and France before going on holiday with Jean and the children in Antibes. In Adelboden the Quartet played for Max Rostal in his summer chalet. 'This is something we shall never be able to afford,' Sigi said looking at it with admiration. We had no idea that within the next ten years we would be able to buy both a beautiful house in Tuscany and a cottage in Sussex.

During the first year in our new house, we lived in the top flat – ultimately intended for my mother – and such middle-floor rooms as were habitable. Extensive work, like the building of a kitchen, still needed to be done on the ground floor. Once the basic structural work had been carried out, we entrusted the finishing off to our old friend Charles Pratt. He had once had his own building business but more recently had been working on his own. Charles had done the alterations to our Mill Hill house, living with us from Monday to Friday and returning to his wife in Selsey for the weekend.

To our grief he died in 1996. He was not just a builder but a splendid friend to us all, including my mother. We had continued to remain in touch with him and his wife Peggy and had begun to feel part of their family. Charles would spend his spare time entertaining the children with stories, particularly those by Enid Blyton. At one point there had to be an extra seat at our kitchen table so that 'Noddy' or 'Mr Plod' or whoever else might be visiting could take part in our conversations, with Charles putting on the various different voices. Once, when Claire was staying with her grannie and Charles was in our house in Mill Hill, I remember sitting on the stairs in fits of laughter listening to him having a prolonged telephone conversation with Claire imitating all the different 'Noddy' characters in turn. In times of crisis he was also a great support. One day Daniel, who was always rather accident prone, somehow managed to shoot a toy arrow backwards into his eye. I was out of the house and it was Charles who took charge and persuaded a neighbour to rush Daniel and Jean to the local hospital.

In November 1966, the Quartet went to York to take up the first of a regular three weeks' residence each term at the university. The arrangement had been financed by Granada Television to enable them to rehearse and play the occasional concert away from the distractions of London life. It was to continue for two years and culminated in June 1968 when the university conferred honorary doctorates on them. It was at the University of York, in June 1967, that I was to give my first academic lecture. Granada Television had organized a conference on 'Music in the North' and one of their producers, Douglas Terry, took the brave decision to invite me to talk about the work I had been doing not long before for the Baumol and Bowen book, *Performing Arts: an Economic Dilemma*. Professor Wilfrid Mellers, who held the chair of music, opened the proceedings and was followed by the professor of economics, Alan Peacock, and then myself on the economic problems of live performance.

In September 1967, the Quartet left for a three-months' tour of Japan and North America. Shortly afterwards I joined them in Japan, travelling out via Bangkok, where I spent a couple of days sightseeing, using the tiny remains of my travel allowance. Britain still had strict exchange controls at this time and foreign travel was severely limited. Sigi met me in Osaka, ugly and crowded. Although by British standards it was not late, maybe ten o'clock in the evening, most places were already shut and it was difficult to get a meal. From Osaka we had a day sightseeing in nearby Nara, a beautiful city with the curving roofs of its sacred gateways and temples resting like the wings of birds among the trees and hillsides. The following day we flew to Tokyo where we stayed in the Imperial Hotel, the fine old building designed by Frank Lloyd Wright, now demolished. The Quartet had already played a concert in Tokyo the week before, and they were now due to give two more. When I took my seat in the hushed Nissei Theatre, there was none of the bustle and eager chattering that precedes concerts in Europe. The Quartet were late starting, but there was complete silence among the waiting audience and no suggestion of the slow handclap that might have started in other countries. We were able to go to a *Noh* play before leaving for concerts in Nagoya and Hiroshima, where we were entertained by a Japanese Christian family. It was still not much more than twenty years since the atomic bomb had been dropped there, killing or making homeless nearly a quarter of a million people. The lonely remaining piece of wall of what had once been a building and the Peace Memorial Park were chilling reminders of the devastation and suffering it caused.

We left Hiroshima by train for Kyoto. Throughout this tour we had with us Henrietta Polak-Schwarz, the elderly Dutch lady who loved music and who had befriended the Quartet from the time it went on its first visit to Holland at the end of the 1940s. Sigi offered to take her to the restaurant car for coffee. I decided not to join them but agreed to look after our luggage, including Henrietta's handbag. We were travelling on the 'Shinkansen', the express train which excited Henrietta's imagination, but also made her nervous. Like all Japanese trains, it was very crowded. When we arrived at what seemed to be a main station, Sigi suggested they might avoid the crush in the corridor by going along the platform. No sooner had they got out than the doors shut and the train moved off. I first realized that something was wrong when I saw our guide and interpreter – his mask-like face normally implacable – trying to rush down the crowded gangway as I waved good-bye to my husband and his companion on the platform outside.

Sigi had a problem. Not only had Henrietta left with me her handbag containing her heart pills and her valuables, but Sigi had left his jacket on the train and had only taken small change with him in his shirt pocket. Moreover, it was not after all a main station but a small one with no signs in English. They somehow made themselves understood and, without any tickets, managed to take the next train to Kyoto. Meanwhile, the rest of us arrived in Kyoto station, packed with people and with long queues for taxis. Our guide was misinformed about the time of the next train, so that when Sigi and Henrietta finally arrived there was no one to meet them. They did not know the name of our hotel, as the original schedule had been changed, but the ever-resourceful Sigi saw a sign marked 'Information' and explained their predicament. The person at the desk turned out to be an admirer of the Amadeus and he agreed to telephone all the main hotels in this town of one-and-a-half million people to trace where they were staying. While he was doing this our guide tracked them down and brought them safely to the hotel in the hills outside Kyoto. We gratefully sat down to a European-style meal and amused ourselves watching Japanese couples trying to use knives and forks.

The old part of the city of Kyoto is very beautiful. Its atmosphere is secretive and subdued. There is the quiet of its formal gardens with their pools and pebbles and tiny plants; the beauty and strangeness of its architecture with its muted green, red and brown colours; its old wooden buildings with the rooms inside elegantly simple. It was not just the language but the culture that was strange to me. While we were in Japan we saw much to admire and much to hate, dangling awkwardly as it did between its old culture and traditions and the American culture that had been thrust upon it after the war. Imprinted on my memory are the pin-tables and fruit-machines and the seething myriads of people in the coastal strip, with children and students spreading out like small insects, all dressed in dark colours, making the garish colours of my summer dresses look out of place.

After a final concert in Tokyo, we flew to Los Angeles. If possible, Sigi and I always took separate planes, for flying in the 1960s was still thought to be hazardous and, as long as our children were young, we took what precautions we could. We left separately from Tokyo, but on reaching Honolulu we found that Sigi's plane had been cancelled and we went on together to Los Angeles where the Quartet were to begin a six weeks' tour of North America. I spent a few days with them before leaving for London and relaxed gratefully beside the hotel pool, allowing Henrietta to indulge her voracious appetite for sight-seeing on her own.

I greatly admired Henrietta but her immense vitality was exhausting. She and her husband, Leo Polak, were both impressive personalities. He was a philosophy professor of international renown, an atheist, an enlightened socialist and an anti-Nazi. During the war he was inevitably soon taken by the Nazis, but Henrietta and her two daughters managed to survive by going into hiding in Holland. One of the daughters was Ans, whose story and marriage to Sylvio Samama have been described in chapter 8. After the war Henrietta and her sister Sara, who had also survived, regained possession of the family factories. Henrietta used her wealth, albeit with a certain im-periousness, to become a patron of the arts and to spread her liberal and often radical views about society.

When we reached the East Coast after flying from Los Angeles, I was met at Newark airport by William and Hilda Baumol, both wearing jeans and with ponchos slung over their shoulders. With an amused smile I watched Henrietta glance disdainfully at William and hand her luggage to him. She continued her journey to Europe and I had a few memorable days in Princeton before going back to London, the proud possessor of one of William's paint-ings. A carving followed by boat shortly afterwards.

I returned home in the middle of October 1967. Our house was still not finished but it was habitable. We had by this time moved downstairs and my mother had already taken over our top flat. Claire had started at her new primary school in September 1966, soon after we moved, and Daniel joined her there the following September not long before I left for Japan. The school was well over a mile away. Lunch presented a problem because there was no room for first-year pupils in the dining-room. The practical headmistress suggested we might consider 'Kosher' dinners. The children were bussed to a central point and to Daniel this meant that he went to 'coaches' dinners! While I was away, my mother and Jean – and Charles Pratt – had looked after the children. What I would have done without them I do not know. By this time my mother was seventy-seven, a little frail but always there to comfort an unhappy child or to cope with emergencies.

CHAPTER THIRTEEN

# I Return
# to Work

_____

With this strong support at home and with both children now at school, I was at last in a position to resume the career I had interrupted when Claire was born in 1958, nearly ten years earlier. The two chapters that follow are mainly concerned with some of the problems which faced me, not so much as the wife of a member of the Amadeus Quartet, but as one woman among many during the 1960s and 1970s who were attempting to achieve parity with men in employment. The first concentrates on the very real problem in the 1960s of getting satisfactory employment and of being taken seriously if, as a married woman with children, you wanted a career. The second, covering the 1970s, tries to give a feel of what happens if you are successful and then have responsibility not only for staff and the development of a work programme, but also often need to be away from home to travel and talk about what you are doing. This chapter coincides with the time when the Amadeus had arrived at the peak of its success and so confronted us, the Nissels, with all the problems that are now being faced by many other professional couples. Although this part of the book is mainly concerned with my own particular story, it needs to be seen against the background of the development of the Quartet and of the competing claims of marriage, children and jobs.

During the early years after my marriage when I was at home looking after the children, I had searched for ways of keeping my mind active. The trouble with suburbia is not so much the people who live there, who are often highly intelligent and imaginative, as the more general environment in which they find themselves and the constraints of keeping within tight budgets. Many of my friends were in a _Catch 22_ situation: if they could get a job, they could afford to pay for child care but, without the extra money, they had no time to seek out or train for a job. It was early in 1973, soon after Daniel was born, that Jean Hubbard came to live with us as a part-time housekeeper and I had the chance to be more relaxed and to go out and about. I had someone to share the cooking, and the shopping could be done quickly without the company of bored youngsters who were fretting to be with their friends.

I began to play an active part in the Labour Party. Sigi and I were both keenly interested in politics and one of our close friends was Arthur Blenkinsop, the Labour MP for Newcastle East. Before we were married, it was through Arthur that Sigi managed to attend the debate in the House of Commons on the Suez crisis following the attack on Egypt by France and Britain on 31st October 1956. Never before had we felt so helpless in trying to influence action by a government with which we fundamentally disagreed.

In the local government elections in 1963 I stood as a Labour candidate in our local Mill Hill Ward and gave the Conservative candidates not a little anxiety in this their traditional territory. We lived in the Hendon North constituency and Sigi and I both vigorously campaigned before the General Election in October 1964. The Labour Party, under Harold Wilson, narrowly won. Sigi was able to join in because, in the spring before the election, the Quartet had no concerts due to Martin Lovett's illness. For someone who was at that time mortally afraid of dogs, he was an intrepid canvasser. He delights in telling of the occasion when an irate Conservative supporter told him that if he showed up again he would set the dog on him. There was also an old lady who, in an upper-class accent, reprimanded him for his politics with the words, 'Norrtie, norrtie'! Mill Hill Broadway, with its shops and flats above, was a difficult patch to cover but he enjoyed pinning down the surprisingly large number of Labour supporters who lived there. In the General Election in March 1966, Ernest Wistrich was our candidate and I was sub-agent for the constituency. A Labour Government was this time returned with a substantial majority, but to our bitter disappointment Ernest narrowly failed to win the seat. We have remained friends with him and his family ever since.

My diaries for these years show that I was involved in a number of other things too, such as a first-aid course, a car-maintenance course, and singing on the all too rare occasions when Imogen Holst's amateur fringe to the Purcell Singers managed to meet. I was an active supporter of our local Parents' Group and became its chairman in 1966. In February 1965, I had the good fortune to be appointed a magistrate for the Gore division of Middlesex.

An Act of Parliament in 1948 required Justices of the Peace to be drawn from all sections of the community and all shades of opinion and, by the time I was appointed, great strides had been made towards implementing the reforms. But the Bench was still predominantly Conservative and women were much in a minority. I took pride in being a magistrate and found the job challenging, with something new to learn almost every time I sat. Dealing with the immensely varied problems of the people who came before me kept my feet firmly on the ground. I hope that I never ceased to treat them as individuals rather than 'cases'. It is important to feel with and understand people who come before you but not to identify with them too closely. A certain detachment is essential for one's own emotional stability. My earlier belief that I could help solve some of their problems gave way to scepticism as I grew older, particularly as the variety of sentences available so often seemed altogether inappropriate. Many years later, when the London Benches were realigned with the Boroughs and I moved to the large Barnet Bench, I was elected chairman of the Probation Liaison Committee. This was at a time when Community Service Orders were being developed. They involved a substantial input from the Probation Service, and seemed a positive and useful way forward for certain types of offender. I was pleased to be in a position to give my strong support.

Interesting though the work was, magistrates are unpaid volunteers and I was anxious to find paid employment. There were two Court houses in the Gore Division, one in Harrow and the other in Hendon. In the mid-1960s we sat only in the morning on about thirty-five days a year so that I could easily manage to do other work. With our two young children, I was particularly interested in education but I did not want to teach, despite the acute shortage of teachers at that time. I applied for a job, part-time at a senior level, with the newly established education unit set up at the London School of Economics under Professor Claus Moser* to continue the statistical work already started by Professor Lionel Robbins' Committee on Higher Education. I received a polite reply saying in effect that they had both senior and part-time posts available, but not (subtle distinction) part-time senior posts.

In July 1964, William and Hilda Baumol – whom I have already mentioned in this connection in chapter 10 when describing our visit to the United States – came to London from Princeton to set up the British section of a study on the arts. They wanted a research assistant and approached Professor Robbins† whom they knew well from the days when William was a postgraduate student at the London School of Economics shortly after the war. Through Claus Moser, my name came up as a possible part-time research assistant and to my delight I was appointed. The study set out to examine the financial problems of the live professional performing arts and to explore their implications for the future. In Britain it was concerned with finding out whether there were any noticeable differences from the situation in the USA, particularly in relation to three matters: the recent financial position of the main performing arts organizations, historical trends in certain long-established bodies, and the composition of audiences.

The study was published in 1966 under the title *Performing Arts: an*

* Later Sir Claus Moser.
† Later Lord Robbins.

*Economic Dilemma*, the dilemma being that the live performing arts cannot increase productivity at the same rate as the economy in general, with the unfortunate consequence that revenues do not keep pace with ever mounting costs. The time taken to play a Mozart quartet varies little and it cannot be performed with less than four players. Higher ticket prices, bigger concert halls, records and faster travel may help to increase revenues but it is uncommon for rewards to performers to keep up with rising standards of living. This problem of increasing relative costs, not only in the arts but in the service industries more generally, was something with which economists were becoming increasingly concerned, and the work of William Baumol in the field was already widely known. During his brief visit William and I interviewed various people at the Arts Council, the Ballet Rambert, the Royal Festival Hall and the Royal Opera House. After the Baumols left, Claus Moser was in charge, and together we visited many other organizations including the Sadler's Wells Theatre, the National Theatre, the Royal Shakespeare Company, the New Philharmonia Orchestra, the London Symphony Orchestra, the London Philharmonic Orchestra and the BBC. Much of my time was spent extracting material from financial accounts. Most of it had to be copied by hand as at that time few organizations had copying machines. I clearly remember studying the income and expenditure figures for the Ballet Rambert, then at the Mercury Theatre, Notting Hill Gate, sitting in a small ice-cold room heated only by a minute gas fire with a broken burner. Even the dancers in the middle of one rehearsal decided the temperature was intolerable, and refused to continue. Such, at that time, were the finances of a well-known dance company.

The longer-term studies of particular organizations included the Shakespeare Theatre in Stratford-upon-Avon, the Bournemouth Symphony Orchestra and the Old Vic Theatre. The latter, which in 1964 housed the National Theatre, was originally under the aegis of the Old Vic Company and its charter stipulated that it 'shall be primarily for the holding therein of public lectures and musical and other entertainments and exhibitions suited for the recreation and instruction of the poorer classes.' The earliest financial records went back to 1911 when the hall was known as the Royal Victoria Coffee Music Hall. The cheapest ticket prices were 2d for the gallery and the most expensive 21/- (one guinea) for the boxes.

I also carried out audience surveys at theatres and concert halls. In the early 1960s, such surveys were still comparatively rare and when he saw the unexpectedly high response rates, William Baumol commented that the English public must be 'starved of nosy questionnaires!' This was my first experience of survey work and for a small fee I persuaded my friends to distribute questionnaires to the audience and collect them up at the end. On one occasion, Claus and Mary Moser agreed to help cover a performance of

*The Crucible* by Arthur Miller at the Old Vic Theatre. Sigi was unexpectedly at home as Norbert had flu, so we asked him to help Mary in the dress circle. The plan was to insert one questionnaire inside every third copy of the cast list which was freely distributed to the audience. At the end of the performance, after I had bundled together the completed questionnaires, I asked Mary and Sigi to hand over their spare ones but found to my dismay that they had none left. Evidently, Sigi in good male fashion had charmed the usherettes to help him fill the cast lists and some of them had filled every cast list instead of every third one. I shamefacedly confessed to Hilda Baumol, who was helping with the study, that the dress circle had been over-represented in the survey.

On Monday 16th October 1967, I returned to Whitehall, to the Central Statistical Office, which was then part of the Cabinet Office. At the beginning of April, Professor Moser had been appointed head of both the Government Statistical Service (GSS) and the Central Statistical Office (CSO), and before I left for Japan to join the Quartet I went to see him in his new office overlooking St James's Park, in the building where I had worked before. Outwardly nothing had altered. There was the same dingy furniture and even the same old battered lampshade which the previous occupant, Sir Harry Campion, had had. But there was a good prospect that there would be fundamental changes.

When a Labour government was returned in 1966, Harold Wilson, who had been my chief when I first entered the Civil Service, was once again Prime Minister. At the time when I first knew him, he had been a professional statistician and in that role had been instrumental in putting economic statistics on a sound basis. As Prime Minister he had realized the importance of reorganizing government statistics in general and improving social statistics in particular. It was thus important to appoint someone who had the capacity to carry through a major reorganization of the service as well as the knowledge and imagination to develop social statistics. The choice of Professor Moser was an inspired one, for he was more than just an academic. He had the ability to handle people and get what he wanted from those in positions of power as well as from those who worked for him. His charm and persuasive powers broke down some of the barriers there were at that time between administrators and statisticians. During the twenty years he was head of the GSS, he helped build up a strong and professional body of high integrity which ensured that policy was backed with sound statistical advice. Although his mother tongue was German, he had a feel for the English language and by the use of simple words could cut through a mass of verbiage in a confused draft.

There was at this point a shortage of the trained statisticians who were needed to improve government statistics. There were of course a number of women like myself who had the necessary background but who, having children at home, would find it difficult and unsatisfactory to work full-time. Indeed, although Claire and Daniel were now both at school, I myself wanted to have time to be a central part of their lives. It took someone like Claus Moser to appreciate that many such women had the academic and technical skills to help fill the gap in the statistical service that years of neglect and the lack of prospects had opened up. He set out to persuade the Civil Service that a four-day week and special leave without pay during the school holidays was a practicable proposition. The next hurdle was pay. Women had achieved equal pay with men in the Civil Service in 1961, so this was not an issue; but those in charge were insisting that I should start again at the bottom of the Statistician/Principal range instead of at the point where I was when I left in 1958. They finally gave way.

It is difficult now, thirty years later when the employment situation is so different, to understand just how exceptional, and how lonely a task, it was at that time for a mother with children to be taken back into the Civil Service after a break in employment. She was not likely to be accepted as some-one who had had useful experience in a different walk of life, skills which might usefully be applied in the office environment. Although I was work-ing four days rather than five days a week, I was merely regarded as 'that part-time woman'. The fact that my fifth day was spent as a magistrate in Court as well as dealing with family matters at home was neither here nor there.

There was the further problem of retraining, for when I had left nearly ten years before, computers had barely existed. Moreover, my former con-temporaries had risen in the hierarchy and did not know how best to use this unusual recruit. I had changed too. With the experience of these years behind me, I looked at my colleagues with different eyes. I could unashamedly un-dress their bodies and look into their minds with an insight that would have been less perceptive in my younger years. Intellectually they were challenging and stimulating to be with. Some showed unexpected flashes of inspiration, wit and humour which drew you to them. Others were more typical of the smooth civil servant, carefully sitting astride the fence. Most, I guess, would have been taken aback by the thoughts that crossed the mind of this middle-aged civil servant – a married woman with children – as she studied them across the conference table.

I had previously been an economic statistician and I was now working on financial statistics. It was far removed from the life I had been leading and no longer kindled much interest in me. Nor could I see a future for me in this field. The status of the statistician seemed to have been eroded over the years. When I had been in the Treasury, I had felt I was in a responsible position, working as a member of a team with a direct influence on policy.

There was no job of comparable status among statisticians in the CSO.

In December, two months after I began work, I started looking elsewhere, in places like the Citizens' Advice Bureaux and the expanding social service departments of local authorities. I was sorry the experiment had not succeeded since Claus had made real efforts to recruit me. Sigi and I had both known him for a long time for we had already met him and his wife Mary in our two separate worlds – the academic and the musical – before we married. Claus's association with the members of the Amadeus went back even beyond the time when they came together as a Quartet in 1948. He himself was a most gifted musician, and chamber music was part of his life. Sigi sometimes played duets with him, the only 'amateur' I have ever known him play with.

When I went to talk to Claus about leaving the CSO, I was surprised by his reaction. He produced a minute from Robert Neild, an economist and special adviser in the Treasury, which he had written the previous year when Callaghan had been Chancellor of the Exchequer, saying that there should be a 'social report or social survey in which trends in each sector should be analysed and discussed so as to produce a general picture of changes in social welfare.' 'Would you be interested in attempting it?' he asked. 'I would like to think about it.' I had so firmly made up my mind to leave that I was caught unawares by this new approach. After the New Year I said I would like to try it, and Claus took the lead in drawing up a programme of work for collecting the necessary statistics for what was to become the CSO's annual publication, *Social Trends*. I thought that the life I had been leading as a housewife and a magistrate, and the experience I had also gained from my political activities which had helped me to find out what everyday people were interested in, might be valuable for this new project. I had my feet on the ground and I might be more suited to the job than civil servants who had spent all their lives within the corridors of Whitehall.

My work quickly became more interesting as there were various plans afoot for developing social statistics. Nonetheless, it soon became abundantly clear that, as a part-time temporary statistician, I could not look forward to a proper career. I would always be exploited as a useful and versatile filler-in for such odd jobs as might crop up.

Reluctantly, for I had stoutly maintained that no woman in her senses who had young children would wish to be employed full-time, I began to consider working five instead of four days a week. Part-timers were severely discriminated against, not only for pensions, but also for all kinds of other benefits. As their leave entitlements were shorter and there was no time off for magistrates' duties, it seemed that the children would hardly see less of me if I were to be employed full-time. The Cabinet Office conceded that, if I did work full-time, in certain domestic circumstances 'we could readily agree that additional absences on the modest scale envisaged could be arranged … as special leave without pay.' So, in October 1968, a year after I had returned, I once again became a full-time civil servant, although in a temporary capacity rather than as part of the permanent staff.

Saturday morning now had to be spent shopping and doing household jobs as well as taking the children to pottery, music lessons or horse-riding. Weekdays began early for me with a pot of tea made from the kettle beside my bed (coffee and a bun were to come later in the office), often beside a sleepy Sigi who was programmed to stay up late at night playing concerts and resting in the morning before rehearsals that did not begin until 10 o'clock. I left Jean with the task of giving the children breakfast and seeing them off to school. There were times when I was able to get a parking pass in Whitehall (regular passes were reserved for more senior staff) and, if Sigi did not need the car, I could leave before the rush hour at around 8 a.m. and be in the office in about twenty minutes. If I were lucky I could then leave before 5 p.m. and be home to have plenty of time with the children. When we first moved to Golders Green, there was a small shop in the North End Road at the entrance to Golders Hill Park, and with the car I could pick up essential shopping on the way. Going by public transport added an extra hour to my day.

The first half hour at home was always tricky. I was still in a kind of no-man's-land between office and domesticity and I just wanted to make the transition quietly. But everyone wanted to tell me about their day. Sometimes they merely needed to vent their personal frustrations on me. I remember I did once flip when Claire and my mother both got at me. I walked out of the house, leaving them to find their own supper, drove fast up the M1 and back through Barnet where I chatted with an old friend. I returned around 9 p.m., calm and collected. I cannot say where Sigi was: he might have been in Australia! I don't think my mother ever really approved of my being a working mother, and she took the opportunity to tell my daughter what a terrible child I had been, so difficult to handle.

At the CSO life was not easy and there were many battles and much heartache to come. It is difficult today to visualize the male chauvinism of the time and the unconscious hostility there was towards promoting women to positions of responsibility. Duplicity, broken promises and half truths soon made my life impossible. I had never set out to be a fervent feminist, believing that slow, determined breaking down of barriers would in the long run be more fruitful. But experience was teaching me always to be on my guard and ready to fight.

I had been told that I was to be the editor of the new publication I was working on. Imagine my shock when, a few months later, I opened the Sunday papers to see an advertisement for the post of editor of *Social Trends* at the more senior level of Chief Statistician.* I applied for the job. Knowing that the dice were loaded against me, I was sorely tempted to don flat shoes, thick stockings and horn-rimmed glasses and tie my hair in a bun for the interview. The CSO did not have the courage or the courtesy to tell me themselves but instead I received a letter from the Civil Service Commission letting me know that someone else had been appointed to the post. I sent in my resignation.

Ron Fry, who was the successful candidate for this higher-level post, had been working for the Greater London Council. He had a formidable task in front of him for he was expected to carry the weight of major developments in social statistics as well as editing *Social Trends*. He knew that without me there was little chance of his getting the publication off the ground in the near future. He was wise and understanding. I was cajoled into withdrawing my resignation on the undertaking that I would be recognized as editor of the publication. Nor would I be part of Ron Fry's staff but I would have my own independent unit. This meant in effect that I was confined to my own patch and isolated from the rest of the work of the CSO.

Meanwhile *Social Trends* was progressing well. It had taken a long time for the various government departments to understand that the purpose of the publication was to look at social policy from a new viewpoint. Above all it was concerned with people and the impact of policies on the everyday lives of those people. This marked a departure from the more traditional approach, which was more concerned with collecting information to monitor the organization and administration of government and the cost to the exchequer. *Social Trends* set out to change the emphasis by looking at the social effects. It set out to show how many pupils or patients there were per teacher or per doctor rather than how many teachers or doctors or nurses there were in total. Some departments, such as the Lord Chancellor's Office, found it difficult to grasp that I wanted to know, not about the Court of Appeal and numbers of High Court Judges, but about the thousands of different types of case which brought ordinary people to the County Court.

Despite the dedicated work of my small staff, the lack of support from the rest of the Office was a tremendous strain. If I had a disagreement with a department there was no one to consult or back me up. All I could do was say, 'We will think about it and let you know.' After a while I might ring back saying, 'We have considered the matter and have decided to publish the table as it stands: if you still disagree, perhaps you would raise the matter formally.' It usually worked. On one occasion the Director of Statistics at the Inland Revenue department objected to my wanting to publish figures they collected showing the ownership of wealth for men and women sep-

---

* At that time the position of Chief Statistician was equivalent to that of Assistant Secretary in the Administrative Class. Amongst statisticians and administrators in the Civil Service, it is now known as 'Grade 5'.

arately, on the grounds that married women 'enjoyed' their husbands' wealth and there was no need for two sets of figures. To him power was not important. The table was published but with a footnote stating that part of the inequality in ownership arose from 'the fact that for married couples a large proportion of the property is owned by the husband although it may be used by both partners'! The cool relations within the CSO took their toll and many were the occasions when, deeply angry, I would spend sleepless night after sleepless night, wondering whether I was going mad and about to crack up, the disordered thoughts going round my head as if it were about to explode. At times it seemed that the whole project would be a failure and it would be my failure. If it succeeded it might privately be my triumph but publicly it would be that of the CSO.

Social Trends was ready for press in the autumn of 1970. It was published on 17th December 1970 and was an immediate success, so much so that the 3,000 copies ordered for the first print were soon sold out. It was runner up for the Library Association Colvin Medal for the best reference book of the year. I suspect that it was only second best because the 'perfect' binding fell apart before any librarian could finish reading it. I remained the editor for five years. Social Trends went on to become one of the most prestigious publications of the Government Statistical Service and now, in 1998, it is in its twenty-eighth year.

At the end of 1970, the initial launch of Social Trends had presented a problem because there had been a change of Prime Minister. Although it was a government publication and in no sense political, it had been conceived under a Labour Government and Harold Wilson had been asked to write a foreword. After the General Election in June 1970, Edward Heath headed a Conservative Government. The CSO was part of the Cabinet Office and we were anxious for him to be associated with the new publication. I was sitting with Claus Moser in his office: 'Do you think, if I could persuade the Amadeus Quartet to play, Heath would throw a party for it at No. 10?' Claus's eyes lit up and we smiled at each other: 'Let us put the idea to Robert Armstrong.' Robert, who was the Prime Minister's private secretary, had been a colleague of mine in the days when I was in the Treasury and we had met together every week to sing madrigals. Robert was clearly taken with the idea and said he would suggest it to his master. I approached the Quartet, who readily agreed.

The party was held on 5th January 1971 at No. 10 Downing Street. The CSO was allowed a substantial say in the guest list and we had a most enjoyable time. Indeed, it was difficult to bring the party to an end. Eventually Heath retired to his flat upstairs together with Sigi and the music critic Edward Greenfield to listen to some of his records. Claus and I were left to try and disperse the guests. Heath later referred to this party in his autobiography:

'We were able to use the dining room for chamber-music concerts. The first was a most unlikely occasion. The Amadeus Quartet played the Haydn quartet Opus 76, no.1, in G major and the Schubert quartet in A minor to celebrate the first issue of a new Central Statistical Office publication, *Social Trends*.'* He then went on to explain the link between me, the editor, and the Quartet.

Heath would have been happy to give us another party the following year but, as official eyebrows might have been raised at the idea of a succession of parties for *Social Trends*, he suggested instead that the Amadeus might like to play to mark the agreement for entry of the United Kingdom into the Common Market. He had hoped that this time the celebration could have taken place at Chequers but, as major building-work was in progress there, it was held once again at Downing Street.

The promised party at Chequers took place in 1973, but was a different kind of occasion. The guests, who included the Amadeus, were nearly all musicians, and they were to be entertained by Isaac Stern and Pinchas Zukerman. It was to be held on Saturday 27th October. On Friday 5th October, the Syrians and Egyptians attacked Israel, invading the Golan Heights and crossing the Suez Canal. That Friday evening was the start of Yom Kippur, the Day of Atonement, the most solemn and sacred day in the Jewish calendar. Most people in Israel had gone home, for it is the one day in the year when Jews throughout the world, even if they are not pious, unite in some sort of observance. The very survival of the country hung in the balance. There was intense anger with the British and the French who embargoed arms shipments to Israel. However, with the help of the United States who sent huge transport planes filled with military equipment, the Israelis drove back the Syrians deep into Syria and encircled the Egyptian Army on the west bank of the Suez Canal.

In these circumstances Zukerman, disgusted with the attitude of the British Government, decided that his place together with other Jewish musicians such as Daniel Barenboim was in Israel itself, supporting and encouraging the people in defending their country. I was hardly surprised when the telephone rang to hear Robert Armstrong's voice on the other end of the line. 'I know it is a difficult and sensitive thing to ask, but do you think the Amadeus would be prepared to play at Chequers on Sunday?' 'I think it is very unlikely, but I will tell them that you have called.' The Quartet contacted Isaac Stern as a fellow Jew to ask for his reaction. He suggested that they should play. He himself would also play but he would use the opportunity to turn the occasion into a memorial concert for Pablo Casals, who had died earlier that year, by showing a film about Casals's recent visit to Israel, thus making some propaganda for Israel at the same time.

* Sir Edward Heath, *Music, A Joy for Life*, Sidgwick and Jackson, London, 1976.

# CHAPTER FOURTEEN

# Juggling Jobs
# and Family

In 1970 I become re-established as a permanent civil servant. This enabled me to cash my endowment policies, repay my marriage gratuity and regain my pension rights. I was allowed to carry over the concession on special leave without pay and I made good use of it by regularly taking short breaks during school holidays.

After the success of *Social Trends*, I found myself travelling a good deal for I was increasingly being invited to talk about it both in Britain and overseas. I became a member of the working party set up by the OECD to exchange ideas on 'social indicators'. It met in Paris no less than four times a year, each meeting lasting about four days. The national delegations changed little and the continuity allowed useful work to be done which could then be fed back into the programmes of individual countries. It was a real working party consisting of people who were flexible in their attitudes and prepared to be convinced by other people's arguments, unlike so many international bodies in which delegates attend to represent the predetermined views of their governments and to state a position rather than have a real debate.

At the beginning of 1971, I was invited by UNESCO in Paris to take part in a discussion on 'cultural indicators' and I was then asked if I would tour East Africa to prepare for a conference of African states on cultural statistics to be held in Addis Ababa in Ethiopia. During my years at the CSO I had been regarded as the general dustbin for anything relating to cultural statistics, and I had a fairly wide knowledge of what was happening both in Britain and abroad. The African visit was a new experience and it brought home to me in a very real way the problems of hotels, travel and altered arrangements which the Quartet faced daily on their endless tours.

At the end of October I left for Dar-es-Salaam in Tanzania. Fog delayed the flight in Rome and I finally arrived in the middle of the night after a detour via Mombasa in Kenya. There was no one there to meet me and I felt very alone, very white and very female. After various meetings during the next day I left not much more that twenty-four hours later for Lusaka in Zambia. The next stop was Nairobi where I had an appointment with a large and impressive Kenyan who was librarian of the National Library. He had wrapping paper covered with 'Papas' cartoons in his room which I immediately recognized as having come from the book publisher Paul Kostin, who at that time lived opposite us. Yes, he knew him and his wife well and had in fact stayed with them when he visited London! He found it difficult to believe that their two daughters, although given the opportunity, did not want to go to university. I had time to shop and came back with a large wooden box containing a couple of Makonda carvings.

In Addis Ababa I again arrived late at night at a time when there was no way of finding out in which hotel I had been booked. I decided to avoid the Hiltons and the Sheratons and go to a hotel overlooking the Palace Gardens that the information desk assured me was good and had a more local atmosphere. The airport bus driver was puzzled, but finally took me there. It was in the middle of the town where building works were being carried out for new offices and conference centres. The local people nearby had no piped water. Women just carried pitchers on their heads. I had an audience with the Honourable Mary Tedesse, the Minister of Education, and had taken pains to remember her surname, only to discover that she was simply addressed as the Honourable Mary. She knew exactly what she wanted. She was concerned that the marvellous heritage of the Coptic Christians might be destroyed by vandals before she could take steps to preserve it. At the Statistical Office I was shown the arrangements for the census of population. Half the complement for the field staff seemed to consist of camels.

I arrived in Cairo late the next evening to discover that all the main hotels had been commandeered to accommodate the heads of African states, who were meeting there. With difficulty I found somewhere to stay and was wakened in the early hours by the muezzin's call from the mosque outside my window. It was Ramadan and no one really wanted to see me; so I visited the Pyramids, the National Museum, which houses Tutankhamen's tomb, and the Museum of Islamic Art. When I left the city, I was relieved that I had a diplomatic visa and that I was being accompanied by someone from the Statistical Office so that I could avoid the milling throng at the airport.

Although a conference on cultural statistics did take place in Africa in 1972, it was on a much reduced scale. These newly developing states, concerned though they were about cultural identity, were not much interested in compiling statistics. Nor, in most cases, was it practicable or useful for them to do so. The report I prepared on my return seemed to me largely irrelevant to their needs. It revealed the superficial approach UNESCO took to many of its projects. Many years later, when I was a member of the UK Advisory Commission to UNESCO, first the United States and then the UK withdrew from the organization, maladministration in Paris being one of the principal reasons.

Just before I left London for my African tour, to my surprise and disbelief I was told that a new post had been created and that I was to be promoted to be a Chief Statistician responsible to the new Deputy Director of the Office, John Boreham,* who was to be in charge of social statistics. I came to have a great respect for him and enormously enjoyed my work. He was highly supportive in every way and you always knew where you stood with him. If he was not going to back you up, he was not afraid to tell you why. When he first arrived, John once described the secretive atmosphere of the office as one in which people not only kept their doors shut but, if you ventured to enter the room, they immediately got inside the drawers of their filing cabinets and quickly pulled them shut too. He had some success in breaking down this attitude.

The direction of my work in the CSO changed and I was now travelling even more, not only to Paris but also to Washington, Geneva, Stockholm, Ottawa and Banff, as well as lecturing or attending courses in Britain. One of my colleagues on my visits to the OECD was Michael Bridgeman from the Treasury. He was shrewd and lively, always good company, and we were a popular team. His wife, June, was also at that time an Assistant Secretary in the Civil Service, and once when we discussed some of the problems of working full-time and having children at home – they had five of them – he said, with a smile, 'June and I regard it as a management job.' I was reminded of this a few years later when I applied for the post of director of the National Consumer Council. The sifting of the several hundred applicants had been put in the hands of management consultants and, although a few women had applied, none were shortlisted. Certain people on the selection panel who knew me asked why my name was not there. The answer was that they did not consider I had had sufficient management experience.

The last time I attended the OECD working party was at the end of January 1974. Tim Reid, a Canadian in charge of the Social Indicators programme in the OECD secretariat, held a party in his home. It was my birthday. The lights went out and in marched his two small children carrying a large birthday cake with candles burning brightly. One of the sad things about Quartet life was that we rarely managed to have family birthdays together and I was touched by the gesture. Tim had a succession of varied and interesting posts after he left Paris and his wife, Julyan, went on to have a distinguished career in the Canadian public service. Sigi and I became firm friends with them and whenever we can, we regularly cross the Atlantic to meet up. Quartet life had brought the Amadeus many marvellous friends the world over and I too was now adding to this precious network, first with the Baumols and now with the Reids.

In July 1974 I wrote my last editorial for *Social Trends*. Although by no means bereft of new ideas, it was time for me to move on. It was fitting that this last issue should include an article on the roles of men and women.

* In 1978 John Boreham (later Sir John) succeeded Sir Claus Moser as director of the CSO and the GSS.

Although it may seem surprising now, there had at that time been little comprehensive statistical analysis based on sex, and the article was widely quoted. My next job, still within the CSO, was to take charge of the branch dealing with the distribution and redistribution of income and wealth. Before moving to this new post I took three months leave without pay.

My final break with the Civil Service came in April 1976 when, somewhat reluctantly, I resigned. Despite all the trauma of the early years and the bitterness which ensued, I had enjoyed my work there. Its value outside the Civil Service was recognized in 1974, and again in 1975, when I was invited to 'The Women of the Year Luncheon'. But I had felt the loneliness of being a woman amongst so many men and I wanted the companionship and support which only other women can offer. I was the only woman in a senior staff of nineteen people. At their meetings there had often been snide remarks about women: even if they were unconscious, they were nonetheless hurtful.

Before leaving I went ski-ing with Daniel in Cervinia in Italy, where I unfortunately broke my leg. I had to hold my leaving party immobilized in a chair with my leg stuck out in front of me – like Sigi on another occasion. Harold Wilson, who had been my very first 'boss' when I began working in the Government Statistical Service in 1942, had resigned as Prime Minister in March, and he kindly agreed to come to the party to wish me well. We succeeded in finding someone to look after the bar who had originally been in the same office with us and trigger off Harold's prodigious memory for facts and faces.

From 1976 onwards I worked more flexibly on a freelance basis. Sigi had been under constant pressure from the Quartet to undertake more and more work, and the strain was beginning to tell. My old colleagues found it difficult to grasp that I was not 'retiring' but was leaving to do something else. One of the reasons for my move was in fact that I knew I would want to go on working beyond the Civil Service retiring age of sixty, and by resigning at fifty-five, when I could freeze my pension, I hoped I would stand a better chance of finding satisfactory work.

I had various projects in mind. One was working in Paris for the OECD secretariat who were prepared to have me for four days a week so that I could be home for the weekends. My teenage children thought it would be splendid for Mummy to have a flat in Paris; but sober reflection told me that the strain would be too great. Tim Reid, who had by this time left the OECD Secretariat, was now with the Canadian Treasury Board, and when they heard I was free I was asked to advise on a possible reorganization of Statistics Canada.

I was also already serving on the Gulbenkian Enquiry into the Training of Musicians. At a dinner arranged by the Fawcett Society in 1975 to mark International Women's Year, Lord Vaizey, who was chairman of the enquiry, had asked me if I would be interested. He was particularly anxious to include someone on the committee who could cast a professional eye over the mass of statistical material which would be part of the evidence. In particular, there was a need to look at the balance between the training of musicians and the prospects for subsequent employment. I readily agreed and not only became a member of the committee but also carried out much of the related research. In February 1976, the committee held the first of its eighteen meetings. The last was to be in September 1977 and its Report was published at the beginning of 1978.

At the time of the enquiry, there were plenty of wind players but a serious shortage of string players. The development of the technique for playing a stringed instrument is linked to physical development, and those who wish to become top-rank players must start at a younger age than those who play other instruments. The problem is therefore one of identifying and encouraging potential players among children of primary school age. The Committee accordingly recommended that the quality and status of music specialist teachers in primary schools should be improved. It went on to recommend that there should be more emphasis on high-quality instrumental training in secondary schools, particularly through the use of peripatetic teachers who were not usually qualified as class teachers. Good class music teachers in schools were, however, critically important and the committee recommended that a small number of further education colleges should specialize in training them. There was in addition a proposal for more satisfactory funding of the existing specialist music schools.

The committee was also concerned about the finances of the music colleges, particularly those in London that were not part of the public sector and hence only had guarantees against loss rather than a more satisfactory type of funding which could lead to 'a positive programme for the development of music training and education'. The committee urged them to seek links with either the polytechnics or the universities in London, and to provide more opportunities for students to take part in joint ventures between the colleges themselves. There were proposals too for improving their almost non-existent residential accommodation. The committee saw the function of the music colleges as providing training for aspiring performers and instrumental teachers, thus leaving the teaching of music in general to the universities and teacher-training colleges. Courses should be lengthened to four instead of three years and backed by local authority mandatory grants instead of discretionary ones. By reducing the yearly intake of students, standards could be raised.

What happened to the recommendations? At the primary and secondary school level, the cutbacks in public expenditure in the 1980s seriously affected music teaching and the situation was to grow worse, not better. Help with private lessons was one of the first cuts made by the local education authorities. Specialist music schools, however, were given 'direct grant' status, entitling them to be independent and fully financed from central rather than local government authorities. The music colleges have lengthened their undergraduate courses to four years and offer degree instead of diploma courses, thus enabling student grants to become mandatory. The earlier Gulbenkian report in 1965, as well as the Gowrie report in 1990, recommended a merger of certain of the London colleges and a reduction of student numbers to help improve quality. Most of them, however, still remain separate, but they have been integrated into the unified higher education funding system. Their financial backing has improved, particularly in relation to other academic institutions. There is more collaboration between colleges, and several are now linked in various ways to universities by a range of joint courses and exchange of teachers. Total student numbers have probably changed little but there are fewer undergraduate and more postgraduate students. There are also many more students from overseas, probably reflecting the improved status of the colleges over the past twenty years.

The Enquiry completed its work in the autumn of 1977. I had in the meantime been asked by the Arts Council to review their statistical needs. My report was published in 1979 by the Centre for Studies in Social Policy (CSSP), which I had joined at the beginning of November 1977 as a Senior Fellow. The Centre had substantial funding from the Joseph Rowntree Memorial Trust, including money for the upkeep of its beautiful little eighteenth-century building in Doughty Street in Bloomsbury. It consisted of a small homogeneous group of researchers who were concerned with social policy, and this common thread enabled us to discuss problems of mutual interest which cut across our individual projects. The year I spent at the Centre, before it was merged with Political and Economic Planning (PEP) to form the Policy Studies Institute (PSI), was one of the happiest of my life.

The eighteen months I spent doing freelance work before joining CSSP in 1977 had given me a little more time with Sigi and the family. In 1976 I had been able to join the Quartet briefly in New York, Evian, Dartington and Berlin. When I returned to full-time work at the Centre the problem of juggling jobs and family was once more thrust upon me. Being a researcher at CSSP was no less time-consuming than being a government statistician, but it was less tightly scheduled.

Meanwhile I myself was travelling rather less, although the late 1970s and early 1980s saw me giving talks and attending seminars and conferences as far afield as Uppsala, Ottawa, Washington, Boston, Michigan and Sofia. My job in a research institute gave me a little more flexibility than in the Civil Service and, during these years of frenzied touring by the Quartet, Sigi and I were able to snatch brief periods together whenever practicable. In April 1978, I joined him for the beginning of a North American tour in New York. It was during this visit that Sigi acquired the nickname of 'sex and violence'. After one of the Amadeus concerts we went to a party in a magnificent penthouse apartment overlooking Central Park. I was amongst people discussing some of the latest films, such as *Clockwork Orange*, when one of us moved over to Sigi's group. 'I hate second violinists,' she said vehemently, or so it sounded to Sigi, much to his embarrassment. Of course what she had really said was that she hated sex and violence, a carry-over from the conversation on films in my group!

After New York I joined the Quartet in Boston and Montreal and we then went our separate ways. I journeyed to Ottawa to stay with Tim and Julyan Reid and give a talk to the Canada Council on the arts in Britain. Sigi and I then met again at the university in Ann Arbor, Michigan, where I was visiting the Institute of Social Research. It was our wedding anniversary. The next day we had lunch with the singer Jessye Norman – Ann Arbor was her 'Alma Mater' – and found her wonderful company. Sigi described her embrace as like being enveloped 'by mother earth herself'.

It was in 1978 that the Centre for Studies in Social Policy was merged with Political and Economic Planning to form the Policy Studies Institute. The new institute had problems trying to develop a focus because the purpose and background of the two original institutes had been very different. The people in them found it hard to mix despite the efforts of its admirable and lovable director, John Pinder. The new institute was a curious body. It reminded me of John Boreham's description of civil servants shutting themselves in their rooms behind tightly closed doors.

One of the projects I undertook arose from my long-standing interest in the use of time which had been stimulated by the often frantic endeavours of women who work away from home to use every moment of the day to best effect. The study set out to measure and cost the time spent by women on the care of their families, particularly children and handicapped elderly relatives who might be living with them. The research, which was jointly funded by the Joseph Rowntree Trust and the Equal Opportunities Commission, was published by myself with Lucy Bonnerjea in January 1982 under the title of *Family Care of the Handicapped Elderly: Who Pays?* * Although it was only a small-scale survey and we were unable to get funding to proceed to a major one, it was a useful pioneering study that has stood the test of time.

After the family study I turned my attention once again to the arts and in September 1983, published a collection of material entitled *Facts about the Arts*. Meanwhile, I had ventured to teach statistics on a part-time basis to first-year sociology students at Brunel University in Uxbridge. At the end of August 1978, I had rather suddenly been asked to stand in for someone and rashly agreed. Term began in October, so that all I could do was take over the existing course and try to teach it. It was not the kind of syllabus I would

* Muriel Nissel and Lucy Bonnerjea, *Family Care of the Handicapped Elderly: Who Pays?*, Policy Studies Institute, No.602; London, January, 1982.

have devised myself. Most of the students had scraped an 'O' level in maths
to enable them to go to university and they did not take readily to a rather
theoretical if elementary course in statistics during their first year, with an
exam at the end. In the jobs they would eventually find themselves in, if they
used statistics at all, it would probably be to highlight in a practical way the
facts underlying a particular situation. Had I stayed for a second year I would
have substantially remodelled the course.

However, at the end of the 1970s sociology departments in universities
were beginning to suffer expenditure cuts and Brunel was no exception. So
I ceased to be Professor Nissel (the courtesy title had no doubt been given
because it was hardly respectable in the late 1970s to be a university lecturer
as just plain 'Mrs' Nissel) and set aside my brief but in many ways enjoyable
teaching experience. I had learnt a lot. Not only had I re-introduced myself
to statistical theory but I had picked up some simple tips about lecturing.
I had soon realized that I was incapable of drawing a 'normal curve' on the
blackboard, and that the best way to do it was to trace it onto a transparency
before the lecture and then project it and use a pointer. Will Baumol, my old
mentor from New York and Princeton, thoughtfully sent both Sigi and me
telescopic blackboard-pointers in 1978 when each of us became professors,
and mine has stood me in good stead ever since.

Throughout the 1970s the Quartet had been as busy as ever, performing
over a hundred concerts a year in all parts of the world. When Jean, our
housekeeper, left in 1970 we had come to rely on *au pairs* who were always
changing. For the most part, their prime motive in coming to England was
not so much to learn English as to escape from family pressures. I always
had the fear at the back of my mind that I would come home one day and
find nobody there except the children. Many of our *au pairs*, however, were
a real pleasure to have, and we are still in touch with a number of them. Our
most loved was Carmen Araluze from Bilbao. She came to us at the end of
1973 and stayed for three years, giving Sigi and myself peace of mind and
the children the continuity that was so important.

In 1973 my mother died. Sigi had returned from a tour of North America
towards the end of April while I and the children were away in Italy, and
found that my mother was not well. He quickly arranged for her to go into
hospital and, after playing a concert in London, flew out to join us. When
we returned home, it was clear that my mother was seriously ill with
pneumonia. She had decided it was time for her to leave this world and was
refusing the drugs offered her by the doctors and nurses at the little Colindale
hospital. She died on 1st May at the age of eighty-three and was cremated
at the Golders Green cemetery. She continues to haunt our top flat and it
does not seem possible that she is no longer there to pop her head out of the
window when I am working in the garden below. Only slowly, as the years
go by, does the enormity of the loss become more bearable, but it never
entirely vanishes.

# CHAPTER FIFTEEN

# Getting Away
# From It All

During the 1970s, when Sigi and I were both fully stretched, we often felt the need to 'get away from it all' during our brief periods of leisure. We began to think about finding a second home to escape from our busy London house.

Towards the end of 1972, we bought an old farmhouse and its adjoining barn in Tuscany in Italy together with Enid and Ernest Wistrich and their friends, Marilyn and Lolek Holzer. We had become friends with the Wistriches through the Labour Party in Hendon North when Ernest stood as our candidate in the 1966 General Election (see chapter 13). In the summer of 1967 we went on a walking tour with them round Mont Blanc, leaving all our children in the charge of our housekeeper Jean and their *au pair* in a chalet belonging to Enid's uncle near Aix-les-Bains.

In the early summer of 1972 we received a telegram from the Wistriches and the Holzers, who were in Italy. It said, 'Have found fantastic property; too big for two families would third care to join?' With the Quartet earning well and with my second income, we had been toying with the idea of buying a house abroad, but in France not Italy as neither of us had more than a few words of Italian. However, the idea appealed to us and in July Sigi and I flew to Pisa to see the property for ourselves.

We very quickly made up our minds and started negotiating with Peter Hart-Nibbrig, one-time chairman of Bols Gin and now a wily seventy-year-old. He had been the owner of the mountainside comprising the hamlet of Compignano since 1958. He and his wife lived in an historic eighteenth-century villa which had once belonged to Napoleon's sister Elisa, and in which his other sister, Pauline, had been imprisoned by the Austrians when she tried to seek refuge there in 1815. Hart-Nibbrig was now selling six farmhouses so that a share of the property could be passed to his son in Amsterdam. His daughter, Christel, wished to remain in her house near the villa in Compignano. All the farmhouses except Campora, the one we bought, were derelict, the occupants having found it more convenient to live down in the valley and come up in their cars to look after their olives and their vines.*

---

* In 1962 Peter Hart-Nibbrig commissioned Girolamo Lera to write a short history of Compignano. It has been translated into English by Catherine Morgan, with an introduction by Don and Beverly Weinstein (Campora Associates, London, 1996).

The view from our house is breathtaking: a wide expanse of hills reaching towards Lake Massaciuccolo and the sea. The only buildings in sight are small huddles across the valley. In clear weather we can see the islands of Gorgone and Capraia, and sometimes, in the faint far distance, the northern tip of Corsica. It is hot and dry in summer but rarely without a breeze, for it sits nearly 1,000 feet up on one of the hills between Lucca and the sea. In spring the nightingales sing and when it is dark in early summer it can be a paradise of dancing fire-flies. A thunderstorm will bring the brown earth to life and restore the rich variety of green of the Tuscan countryside: the grey green of the olive trees, the feathered fronds of the mimosa, the indented fig leaves, and the sombre green of the cypresses against the backdrop of holm oak and sweet chestnut. The cicadas scrape, footsteps on the grass bring the smell of mint, and the sun opens the faces of the deep blue wild chicory.

On arriving at the house one notices first the scent – of jasmine – not heavy but lightly floating up towards the sky. Then you see the purple flowers of the wistaria hanging down over the marble-topped tables on the terrace, leafless in spring but dense with shade in summer. The house itself is a jumbled mass of stone and brick, built and rebuilt over the centuries with a blocked-up window here, a door there, a new opening here and another one there.

One of Peter Hart-Nibbrig's main concerns was wild life. Compignano with its 174 hectares was large enough to be declared a game reserve and, with the help of gamekeepers, he kept the area free of random hunters shooting birds, regrettably a continuing and favourite pastime of Italians. Word about the sanctuary got around amongst the feathered fraternity and we waken to the sound of birds. In late spring swifts nest in the nooks and crannies of the old walls. After the land was split up, we were unsuccessful in trying to get the area classed as 'una Oasi di Pace' (Oasis of Peace) and were unable to continue to patrol the land. But birds still risk their lives to stay. The beautiful hoopoe, with its long curved beak and colourful crest, occasionally takes up residence. Swallows we have in plenty and they swoop in their hundreds over the swimming pool in the evening, open-mouthed, searching for insects, and waiting for me to finish my evening swim so that they too can take a dip. Sometimes, getting bored with waiting, they follow me as I turn in the water and touch down behind me. The speed and accuracy of a swallow's flight is astonishing: only a swallow can manage to fly in through one of our sitting-room windows and decide, without getting confused, that it is no place to roost and then fly out again through another window, perhaps coming back in again to take a second look to make quite sure.

The wood, which used to reach almost to the foot of the barn next to our house, was destroyed by fire in 1980. Fire is always a hazard and in 1988 it broke out again, this time in the woods on the edge of an adjoining property. The wind was blowing in our direction and it threatened to leap across towards us. After what seemed an eternity of unsuccessful attempts by the local fire brigade to get it under control, a helicopter with a water bucket attached moved in and, by means of sortie after sortie to our swimming pool, eventually more or less put it out. It continued to smoulder and flare up from time to time, and the smell lingered for days.

A place is only a home if it is rooted in people. Coming back to Compignano and Lucca is like visiting old friends. The shopkeepers remember you and give you warm greetings. From time to time we see Lelio Deghé, the gifted architect who transformed our house, and his English wife Susan who helped us furnish it in Tuscan style. Our real friends are those who make it possible for us to live there, particularly Gabriella Francesconi, our agent. Elegant, good-looking Gabriella, an eternal student when we first met her and now gracefully easing into middle age. She is kindness itself and quietly competent. No words can describe the debt we owe her. Also Mafalda Lucchesi, who worked in our house and on our land until she finally retired in 1995 at the age of seventy-six. She speaks her own variant of Tuscan Italian in a harsh voice and with such speed and complexity that few of us can understand her. She is forthright to the point of aggressiveness. In what we describe as her 'Si' or 'Non' mood, she could send us all scurrying out of earshot into the far reaches of Campora. But she has a heart of gold and she worked with incomparable physical grace. No mean feminist but, with her shapely figure and her well-tended hair, delightfully vain. Today the scythe and the broom have given way to the splutter and strident buzz of the grass-cutter and the vacuum-cleaner.

The many hundreds of people who have stayed in Campora will know that it is now very different from the original two simple farmhouses we bought in 1972. It took years to convert and put in good running order. There were a lot of problems, not least the continual frustration of machinery not functioning properly and of money being over-spent or spent to no good purpose. One of our favourite stories is of the time when Sigi asked the electricians if there was any hope of the new cable being installed and in working order by Saturday, the day we were expecting a number of visitors. 'S-i-i,' was the slightly doubtful reply; so Sigi checked, 'This Saturday?' 'Oh no, some Saturday'! At one point we were all so daunted that we even thought of selling the house, but then we realized we had spent so much time and energy in getting it into good shape that it did not make sense to get up and leave.

We three couples – the Wistriches, the Holzers and the Nissels – owned the property communally with each of us having a one-sixth share. This 'sextet', like the Quartet, was a kind of marriage. When we embarked on the venture there was scepticism. Was it likely that six people could collaborate to carry out such an undertaking? What makes such an enterprise tick, and how does it endure? In the event we were all joint owners in this co-operative for seventeen years and it was only the death of Marilyn Holzer in 1987 that eventually led her widower, Lolek to sell. The barn, which the Holzers used to occupy, together with a large part of the land, now belongs to an Italian family.

There were resentments within our co-operative which were not always satisfactorily resolved. But, as with the Amadeus Quartet, there were certain factors which helped us to stay together. In 1972 we all had children aged between eight and fifteen; we were politically on a similar wavelength; and we all loved music. Marilyn Holzer had been a child prodigy and was a professional pianist until she was handicapped by a stroke. The parents of both Ernest Wistrich and Lolek Holzer came from Poland and Enid Wistrich and Marilyn Holzer too were Jewish. Enid's family was also originally from Poland; Marilyn came from New York. Jewish friends have been very much part of my life although, as with the Quartet, there have been occasions when I have suddenly felt myself totally alien, standing apart, a 'shiksa' in a culture that is subtly different in its philosophy and humour.

Campora has been a marvellous holiday home. Every year the children brought their friends and we would pile into the Volvo, often putting it on the motor-rail in Boulogne, and meet Sigi at the end of a tour somewhere in Europe. Our first visit was in April 1973. I had three children with me, Claire, Daniel and his school friend Anthony Maher, and an old colleague from Oxford days, Mary Usherwood. We hired a car at Pisa airport and found our way to Lucca where we stopped on the road that used to run along the top of the wide city walls and asked a friendly Italian how to find our architect's office. He kindly took us right there through the maze of winding streets, and showed us where to park. It seemed a good beginning. However, although we had been assured that the house would be liveable, it was not. There were a few naked light bulbs but no water, so we had to fetch it in buckets from the nearest house two or three hundred yards away. There was a staircase without a rail and no glass in the windows. Moreover, despite it being spring, it hailed and the bedding we had brought was by no means adequate. One night, when everyone else was in bed, I snuggled beside the fire left by the workmen in the old kitchen and turned on the radio. It was the Amadeus Quartet playing Beethoven's Opus 132. That was a good omen.

The Quartet have visited our house both socially and during concert tours. They first stayed in February 1974 when they were touring Italy. The visit was a near disaster as it was very cold and the central heating broke down. It was also during the oil crisis, triggered by the OPEC countries when they collectively raised the price of oil. Italy had cut back petrol consumption by limiting the use of cars to alternate Sundays. The concert in Lucca was on a

Saturday and, as concerts always started late in the evening, we had scant time for a meal afterwards if we were to reach Campora before midnight banned all private cars that Sunday in Tuscany.

The next problem was how to get the Quartet to Perugia where they had a concert on the Sunday. Although it was only about 150 miles away, there was no possibility of obtaining a car to take them all the way there. It was difficult to reach by public transport but, as this was their only hope of getting there, we arranged for a couple of taxis – which were allowed to drive for short distances – to come up to Campora in the early morning to take them to Lucca station. From there they took a train to Florence where they had to change for the line to Terontola, the nearest mainline station to Perugia. There they were met by a local taxi, but the train was two hours late and they still had some thirty miles to go before they reached Perugia, just in time for the concert that evening.

The concerts in Perugia always drew a large and enthusiastic audience and I went there to listen to them on a number of occasions. Signor and Signora Buitoni were the mainstay of the local Chamber Music Society and we were regular visitors to their house after concerts. The Signora was a most likeable person, formidable but kind and tactful, and a friend to many artists. She regarded herself as a socialist and we had many interesting talks together about politics and women's issues.

Susi and Martin once came to Campora with their caravan; and shortly after we moved there Norbert built a house nearby at Barga. From time to time we visit each other. In 1975, when Norbert broke his thumb and Sigi had time on his hands, he invited Peter to stay. The two of them together enjoyed a restful holiday, studying new works and keeping each other company. Peter and Margit also came again in 1978. They paid us their last visit in 1987.

Originally neither Sigi nor I spoke any Italian. As a gifted linguist, he quickly began to pick it up in his negotiations with plumbers, carpenters, electricians and the like. This was a male world and, living on an isolated hillside with little opportunity to meet Italians, my best chance of learning Italian was by joining a class at the local institute in Hampstead Garden Suburb. Some while later I took a couple of short courses at the British Institute in Florence. Unlike with German, I was not inhibited by Sigi from speaking bad Italian and I have become knowledgeable enough to understand and take part in simple conversations and enjoy a meal with Italian people. Sigi has spent rather more time in Italy, playing concerts, teaching and sitting on juries, and though he seems fluent, he knows that speaking good Italian is beyond even his grasp.

We bought our Italian house because we had good friends who did the initial exploring and wanted us to join them. At the end of 1974 we also became the proud owners of a cottage in Sussex. When we acquired our house in Golders Green, which backs onto Hampstead Heath, we thought we would never feel the need for a country cottage. However, as the children grew older they loved to roam in the kind of wide, open space that the Heath could not offer.

One morning in the late autumn of 1974, Sigi woke up and said, as we sat in bed drinking tea: 'Why don't we put our money into something we can enjoy rather than tie it up in stocks and shares which don't seem to be very profitable?' 'You mean a cottage?' 'Why not?' House prices in England had come down steeply in the past year, and so I immediately contacted agents in Sussex and went down the following Saturday to view four possible properties. One of them, nestling at the foot of the South Downs in the Cuckmere valley near Alfriston, seemed almost ideal. It was between Eastbourne and Lewes, close to Glyndebourne and only five miles from the sea. Sigi and I loved walking and we would be able to stride out from the cottage without having to get into the car. Unfortunately, there was no immediate possibility of Sigi seeing the house, for the next day, which was a Sunday, the Quartet was playing with Clifford Curzon at the Royal Festival Hall and then on Monday they were due to begin a tour of Germany lasting until the middle of December. Not only would I not be able to get Sigi's opinion about the house, but it was almost the first one I had seen. It is always difficult to buy something without having had the opportunity to look around and find out what else is on the market. But I was sufficiently sure about this one to go down once more and make an offer. As with our London house, Sigi was back in London in time for us to exchange contracts.

The cottage had originally been three tiny thatched cottages. They had been converted by an architect in the early 1960s, and he and his wife had retired and lived there until they died. Unlike Campora and our London house, it was in very good order, complete with carpets and fitted cupboards, so we could move in quickly. I was working full-time and, apart from making curtains, could spare little time for furnishing and equipping it. By Easter 1975, we had sorted it out sufficiently to have our first holiday there, and from then on we visited it regularly at weekends. It is big enough to entertain friends and, during that first summer, we and our children had a continuous stream of visitors. Claire, just turned seventeen, was away at school in Dartington but Daniel, aged twelve, was at school locally in London, first at Hendon Prep and then at Highgate, the local 'public school'. He often came down and soon became expert at flying radio-controlled model gliders from the 'Long Man' bowl just above us. When Claire went to the University of Sussex, she lived in the cottage. We are as attached to our Sussex cottage as we are to our other houses and we have made good use of it. Daniel now owns it and the garden contains a swing for our grandchildren.

We have had a succession of Dalmatians and they have all loved chasing across the Downs; two of them would fearlessly go into the sea whilst the other, the gentle liver-spotted bitch who gave us nine puppies, would anxiously stay on the shore, barking at the water. Italy, however, was barred to dogs because of British rabies and quarantine restrictions. Our Dalmatians had to stay in London during our visits to Tuscany. Whilst we were away, and also during the long day when I was at work, we had to have someone who could feed them and take them out for walks. When we no longer needed *au pairs* for the children, Domenico Vivona lived in our house as friend and dog-watcher. He has been immensely helpful. Born in the early 1950s, he grew up in the sincere belief that we should not under any circumstances kill other people and, when faced with compulsory military service in Italy, he became a conscientious objector. Instead of doing military service, he was allowed to work for the 'Gruppo Abele', an organization founded by a priest to help young people, particularly drug addicts and prostitutes. It was based in Turin and he used to take groups of young people daily out into the country to work on the land. He came to England to study English and has remained with us, another perpetual student, a poet and a recluse. One summer in 1989, when staying in our cottage he wrote a poem comparing Alfriston with Trapani in his native Sicily:

'Alfriston'

Although Trapani is far apart
from this Cuckmere country,
the hills are yellow with cut hay
in the summer of '89;
a slice, a share that unify
that bind together the sky
and earth,
as though we need a confirmation
that wind and stone are only one.

More flints here,
no olives,
but hanging from the walls are flowers
that sing and drink the sunny air
ever oblivious of the evening –
webs          spiders          spinning.

Domenico Vivona

# CHAPTER SIXTEEN

# Staying at
# the Top

The phone rang, and I answered. It was Bamber Gascoigne, who for many years had hosted a popular BBC programme called 'University Challenge' for which different universities fielded teams to compete against each other answering general-knowledge questions. He wanted to tell us that they had just recorded the first of the new season's programmes, and one of the questions had been: 'Who are the following: Norbert Brainin, Siegmund Nissel, Peter Schidlof and Martin Lovett?' The buzzer was pressed: 'The Tolpuddle Martyrs.' Joyce Marlow's book where she describes what happened to the six Dorset agricultural labourers who agitated for better pay and conditions and were subsequently tried and transported to Australia, was a 'must' for Sigi's next Christmas present. Staying at the top of their profession did bring a certain distinction to the Quartet!

The 1970s were celebration years. In February 1970, Sigi, Peter and Martin were awarded the Order of the British Empire. Norbert had already received the award some eight years earlier. All four members of the Amadeus Quartet were now OBEs, or 'other blokes' efforts' as they are frivolously known. In January 1973 they celebrated their twenty-fifth anniversary with a concert at the Royal Festival Hall, followed by a reception attended by the Prime Minister, Edward Heath, and many of their musician friends. DGG at the same time presented them with the much treasured award of the Golden Gramophone. Later, in June, they were given the Grand Cross of the Order of Merit at the German Embassy. Another award, which aroused many emotions, was the Grand Cross of Merit for Literature and the Arts from the Austrian Government. Martin was particularly pleased that his three ex-Viennese colleagues should be thus recognized by the country that had once rejected them.

Appendix I sets out the itinerary of the Quartet during their twenty-fifth anniversary season in 1972–3, together with the programmes they played. There were major tours of Germany, Australia and New Zealand as well as rather shorter visits to North America, Japan and South Korea. Within Europe, in addition to between twenty and thirty concerts in Britain itself, they played in France, Belgium, Holland, Switzerland and Austria. They made a series of three visits to Munich in Germany to record Haydn quartets. Two anniversary films were produced, one for the BBC in London and the other for London Weekend Television whilst they were playing concerts in Vienna. The BBC film, produced by Humphrey Burton, not only focussed on the Amadeus playing but portrayed something of our home life. The Nissel interview was interrupted by our boisterous Dalmatian bounding in, and the film then showed the four Nissels fiercely facing each other across the table-tennis net. For the London Weekend Television programme, Derek Bailey cleverly interviewed each Quartet member as they gently swung round on the big wheel in the Prater pleasure gardens in Vienna.

The works included in Appendix 1 largely reflect what the concert agents wanted. For the most part it was the mainstream composers such as Haydn, Mozart and Schubert, with Schumann, Mendelssohn, Verdi, Dvořák and Smetana occasionally interspersed. Less frequently the Quartet played Bartók, Britten, Tippett and Seiber. Beethoven programmes, and whole Beethoven cycles, were increasingly in demand. Although the programmes were conventional, the Quartet made a point of not repeating them exactly on any two successive occasions.

The pattern of their concert-giving had been changing. During the 1960s and 1970s, much of their time had been spent in Germany, where each year they gave some twenty to thirty concerts, or about the same number as in Britain. In later years, France and Italy became increasingly important. They went on their first tour of South America in 1970 and after that it figured regularly in their schedule every three or four years. North American tours, involving around thirty concerts, used to take place every other year but they began to be interspersed with brief visits in the spring to the East Coast. They visited Japan, Australia and New Zealand in the 1960s and again in the 1970s. Although they never repeated their prolonged world tour of seven months in 1958, they were often continuously away from home for as much as two months.

They first went to the East German Republic in 1978. The Quartet had been to East Berlin on a number of occasions, either to play concerts or to record for the radio station, usually flying first to West Berlin and then getting East German visas to cross the border. However, on this occasion, they went by train after playing at Schloss Elmau in Bavaria, which had a common frontier with East Germany. Their first concert was in Karl Marx Stadt (Chemnitz) and special arrangements were made for them to be collected and driven to their hotel. Buses were not allowed into the small frontier town so they had to take a local train that was used by frontier officials and railway workers. This meant spending a few hours trying to keep warm in a nearby hut in the bitter cold. To get there they had to climb an icy embankment and they were helped by the East German guards who carried their instruments and suitcases. During this visit they also played in Leipzig and Dresden as well as East Berlin. In Dresden, to their dismay, they were greeted by musicians ringing up in despair saying they had been unable to get into the concert. The hall had been block-booked by the Communist Party. Although all four Quartet members were fluent German speakers they were accompanied by an interpreter, her real function being to keep an eye on them. They teased her by asking whether they needed an interpreter to translate the local Saxon dialect into proper German. Just before she left them at Checkpoint Charlie to go into West Berlin, she told them that her husband was a Protestant Minister. The Church at that time formed part of the resistance movement and he might well have been involved.

Not only did the countries the Quartet visited change during the course of their career, but so also did the towns where they played. More and more frequently they performed in the world's top cities and less and less in provincial towns with small enthusiastic music clubs. Their every note would be subjected to an intense scrutiny. In 1980 these towns included Edinburgh, Paris, Berlin, Amsterdam, Brussels, Stockholm, Copenhagen, Oslo, Naples, Florence, Sofia, New York, Detroit, Los Angeles, Toronto, Montreal, Vancouver, Buenos Aires, Rio de Janeiro, São Paulo and Santiago. They played only a handful of concerts in smaller places like Blackburn, Chichester, Rochdale, Bielefeld, Louvain, Cervo, Pavia, Bergen and Charlottesville.

During the 1970s and 1980s, pressure from within the Quartet to accept more work continued unabated, and their schedule entailed an immense amount of touring. In 1980 they played over a hundred concerts and made recordings of two late Beethoven quartets, Opus 132 and Opus 130, and of two Schubert quartets, in B flat and E flat. They also taught for eight separate weeks at the Hochschule in Cologne.

As well as playing, Sigi was still looking after all the negotiations and contracts for their engagements and preparing the material for their tax returns. This often involved chasing up fiddly but important details. For example, there was at one time in Germany a 'withholding tax', or income tax, which was to be deducted at source by the various organizations concerned. The law was subsequently changed to make artists resident outside Germany responsible for paying tax in their own countries. As the law was retrospective, thus enabling the Quartet to reclaim tax for a number of years, this meant Sigi had to contact the many organizations concerned in innumerable different places. Incidentally, it also threw up many instances where tax had been deducted from payments to the Quartet but had not been paid over to the tax authorities.

Sigi was very conscientious and scrupulously honest, so it was hardly surprising that during the 1970s, when he was in his fifties, the strain had begun to tell. Fortuitously the situation was greatly improved through a change of accountant. Sigi had not been happy with the firm who up to that point had been responsible for the Quartet's accounts. Not only did he find them unfriendly but he was always afraid that if he unwittingly made a mistake in the figures he submitted to them, they might not pick it up. It so happened that one summer the Holzers had an accountant friend staying with them in the barn in Campora at the same time as we were there. After sympathetically listening to our problems, he suggested we might approach a partner in his firm who was not merely an excellent accountant but also an enthusiastic music-lover. Accordingly, in 1976, Geoffrey Golbey became our accountant. With his short figure, his round boyish face and his East End Jewish accent, he soon became a familiar figure in our house, poring over the figures Sigi had painstakingly prepared. Sigi still had to provide him with this basic material of course, but from that time onwards there was someone to process them with care and understanding as well as professional knowledge.

The next step was to relieve Sigi of some of the burden of administering the Quartet's engagements. In 1979, the Quartet – with their four wives – were invited to play on a cruise in the Aegean on the *Mermoz*, a French boat belonging to the Paquet line. This gave us an opportunity to discuss plans.

Katinka, Margit, Susi and I joined the boat at the start of the cruise in Toulon and the Quartet arrived one day later in Rome. They had been giving a couple of concerts in St Jean de Luz on the coast near the Pyrenees, in the south-west of France, and the only way they could join the boat was to take a plane at Lourdes which had come from Dublin and was continuing on to Rome with a load of pilgrims. They played a concert in Rome as soon as they arrived that evening. Some days later they gave another concert, this time on board ship. We went through the Dardanelles into the Bosphorus as far as Istanbul, and on the way back we stepped ashore for concerts in Sicily and Corsica. Most of the passengers were French, with a sprinkling of Americans. They were wealthy and tended to wear the kind of glamorous outfits round the pool that I would reserve for the evening. The food, not surprisingly, was marvellous. Fellow artists included the violinist Gidon Kramer, the cellist Yo-Yo Ma, the baritone Hermann Prey, the pianist Peter Frankl and the trumpeter Maurice André. One memorable evening we heard Hermann Prey singing in the open air at Epidaurus in the Greek amphitheatre that had been built to seat 14,000 people. Sigi and I climbed to the very top where his voice came soaring up, clear and strong.

During the cruise, the Nissels made it clear that their life was becoming intolerable and that something had to be done to relieve Sigi of some of his work. The others agreed that we should try to find a good administrator. As soon as we returned to London, Susi got busy. One evening in the Queen Elizabeth Hall, she met Michael MacLeod, a friend of the sister of one of her

# TEATRO ALLA SCALA
ENTE AUTONOMO

**STAGIONE D'OPERA E BALLETTO 1979**
(390° dalla fondazione del Teatro)

Abbonamento ciclo Schubert
e Fuori abbonamento

## MUSICHE DI FRANZ SCHUBERT
II

### LUNEDI 19 FEBBRAIO 1979 - ORE 20.30

# QUARTETTO AMADEUS

**NORBERT BRAININ**, violino     **SIEGMUND NISSEL**, violino

**PETER SCHIDLOF**, viola     **MARTIN LOVETT**, violoncello

### PROGRAMMA

**FRANZ SCHUBERT**     **QUARTETTO IN SI BEM. MAGG. op. 168 D. 112**
Allegro ma non troppo
Andante sostenuto
Menuetto (Allegro)
Presto

**QUARTETTSATZ IN DO MIN. op. post. D. 703**

**QUARTETTO IN LA MIN. op. 29 D. 804**
Allegro ma non troppo
Andante
Menuetto (Allegretto)
Allegro moderato

---

**PREZZI (Tasse comprese)**
Posto unico numerato di platea e di palco L. 3.000
Posto numerato di I° galleria L. 2.000 - Posto numerato di II° galleria L. 1.000 - Ingresso in piedi L. 500
Abbonamento per l'intero ciclo di 8 concerti - Posto unico di platea e palco L. 24.000
Giovani fino a 26 anni sconto 50% su tutti i prezzi

I biglietti dei posti riservati e segnati nei grave possono quelli delle spezzale pero L 20, il ritiro presentazione
A termine di legge e vietato durante lo spettacolo effettuare, anche parzialmente, riprese filmate e registrazioni e scattare fotografie in sala o nei ridotti
Durante l'esecuzione dei concerti i vietato accedere alla platea e alle gallerie. Il pare venite muoversi dai propri posti prima delle fine di ogni pezzo
In platea non si cumo posti in piedi
Le gallerie si aprono alle ore 19.30; platea e palchi alle ore 19.45.
Informazioni e prenotazioni alla biglietteria del Teatro telefoni 887041/2/3/4, orario dalle 10 alle 13 e dalle 15.30 alle 17.30 (lunedi chiuso)

Non riaperta palchi e nei ridotta galleria (ingresso dal Museo Teatrale)
Dal 25 novembre 1978 al 28 febbraio 1979 (orario: 9-12, 14-18 - domenica esclusa)
MOSTRE VIVALDI in collaborazione con ASSESSORATO CULTURA COMUNE VENEZIA
"IL CIMENTO DELL'INVENZIONE - IL SECOLO VIVALDI E IL MELODRAMMA 1650-1750"
"VIVALDI DRESDEN BACH - INFLUENZE ED EFFETTI" - Catalogo ELECTA EDITRICE

Programme for the Quartet's concert at the Teatro alla Scala, Milan, 19th February 1979

pupils, who had gone backstage in search of a ticket for an Amadeus concert which had already been sold out. He had recently come to London to administer the newly established National Centre for Orchestral Studies at Goldsmiths' College for Basil Tschaikov. For the previous four years he had been in Edinburgh working for Leonard Friedman, who had founded and directed the Scottish Baroque Ensemble. He had therefore already met both Norbert and Peter when they had been engaged as guest artists. Susi remembers how she had a hunch and asked whether he would like to work for the Amadeus Quartet. When he said he would love to, she arranged for him to come to tea. The Amadeus asked him whether he could look after their affairs as a sideline to his main job with the NCOS. Michael seized the opportunity.

Thus began their nine years' association brought about by Susi's initiative. With his quick incisive mind, Michael in effect became their chairman, cutting through discussions that were going round and round in endless circles, with constant arguments about how many concerts they should give, where they should play, the fees they should charge, the works to be played, how much should be spent on publicity, etc. He himself said that 'one of the reasons why I was asked to do the job was that there were four people who had spent thirty years either on a concert platform, or on an aeroplane or in a hotel, and to a certain extent there was a kind of slightly childish helplessness about them, reflected in the very fact that they came to the conclusion that they needed someone to help sort things out. When they brought me in, I admired them for this. They gave me respect right from the beginning, and when I said I think we should do this, that, or whatever – not that I imposed my will on them at all – they listened to me. There is this recurrent pivotal thing. Quite often with a quartet there can be a vote or a feeling of two and two: with five people I could at least express an opinion and get a decision.' Sigi had found the eternal arguments and squabbling within the Quartet extremely burdensome and, in retrospect, he thought that the new arrangement added years to his life.

Michael was a great diplomat following, maybe, in the steps of his father who was a Scot in the British Diplomatic Service. For him it was mainly a question of how to approach the Quartet – as a group or individually. Sometimes, if he had to raise an issue with all four of them simultaneously, he would choose his moment before saying, 'This is the problem; what are we going to do about it?' At other times, he knew that the best way to sort things out was to speak to each of them separately. He lived in south London, so he might go on his motor-bike first to Hampstead where the Lovetts lived and find out what Martin's views were on what should be done. He would next move on to Sigi, and then to Peter; and end up at Norbert's house out in Bushey Heath. 'I would already have the other three's views so, if there was any difference of opinion, I could say to him, "Well, the others all think this." And if I also said to him, "I too think it is the sensible way forward," he would invariably say yes.'

Meanwhile our children had been growing up. One never ceases to worry or at least be concerned about one's children, whatever age they may be. However busy Sigi or I might be professionally, they were always in the forefront of our minds. Inevitably there were stormy scenes from time to time and I feared that I might at some point lose my temper and throw one of them out of the house. It didn't happen and we are now, all four of us, the best of friends. Above all we have a shared set of values.

Claire spent three sixth-form years from 1974 to 1976 at school at Dartington Hall and then went on to the University of Sussex to study geography. After that she began doing social research, a career which began for her at an early age. When she was only eight, she had already had a gift for putting people at their ease and making them laugh. At Christmas she had taken our new tape-recorder, then a novelty, and started interviewing people. She boldly went onto Hampstead Heath. 'Please, what do you think of snow?' a small voice asked. 'Would you sing me a carol?' Many years afterwards, when she worked for Michael Young, he sent her a copy of his book, *Life after Work*, with his thanks to 'one of the best interviewers I have ever known'.* Her research, much of it in the voluntary sector, focussed particularly on people who used public services. Later, the compassion she had for them led her to campaign from within by working as a manager in the National Health Service. Her forthright determination and fearlessly blunt approach usually succeeded in getting things moving. She finds nothing more frustrating than being stuck in a project that is in a muddle and has no useful purpose, for she has a perceptive mind and can rapidly sum up a situation. She is a good judge of people and with her generous nature genuinely cares about them and their problems. Small, vivacious and good-looking, she lives in the country in the Wye Valley, in a newly built house designed with great artistic flair.

At the age of seventeen, Daniel also went to school at Dartington. I had met many pupils from the school and had been been impressed by their self-confidence and poise. They talked to me as one human being to another with none of the obsequiousness towards adults that is sometimes found in pupils from English public schools. The atmosphere at Dartington could not have been more different from that at Highgate where Daniel had been previously. When I went with him for his interview, I was greeted by John Whittick, the headmaster: 'Hello Muriel, how nice to see you again!' At Highgate, I did not exist: all communications were addressed to Mr Nissel.

Both our children gratefully remember Dartington. Boarding-school allowed them to pursue their secret lives away from the watchful eyes of their parents, and many of the friendships they made there have been lasting ones.

---

* Michael Young and Tom Schuller, *Life after Work*, Harper Collins, London, 1991.

Although Dartington pupils were materially privileged, they were mixed in ability and background. Whereas for the intellectually inclined the school offered the prospect of university and a professional career, for others its attraction was that it gave them the chance to break away from the rigid bounds of more conventional schools and develop imaginatively in other directions.

This was particularly important for Daniel who is gifted in many different ways. He is musical and, like his father, has an ear for languages. At Dartington he began to study art for the first time and gained an 'A' level in it. His artistic bent is combined with an exceptional spatial sense and a capacity to understand how things work. But even Dartington failed him. Like so many of his generation, he was confronted with the gaps in training facilities for those in the sixteen- to nineteen-year-old age group whose interests and potential lay in their technical abilities. Neither public nor private educational institutions had anything satisfactory to offer him. Some years later, mainly through the strength of his well-balanced personality and his ability to seize an opportunity when it was offered, he studied stage management at the Bristol Old Vic Theatre School. This, combined with a firm grasp of the potential of the computer which he had taught himself to use, has made it possible for him to build up a successful career, initially in the theatre and later in the commercial world mounting exhibitions and conferences. He has great charm and, like his sister, can act as a calming influence putting people in all walks of life at their ease. He is now married to Eileen and is a model father to his son and daughter and to his stepson.

At the end of 1980, Sigi and I went to Israel for a couple of weeks together with Claire and Daniel. Along with the other members of the Quartet, Sigi was a 'friend' of the Rubin Academy of Music and had been invited to visit them. We spent Christmas in Jerusalem and visited Bethlehem where we were distressed by the commercialism and 'unholy' atmosphere. Sigi had many friends in Jerusalem and they set out to make us feel welcome in this fascinating city, which is shared by people of many faiths, and nestles on the hills overlooking Jordan across a narrow strip of the West Bank. We walked up the Via Dolorosa, winding our way through the narrow cobbled alley-ways of the markets in the Old City, and visiting the Stations of the Cross and the Church of the Holy Sepulchre where so many different Christian sects struggle for their square inch of ground.

Claire was at this time obsessed with living in the 'here and now', and showed an active lack of interest in the historical influences which had shaped her father's background and had been behind the making of the Jewish state. She was indifferent to Masada but enjoyed her 'swim' in the Dead Sea. Some things, though, did impress her, such as the Schiller kibbutz at Rehoveth near the Weizmann Institute of Science, where a distant cousin of Sigi's, Naomi

Kermisch, had gone late in 1938. Naomi left Vienna for Sweden and had then made her way to Israel. Her gentle husband, Zvi, had emigrated much earlier, and had helped to establish the kibbutz in which they were still living. He had been a member of the Hagana, an underground group set up to fight the British, and at one stage had been imprisoned and shared a cell with Moshe Dayan. When we met him, he was an old man but still making himself useful by helping to look after the community shop. Their family consisted of a son and two daughters but, to their parents' disappointment, none of them had remained in the kibbutz. When we visited them, their son, who was training to be a dentist, was doing military service.

We then took a bus to Haifa where we were entertained by an old friend of mine, Gershon Avner, and his wife Yael. Gershon's father, who had emigrated from Germany in the 1930s and started a textile business in Tel Aviv, had sent his son to the University of Exeter to learn English and then to Oxford where I knew him as George Hirsch. He returned to Israel where, after a spell in the Foreign Service, he became secretary to Golda Meir and later an ombudsman. When we met him in 1980, he was Chancellor of the University of Haifa. He drove us round the Golan Heights and from their dominating position we looked down on, and subsequently visited, various kibbutzim in Galilee. Throughout the tour, Gershon gave us a beautifully articulated running commentary on the political background and current problems in the area.

We went to Eilat for the New Year, hoping to relax and swim in warm sunshine. Instead it was cold and windy, and we huddled on the beach watching a crowd of ships on the Jordanian shore opposite unloading arms and equipment destined for Iraq in its war against Iran. Our apartment on the desert fringe was shoddy and not very welcoming. What is more, Sigi had a nasty cold and was not at all well. We had planned a celebration on his birthday but I developed raging toothache. What do you do in such circumstances in Israel on Shabbath? Sigi went off to the local hospital which recommended a Romanian dentist who approached me with shaking hands and unsteadily poised a drill over my mouth. He dealt with the aching tooth and the following week my London dentist told me that he had done a good job.

The day after we returned to London, Sigi left for Schloss Elmau. I was worried as he was still not well and he was very depressed. Norbert, Peter and Martin were all workaholics and, although Michael MacLeod had taken a huge weight of the administration off Sigi's shoulders, the sheer efficiency with which he worked meant that it was possible to fit in more and more concerts. Sigi had resisted but he was caught in the Quartet's net and had been unable to make his views felt. Something had to snap somewhere. It was a shock but no surprise when Norbert rang me on 12th January 1981 to say that Sigi had had a heart attack and was in hospital in Garmisch-Partenkirchen.

# CHAPTER SEVENTEEN

# *The Last Years of the Quartet*

---

Immediately I heard about Sigi's heart attack, I flew out to Munich, and I was met that same evening by our old friend, Dr Finny Prager. It was a relief to be welcomed by her kind face. She and one of her sons drove me through the snow the fifty or so miles to Elmau, where Sieglinde Mesirca assured me that I would be able to see Sigi in the hospital in the morning.

During our recent visit to Israel Sigi had not taken his violin with him and he had been unable to practise. He had been worried because he was due to play a concert the following Sunday, shortly after he arrived in Elmau. When he reached Munich railway station from the airport he had found that he might just be able to catch a train leaving almost straight away for Post Klais, the local station for Elmau. He ran pushing his trolley and sank breathless into a compartment as the train pulled out of the station. The brief sight of Munich had brought back memories of that dreadful moment as a child when Monday morning dawned and he had to go back to the school he so much hated. He got to Elmau in time to practise before dinner. In spite of all the friendly reunions and the busy hustle of arranging rehearsals, he remained depressed; he remembers how a sense of disquiet descended on him 'like a black cloud'. He had also been given a room he found gloomy.

He felt very short of breath during the rehearsal the day after and everything was a tremendous effort. When he went back to his room after the concert the following evening a deep oppression seemed to settle on his chest. It was not a sharp physical pain but more like a clamp over his heart. He spent the night walking up and down, and as soon as morning came he contacted a fellow guest, Dr Westerkamp, and told him that he did not feel well and might have had a heart-attack. The doctor thought it could be the after-effects of the bad cold he had had, and suggested that they paid a visit to the hospital the next day. During lunch Sigi told Dr Westerkamp he could not wait and wanted to go to hospital at once. The hospital took a cardiogram which confirmed that he had had a very recent heart attack, though the precise time it had occurred was uncertain. Sigi recollects how he heard the news with a mixture of shock and relief. He thought, 'If I survive and I am well enough, then I will be able to insist on reducing the number of concerts.'

After I arrived in Elmau on the Tuesday, I somehow managed to drift off to sleep from time to time that night, and I went to see Sigi early the next morning. We greeted each other almost unable to believe that we were together again. We were filled with a strange mixture of excitement and relief that for the moment everything was all right, but at the same time an awareness that of course it wasn't and that there was to be much uncertainty and anxiety in the long haul to come.

I stayed in Elmau until the following Sunday, long enough to know that Sigi was no longer in any immediate danger. Norbert, Peter and Martin improvised a couple of concerts without him and then went home. The sadness hanging over me lifted for brief instants when I talked with fellow guests or listened to the pianist Graham Johnson and the singers Neil Mackie and Linda Russell, also in an improvised concert because Peter Pears had had a stroke and was unable to be there.

Two weeks later I flew back to Munich and stayed in a guest-house near the hospital. I had a lonely sixtieth birthday dinner but I was able to spend the day with Sigi in his room overlooking the Olympic ski-jump and ski-runs on the Zugspitz. After another month, at the end of February, I went out again, but this time I stayed at the Lauterbacher Mühle rehabilitation centre on the Ostersee south of Munich where Sigi was to spend nearly six weeks before returning home. I scarcely recognized my husband. He greeted me in a track suit and training shoes, several stones lighter than when he had left London. He found the centre immensely helpful for, apart from diet, there was a strict regime of exercise, autogenic training – which is a form of relaxation – and medical tests to monitor the progress of his recovery. Above all it gave him the self-confidence to judge just how much physical exercise he could safely take. Walking was encouraged, at first under supervision to ensure that patients were not over-ambitious. When I arrived, we walked on the ice on the Ostersee in brilliant frosty sunshine but by the next day a thaw had set in and it was no longer safe. We explored the pine forests instead.

While Sigi was ill, DGG had been most kind and considerate. Their representative, Steven Paul, brought him a Walkman and a collection of tapes which gave him great pleasure. This small tape-recorder was a new invention at the time and the sound that came through the earphones was a revelation.

At the end of March an old friend, Derek Kartun, drove out to Germany and brought Sigi back home in his car to avoid the possible dangers of flying. In London there were still tests to be done. The need for a heart-bypass operation had not been ruled out, and towards the end of 1982 he was advised to undergo it. Since he wished to minimize the upset to the Quartet's activities, he hoped he might be able to have the operation at the end of the 1983 season. Throughout his illness his colleagues had been most co-operative and supportive and on this occasion Norbert insisted that Sigi's health must come first. 'Have it done as soon as possible,' he said; 'I couldn't bear it if something happened because you delayed it.' So in the middle of February, Sigi was operated on by Magdi Yacoub* in a small private hospital in Ealing. He returned to the Lauterbacher Mühle to recuperate early in March. Britain's rehabilitation facilities could offer nothing comparable.

In the years that followed the other three members of the Quartet continued to be unwaveringly loyal. After serious discussions it was finally agreed that they should limit their concerts to forty a year. Why forty? It was an arbitrary figure, and there was always the temptation to add just one or two extra ones.

The limitations on their activities inevitably presented the Quartet with problems. In February 1981, while Sigi was in hospital, Norbert, Peter and Martin had recorded Mozart's first and second piano quartets with Walter Klien, and a year later they recorded Mozart's Divertimento, K563. From time to time they were to tour without him, playing string trios and piano quartets. In May 1986 they went to Australia and on another occasion they visited South America. Once when they were playing in Turin, Sigi went with them but did not play in every single concert, sometimes remaining behind in the hotel to practise instead.

However, the whole Quartet continued to play throughout the world, not only in Europe but on the west and east coasts of North America and in South America, Japan and Australia. In January 1982 they celebrated their thirty-fifth anniversary with a performance at the Wigmore Hall of quartets by Haydn, Beethoven and Britten. This was followed shortly afterwards with an all-Beethoven concert at the Festival Hall. In the spring they were engaged to give a Beethoven series at the Tully Hall in New York. They had already discussed and fiercely argued about the possibility of putting on the series themselves in the Carnegie Hall. In spite of the doubtful prospect of breaking even on such a venture, they felt the need for greater publicity in New York and for the wider impact throughout the USA of successful reviews. But their agent, Mariedi Anders, persuaded them that the prestigious chamber-music series at the Tully Hall was an equally satisfactory and more reliable way of achieving the same ends. They would also receive a fee.

The next year they played at the Royal Opera House in Covent Garden at a concert introduced by Dame Janet Baker in aid of the Edward Boyle Memorial Trust set up 'to encourage young people of real promise'. Lord Boyle, who had been Vice-Chancellor of the University of Leeds, was a great music-lover, as well as being a statesman and educationist. When we were in New York some months later, I went shopping. Our visits to the USA were

* Later Sir Magdi Yacoub.

The Royal Opera House
Covent Garden
General Administrator: Sir John Tooley

A Gala Concert in aid of the
Edward Boyle Memorial Trust
Sunday 6 February 1983 at 8 pm

In the presence of
Their Royal Highnesses The Duke and Duchess of Kent

Artists Appearing

The Amadeus String Quartet
Norbert Brainin, Siegmund Nissel, Peter Schidlof and Martin Lovett

Dame Janet Baker

Vanya Milanova

Murray Perahia

Kathryn Stott

Silk programme designed and printed by Michael Szell

Programme for the Quartet's Gala Concert at the Royal Opera House,
6th February 1983

always a good opportunity to refurbish my wardrobe, for I had time to spare and clothes were cheaper and more interesting there than in London. When I returned to the Baumol apartment in Greenwich Village and showed off my purchases, imagine our surprise when we found that in the text of my black and white shirt designed from newspaper cuttings there was a press review of this very same concert. It referred not only to Janet Baker's singing of Schubert songs accompanied by Murray Perahia but also to Murray's rapport with the Amadeus Quartet in Mozart's G minor piano quartet. Fame indeed.

On 25th November 1983 they were each awarded the honorary degree of Doctor of Music by the Chancellor of the University of London, HRH Princess Anne. Peter was a little late for the ceremony after being caught in a traffic jam. When they were invited to play at a similar occasion at the university a few years afterwards, Princess Anne teasingly pointed out to Peter that on this occasion, unlike the previous one, he was punctual. She went on to assure him that they would not have started without him.

Immediately after receiving the awards at the University of London they paid a second visit to East Germany. They had been invited to Leipzig by the conductor, Kurt Masur, to celebrate the 150th anniversary of the Gewandhaus Quartet. This quartet, which had of course had a succession of different members, was named after the building of the same name which had been transformed into a concert hall and was home to the Gewandhaus Orchestra as well as to the Quartet. Kurt Masur, who was an international figure, lived in Leipzig and became a focal point for resistance to the Communists before the Berlin Wall came down.

The many important events in these years included, in December 1984, a performance by the Quartet in Kensington Palace in the presence of the Prince and Princess of Wales in aid of the Royal College of Music Centenary Appeal. In the spring of 1985, and once again in 1987, they played at the Carnegie Hall in New York. They were pleasantly surprised to find how good it was acoustically despite its size.

Then on Sunday 5th July 1987, they sat down together on the platform at Cheltenham for the last time. In his usual fashion, Peter gave a slight grimace, more like a wince, Martin was his serious implacable self, Sigi sat there unmoving, Norbert gave a slight nod of his head, their bows moved together and they began playing Beethoven's Opus 18, no.4.

Appendix 2, showing their itinerary for this final season in 1986–7, gives a typical picture of the Quartet's activities in their last years. Although they played only forty-two concerts, at least half of them were in the world's top concert halls, including the Carnegie Hall in New York, the Teatro Colon in Buenos Aires and the Barbican and Royal Festival Hall in London. They did two complete Beethoven cycles, in Munich and Turin. There was also a tour without Sigi in Australia, when the other three members played string trios and piano quartets with Maureen Jones.

The most striking change in the Quartet's engagements towards the end of their career was the substantial increase in their teaching activities and the sharp reduction in the number of recordings they did. In 1980 and 1981 they re-recorded three Schubert and three late Beethoven quartets, but after that their long association with DGG more or less came to an end. However, their last season included four days' recording for Decca. It was the first session of what was intended to be a complete re-recording of all Beethoven's string quartets, something very dear to their hearts. Their understanding and interpretation of these quartets had changed greatly since they first started playing them in the 1950s and they were anxious for this to be recorded for posterity.

Fewer recording sessions and fewer concerts meant that there was more time for teaching, and from the end of the 1970s it had begun to take up a greater share of their already busy lives. In their last season they devoted eighty-two days to it – they spent more than two weeks both teaching and playing at the summer festival in Città di Castello in Italy, and then, during the rest of year, taught at both the Musikhochschule in Cologne and the Royal Academy of Music in London.

The changing pattern of the Quartet's activities was reflected in their earnings. These are set out in Appendix 3 for the 1972–3 season, their twenty-fifth anniversary year, and for 1986–7, their final year. By far the biggest change in their income came from teaching. Whereas it did not figure at all in 1972–3, by 1986–7 it was well over forty per cent of the total. Income from concerts on the other hand, which had accounted for some two-thirds of total earnings in 1972–3, had shrunk to two-fifths in the later period. Recordings, which had been enormously important in the earlier period, bringing in about a quarter of their total income, continued to remain significant in the later period. Although the Quartet did little new recording in their last years, sales of their past work remained high. Radio and television broadcasts, together with their repeats, which had also been significant in the early days, were minimal.

In the 1972–3 season, when the Quartet gave just over a hundred concerts, their total earnings, after deducting expenses, were some £70,000. In 1986–7, they were over £300,000. However, between the two seasons inflation had taken hold and prices generally had risen more than four times. The figure for 1972–3, expressed in terms of the prices prevailing in 1986–7, would thus have been much the same as that for the later season. An income of nearly £80,000 each at the end of their career in 1986–7 would have been beyond their wildest dreams in their early days.

The Nissels were undoubtedly well off, particularly as we had the benefit of two incomes. Our outgoings were high since we owned three houses, and their upkeep, together with insurance for them and for Sigi's violins, was considerable. Moreover, in their sixth-form years both children had gone to boarding-school. But as we grew richer, our life-style did not change much. Sigi and I had both been brought up to watch our spending carefully, and the war years had further instilled into us the importance of never wasting anything. With the children he was always 'Daddy Dustbin' because he would clean up any food they spurned. Taxis were still a luxury if a bus or train – or walking – would do instead. What we did do was save money, and we were thus able to give our children a good start to their adult lives by helping them set up home for themselves.

Although my income was modest in comparison with Sigi's, during the ten years from 1968 onwards when I had been working full-time, it was fairly substantial. Once I reached the age of sixty in 1981 I began to work part-time. In 1986 I left the PSI and after that, with papers and books at our home and a computer at my desk, I worked on a freelance basis.

Amongst the various projects I undertook, one of the most interesting was a history of the General Register Office, which was commissioned for its 150th birthday in 1987. Up to 1837, the main population records had been the parochial registers of baptisms, weddings and funerals, and the new office was set up to keep official records of births, deaths, and marriages. It was also given the task of conducting censuses of population. The story was a fascinating one, with all kinds of unexpected sidelights such as the use of notifications of deaths to trace the origins of cholera outbreaks during the nineteenth century. It was fun to write and I had tremendous co-operation both from the Office of Population Censuses and Surveys, who dug out old documents and illustrations with enthusiasm, and from Her Majesty's Stationery Office, who proudly displayed it at the Frankfurt Book Fair.*

Shortly afterwards I became the statistical consultant to the Carnegie Inquiry into the Third Age, a major inquiry that lasted some three years. It covered all aspects of the lives of those around the age of fifty who had established their families and their main job or career and were pondering what the future might hold for them, and what might be done to help them. A few years later, as the original editor, I was asked to write a signed intro-ductory article for the twenty-fifth anniversary of *Social Trends*. My review of the period from 1970 to 1995 inevitably included the years in the 1980s when severe cuts in public expenditure on Government statistics and the pressures that ensued had had, in my view as a professional statistician, an unfortunate impact on the content of the publication. It had led it to concen-trate on 'Mr and Mrs Average' at the expense of analysis of one of the major

---

* Muriel Nissel, *People Count: A History of the General Register Office*, HMSO, London, 1987.

social changes of the time, the growing inequalities in income. The article was unexpectedly withdrawn just before publication and the implied censorship, which threw doubt on the integrity of the GSS and threatened further muzzling, was quickly picked up and strongly criticized by the press. The article was subsequently published in the *Journal of the Royal Statistical Society*.

When the Quartet ceased to exist in 1987, Sigi continued to be extremely busy. He was much sought after throughout the world as a teacher and as an adjudicator at chamber-music competitions. He had always loved teaching and for him a whole new career opened up. From time to time he played chamber music: never quartets, since that would have been unbearable, but sextets. Norbert and Martin played together for a while in the Amadeus Trio, mainly with Arnaldo Cohen and Pludermacher, but also with various other pianists. They too were in much demand as adjudicators at chamber-music competitions but, as with Sigi, teaching was their main occupation. The lasting legacy of the Quartet is to be found not only in memories of how they played and the recordings they made, but in their coaching of string quartets, through which they passed on the wisdom and experience gained in their forty years' playing together.

# CHAPTER EIGHTEEN

# Teaching:
# An Amadeus Legacy

Teaching requires special gifts which performers do not necessarily have. The members of the Amadeus all knew how to teach. 'Those who can, do; those who can't, teach.' This gibe, often used to taunt musicians, cannot be levelled at the Amadeus, for they had already been much in demand as teachers when they were at the top of their profession as performers. As early as 1965 they had taught both in the Summer School in Aspen in Colorado and at Stanford University, and in 1968 they had taught for a brief spell at the Van Beinum Foundation in Holland.

At the castle in Breukelen where the course was taking place, Queen Wilhelmina quietly took her place and listened. One of the quartets participating had been given permission by the Romanian Government to attend the course. The problems they encountered were typical of those facing musicians who lived behind the Iron Curtain. After the course, the first and second violinists, who had family ties in Romania, returned home, but the viola player and the cellist decided to stay in Holland. Later the second violinist, Alexandru Todicescu, and his wife managed to escape to Holland, and eventually he and the viola player, Laszlo Kiss, emigrated to Australia to help found what became the well-known Sydney Quartet. Stefan Metz, the cellist who remained in Holland, joined the Orlando Quartet; he never forgot his lessons with the Amadeus and subsequently invited them back to teach at the Orlando Festival organized by his quartet.

From 1966 to 1969 the Amadeus taught chamber music once a month to the BBC Training Orchestra in Bristol. This orchestra was the brainchild of William Glock, who was Controller of Music at the BBC. He considered that orchestral players would benefit from experiencing the independence that playing chamber music could give them.

They started teaching at the Musikhochschule in Cologne in the autumn of 1978. Sigi had already been approached by the Conservatoire in Frankfurt, but negotiations to involve all four of them had not been successful. He had no wish to teach separately from the rest of the Quartet, nor would it have been practicable for him to do so. Norbert then began to investigate the possibilities in Cologne. It so happened that the Prime Minister of Lower Saxony, Johannes Rau, was a music-lover and, partly through his initiative, funds were made available to make it possible for the Musikhochschule to engage them. At the end of October 1978 they began teaching eight times a year for a whole week. When Peter died, the arrangement continued for the three remaining members until the government retired them on the grounds of age. Some years later, the Alban Berg Quartet took over, although they had previously declined the post because they saw no good reason why eminent musicians should be ousted because they were growing old.

The Musikhochschule became a popular centre for young quartets. Not only was the Amadeus based there but so was their old teacher and mentor, Max Rostal, now venerably capped with a white wig. Moreover, the government made generous grants available, thus enabling quartets both from Germany and from other countries to have lessons at very low fees. Numerous quartets and many individual students taught by the Amadeus are now in thriving chamber-music groups making their way in the profession all over the world. Two of the quartets, the Auryn and the Carmina, both played at Peter's funeral.*

In September 1986 the Amadeus also began teaching at the Royal Academy of Music (RAM) in London. They had explored the possibility some years before, but they had expected to be paid at something near the rate they received when playing concerts, and at that time the finances of the RAM were insufficient. However, in 1986 Sydney Griller, who was in charge of chamber music there, was due to retire and the Academy was looking for a replacement. Sydney and the other members of the Griller Quartet had been familiar figures in England during the war but had subsequently left to take up a residency at Berkeley in California. When the Quartet broke up, Sydney came back to London. The RAM approached the Minister of Education, Sir Keith Joseph, whose daughter was a student at the Academy, to see whether additional finance might be made available to employ the Amadeus. The approach was successful and an arrangement was made whereby each member would teach for twenty-seven days a year. Although Peter died within the first year, Norbert, Sigi and Martin continued until eventually cuts in expenditure forced the Academy to retain only Sigi. Many of the groups they taught, such as the Gould Piano Trio, the Leopold String Trio and the Duke, Emperor and Vanburgh Quartets, are also now well established in the profession and a number have been first-prize winners in international competitions.

The RAM could never become the kind of centre for chamber music that developed in Cologne. Whereas quartets from all over Europe were

---

* As well as the Auryn and the Carmina, many others are already well known. They include the Fontenay Piano Trio and the Cherubini, the Danel, the Henschel, the Latin American, the Parisii, the Verdi, the Voces and the Ysaye Quartets.

encouraged to come to the Musikhochschule and have lessons with the Amadeus, the scope in Britain was much more restricted. The Gulbenkian Enquiry into the Training of Musicians, which had reported in 1978, and of which I had been a member, drew attention to the importance of providing more opportunities for students to take part in joint ventures between colleges. Little happened because of the continuing rivalry between the different institutions. The stupidity of this short-sighted approach meant that, even within London itself, students could not have lessons in a chamber group they might have chosen to put together whilst playing in youth orchestras or at music courses unless they happened to be at the same college. Indeed, when the Amadeus first started at the RAM, only current students were entitled to be taught. It was not until later that a concession was made so that ex-students, such as those in the Vanburgh Quartet and the Leopold Trio, could also come for tuition.

In addition to their regular work in Cologne and London, the Quartet were much in demand for various courses. They taught at the Britten-Pears School for Advanced Musical Studies at the Maltings in Snape* in 1979 and in Berne and Paris in the 1980s. In 1984, 1985 and 1986, they both played concerts and taught at Città di Castello.† For a while after Peter's death, Norbert, Sigi and Martin, and then Sigi alone, continued teaching there.

In Cologne, although they went as a quartet, they always taught individually and the students could choose whom they wished to have lessons from. At the RAM the arrangement was different in that they tried to spread their teaching days over the term so as to give students the maximum chance of benefiting from the Amadeus' experience. Some well-known quartets, such as the Chilingirian and the Lindsay, have managed to teach as a group, but the Amadeus never attempted it. They were so used to discussing musical points amongst themselves when they were rehearsing that they thought they would probably start arguing about interpretation instead of teaching the students. They also felt that everyone would be more relaxed if they taught them separately.

Each member of the Quartet had a different approach, reflecting their different personalities; but as they were all teaching against the background of what they themselves had been aiming at with the Amadeus, the end results were similar. Peter was a great teacher of the viola and people who had lessons from him revere him as a saint. Norbert's strength lies in his ability to inspire people. He was a remarkable quartet leader with an intuitive approach and understanding of what the music was about. Likewise, when he is inspired, he can convey that to his students. He often sings to them or

* The Camerata, the Nossek and the Takacs Quartets all studied with them at the Britten-Pears School.
† One of the groups was the Manfred Quartet who were subsequently winners in the prestigious Banff and Evian competitions.

picks up his violin to demonstrate a point, particularly if he is discussing a first fiddle part. This holds certain dangers, as what students choose to hear may not necessarily be what is intended. It needs to be supplemented by clear and consistent explanations of balance, articulation, interpretation of mood and choice of tempo. Martin and Sigi cannot use their instruments in the same way as Norbert and have to convey what they want differently. They know what the music should sound like and both have learnt how to explain it verbally. They can also suggest what they want and help students to understand the shape and purpose of the music by singing, conducting, moving around and generally cajoling.

After Peter's death, Norbert, Sigi and Martin, together with a group of devoted admirers and friends, considered commemorating the Quartet by setting up a competition. One problem was that there was already an established competition held in Britain every three years under the aegis of Sir Yehudi Menuhin, and there was hardly room for a second one. Moreover, that competition was about to move from Portsmouth to London. Sir Claus Moser accordingly wrote to Sir Yehudi suggesting that the existing competition might be merged with the proposed Amadeus competition. This was not acceptable, and a compromise was reached whereby one of the remaining members of the Quartet – it was agreed between them that it should be Sigi – would become a permanent member of the board of the Menuhin competition. In future, the competition would be known as the London International String Quartet Competition, and each of the three Amadeus players in turn would be on the jury of the competition. There would also be a special Amadeus Trophy. Organizing competitions, even at three-yearly intervals, is a major undertaking and the arrangement was a very agreeable solution.

Instead of a special competition to commemorate the Quartet, a general fund – the Amadeus Scholarship Fund – was set up to help young string quartet players. The Fund has charitable status and is governed by a committee with Sir Yehudi Menuhin as its president. Sir John Burgh was the first chairman and he was succeeded later by Oliver Prenn. The administrator is Brigitte Eisner, who is a professional cellist and a long-standing friend and admirer of the Quartet.

Although at one time it was hoped that sufficient capital might be forthcoming to create an endowment fund, this did not materialize and money has to be raised annually. The list of benefactors is a long one, with some people giving large sums and many small amounts. One donor is particularly appreciated because of her association with Haydn. Norbert happened to find out that Sotheby's were auctioning the original manuscripts of the Opus 50 quartets nos.3, 4, 5 and 6. He mentioned this to Oliver Prenn, who then wrote to Sotheby's asking if they would forward a letter to whoever might own the manuscripts suggesting that some of the proceeds might be donated to the Amadeus Scholarship Fund, thus enabling Haydn's music to help young chamber-music players. The owner – who was selling the manuscript – lived in Melbourne in Australia. By coincidence Sigi was about to adjudicate at the Melbourne International Chamber Music Competition for piano trios and string quartets, and so Oliver Prenn let her have an address at which Sigi could be contacted. She and her husband invited him to visit them and kindly agreed to make a yearly donation to the Fund.

They have both been to London since, and we have had the pleasure of entertaining them in our home. They told us that in 1852 the manuscript of Haydn's Op.50, nos.3, 4, 5 and 6, was brought to New Zealand by an early settler from London. He had a deep interest in music played by small groups, and it is likely that he sometimes performed these quartets with other musicians in the young colony. His granddaughter was given these autograph scores and she kept them at her high-country sheep-station where she lived for many years. She later gave them to her sister in Australia. This family has many musical interests and after the sale of the manuscript a fund was established to help young musicians. Sigi invited one of them, an opera singer, to attend a masterclass of the Kim Quartet, and the family in Melbourne were able to listen to it via his mobile telephone.

The Amadeus Scholarship Fund has been used to finance students attending the Amadeus International Summer Course, which is held for two weeks in London under the aegis of the Royal Academy of Music with the members of the Quartet as teachers. In the early years it was run in association with Regent's College but it was later taken over by the Amadeus members themselves. Robin Anderton is the administrator of the course. Before her marriage, Robin had looked after the Amadeus when she had been on the staff of the concert agents Ibbs and Tillett. Blonde, round-faced and plump, she remains cheerfully unruffled as she most efficiently deals with every crisis. The students love her and she in turn enjoys working with them.

A dozen or more quartets from all parts of the world attend the course each week. Teaching usually takes place at the RAM, and accommodation is in nearby institutions. Some participants are able to meet at least part of their expenses, often with help from scholarships awarded in their own countries, but most of them depend on full scholarships from the Scholarship Fund. Appendix 5 gives details of the quartets who have attended in the last nine years. Nearly ninety different groups are listed. Many stay for the full two weeks, and many come again for a second or third year. More than a dozen of them had already had lessons with the Amadeus when they were teaching at the Cologne Musikhochschule. Although the individual members of a quartet frequently come from different countries, the number of nationalities ascribed to the groups adds up to more than twenty. The largest contingent comes from Germany, followed by those from the UK, France, Italy, Poland and Japan. As many as sixteen quartets have come from eastern Europe.

What has become of all these aspiring quartets? Several of them are already well established and developing successful professional careers. Some gifted ones have only been in existence a short while and time alone will tell whether they stay together. Many have won first prizes at international competitions. Others are teaching as well as playing. A short account of the achievements of the various quartets who have been on the Summer Course is also given in Appendix 5. It is an impressive record and a tribute to the lasting reputation of the Amadeus and their teaching abilities. As Gina MacCormack, one of the talented young violinists attending the course has put it: 'It is the most wonderful experience to be at the receiving end of forty years of quartet-playing wisdom, and when it is imparted (or should I say "shared") with such obvious enthusiasm and affection for the music, and spiced with anecdotes from such interesting lives, one cannot help but be totally inspired. No wonder one keeps coming back for more!'

From time to time Norbert, Sigi and Martin play sextets with members of the groups they have taught, and Martin regularly plays in the Schubert cello quintet. Each of them continues to teach privately at home. Very often quartets come for advice shortly before entering for international competitions. Norbert, for example, taught the Ygdrasil Quartet from Sweden who were prize winners at the London International Competition; and Sigi taught the Vanburgh and the Emperor Quartets and the Gould and Jean Paul Piano Trios, before they won the London, Evian, Melbourne and Vittorio Gui competitions.

Teaching can be a strain, though it is a strain of a different kind from playing on a concert platform. It requires intense concentration: it is a waste of time for teacher and student alike to sit there and let the music flow in one ear and out of the other without submitting it to the closest critical examination. It also calls for sensitive understanding of each individual. Students can easily be discouraged and an unkind word may destroy their self-confidence and wreck a career. Then there is the problem of judging a student's capability and maybe having to say frankly that it would not be worth their while trying to pursue a career as a chamber-music player. For the most part, however, when the members of a quartet are of very different standards, things usually sort themselves out: those who are not really good enough know it, and so do the others in the group.

Teaching the most gifted ensembles is exhilarating and exciting. Teaching moderately gifted ones, who are likely to have good but not outstanding careers, is a challenge. Teaching the ungifted can be wearying and difficult. Sigi has described teaching a top-class group as like rehearsing with the Amadeus when they came together to try and interpret the music. For him it is an inspiring experience and gives him the feeling that he could teach for hours on end without getting tired.

# CHAPTER NINETEEN

# A Dedicated
# Life

---

When Peter died in 1987, the Amadeus Quartet had continued unchanged for nearly forty years. This was unique. Other contemporary quartets of international standing have all celebrated anniversaries with different players. They include the Alban Berg, the Budapest, the Hungarian, the Italiano, the Juilliard, the Netherlands, the Smetana and the Tokyo quartets. All four members of the Budapest Quartet – who had their début as early as 1917 – were different when the quartet finally folded in the 1960s. At the time of their thirtieth anniversary, the Juilliard retained only one of its original members, Robert Mann, the first violinist. Even the Quartetto Italiano, who were active for around thirty years, had a new viola player towards the end.

How is it that the four members of the Amadeus remained together for so long? Some answers have already been given in the book, but above all it was because of the outstanding quality of their playing and the fact that they had dedicated their lives to the Quartet.

In a BBC broadcast entitled 'A Second Violin Speaks', Sigi compares a string quartet with a bottle of wine. The first violin is the label, the cello is the bottle – it holds the stuff – and the middle parts are the wine itself, determining the quality of the product and giving colour and flavour and enduring reliability.

The Amadeus Quartet was vintage wine of rare quality, and the eloquence of Norbert's playing was the label by which the Amadeus was known. Day in, day out, he had to play the most difficult parts, in many cases even more difficult than the normal repertoire concertos of soloists. That takes nerve and skill and musicianship of a particular type. Any off-moment or off-evening was only too painfully obvious to him, his partners and the public. Norbert not only had just the skill, aplomb and fire that were needed but he also had tremendous musical personality and the sheer sound of his playing reflected wonderful imagination. When the cellist Robert Cohen recorded the Schubert quintet with the Quartet towards the end of their career, he described Norbert's way of playing as being that of a free spirit. 'However restricting quartet playing may be, he always finds the absolute freedom within the music and it's a fantastic source of inspiration to be with him and to see that kind of freedom within very strict confines.'

Such freedom is only possible against a background of firm discipline in the other parts. Martin, with his acute awareness of phrasing, was able by his playing of the bass notes to give impetus to the rhythm and pulse in a most musical way. An example is the first movement of Haydn's Opus 33, no.2, and even more striking, the slow movement of Beethoven's Rasumovsky quartet Opus 59, no.3, where the pizzicato of the cello gently but firmly shapes the whole movement. The cello, or the bottle as Sigi described it, is concerned with form and harmony and all they imply. Such was Martin's role, and he brought to it superb musicianship and a profound understanding of chamber music. Robert Cohen described Martin as the great lyricist of the Quartet: 'when he strokes the cello ... he inspires great beauty in a very simple and lyrical way.'

The middle strings have a particular responsibility for the overall balance, and it is significant that when Haydn and Mozart played together, it was Dittersdorf who regularly played the first violin, Haydn the second, Mozart the viola and Wanhal the cello. More often than not quartet movements open with longer, more sustained notes from the first violin and shorter quaver ones from the middle parts, who thus set the mood and tempo. Intuitively Peter and Sigi understood how to do this.

Many people have said that they only had to hear the opening bars of a work, maybe merely the opening chord, to know that it was the Amadeus they were listening to. The rich smooth sound of the Quartet was once described by a BBC interviewer as an instantly recognizable trade mark, 'like the phut of a Rolls Royce'. It has sometimes been suggested that the unity of their playing stems from their background and training. Three of the four members came from a similar musical background in Vienna and all three had studied with Max Rostal who also came from central Europe. The lilt and variation of tempo in Viennese folk song and *heurigen* music was in their blood, and it must certainly have played its part in their interpretation of composers like Schubert and also of many of Haydn's works. It applied much less to Mozart and scarcely at all to Beethoven.

Norbert, however, saw the essence of the Amadeus sound as an aspect of their meticulous attention to balance and to the texture and appropriate sound for a particular work or movement. Sigi's experience of playing second violin, where the musical line is often in a register that is not as favourable as that of the first violin, underlines this when he says that the solution is not to play louder, for that would spoil the character of the music, but to project one's playing in such a way that clarity comes across in the balance. In a talk given at an ESTA (European String Teachers' Association) conference, Norbert emphasized that it was this balance which gave a quartet 'the ability to engage the ear of an average concert goer'. He bemoaned the fact that any slight imbalance would hardly ever be noticed by either public or critics, whereas 'the slightest failure in an exposed passage would be pounced on by them and the media and exaggerated beyond belief, simply because this is what they can actually hear without the burden of too much knowledge.' He went on to say that he remembered that when the Quartet was practising in its early days, 'we would say you are too loud or too soft, this and that. But that is not the whole story: the texture of the sound, the appropriate sound for the appropriate work, or the appropriate movement, is of course very important and this is something one cannot really talk about much. What one would do at rehearsals is – after we had played a few notes – I might say: "No, let's try it again." After about the fourth time we might get it right.'

Sometimes playing it again led to more vociferous comments. 'You're playing flat,' shouted Peter, 'let's try it once more.' The shouting began again, 'It's still out of tune;' 'No, it's not.' Then they all joined in the general hubbub and a fearful din came from the music room in our house in Golders Green. Their arguments could well be about tempi, tone quality, or being too soft or too loud; but, whatever it might be, the intensity of feeling and the determination of each member of the Quartet to get it right was such that even at the very end they were still not only arguing but getting very angry with one another. During their last recording of the Beethoven quartets, there was just such a flare-up in the slow movement of the *Harp* quartet. Norbert and Martin were arguing quite viciously and then, when Peter criticized Norbert's playing of the movement which he thought should have a certain character, Norbert – always sensitive to criticism from Peter – flew into a temper, packed up his fiddle and walked out. The others said, 'If you want to go, go.' This was the first time they had recorded with Decca and the technicians were aghast: what do you do when one of your artists walks out on you? Don't worry, said the other three; he'll be back. In a brief while he was, and the recording continued as if nothing had happened.

In an interview in December 1981, Bernard Levin, the writer and broadcaster, asked the four of them whether they quarrelled, particularly in their early years, and they all replied, almost with relish and enthusiasm, 'Oh yes, we're still doing it.' They explained that they continued to have major disagreements and quarrels which were basically musical. Sometimes after spending an hour or more on a small point in a work they would leave it unresolved, but at the concert a truth about the part that had been under discussion would be revealed. They would argue and discuss until they eventually agreed. They could then all play with conviction and that was for them the hallmark of democracy within the group. For Norbert, argument wasn't just a matter of expressing one's personality or letting off steam: it was essential to what they were trying to achieve. 'If you cannot argue, you are lost. You have to learn to put over your point of view, because without this you are absolutely useless in a string quartet. What I am saying now is probably the exact opposite of what many people believe it to be like. Everybody thinks that you have to sink your individuality; you have to compromise. No. Not at all, because if there is anything that any one of you doesn't like, it just falls apart.' He was often asked whether, as leader, he was a sort of umpire when resolving differences within the Quartet. 'Certainly not,' he would say. 'In a group of equals it would be unthinkable for one or two or three members to force a decision upon an unhappy rest of the group and a disunited string quartet would be no good at all. If you get to the stage when you cannot resolve your disagreements about things that are extremely important to you, then you have to split up.'

The Amadeus contained four strong characters and each played his part. Sigi and Martin had more organized minds than Norbert and Peter and the arguments between the four of them reflected these differences. Peter was just as great an instrumentalist as Norbert, so that arguments between them were more likely to be musical than technical. Bill Pleeth remembers that 'Norbert would argue like hell and get stroppy, and then he would give in and perhaps say, "you are quite right."' Peter hated conflict and complications, and some have described him as one of the two peacemakers in the Quartet. The other was Sigi, who was more apt to sit back and see how things developed. When roused, however, he would enter into the fray with equal ferocity. It was a revelation in the early days of our marriage when I unexpectedly heard a tremendous fracas taking place on the telephone: my husband was shouting uncontrollably at the person on the other end – Norbert.

Other quartets, like the Chilingirian, resolve their differences less vehemently and try to show what they mean by playing rather than talking about it. But Levon, their first violin, wisely recognizes that seemingly musical arguments may hide more deep-seated personal problems. 'You can have a big argument about a non-event because you feel bad or you are annoyed with someone who has nothing to do with the quartet, so you want to take it out on somebody.' Sigi certainly understood this. 'Norbert usually got back at me during rehearsals because we had had a business argument beforehand.'

Despite the tensions during rehearsals, when they came together on the platform the Amadeus merged their personalities and played with intense concentration and dedication, lifting the spirits of all who heard them. Sigi, who had once watched a brain operation being carried out by a surgeon and his team in a hospital, has suggested that the four members of the Quartet on the platform likewise became as impersonal as the team in the operating theatre. But when you met them afterwards, they were again human beings. Robert Cohen paid similar tribute to their immense powers of concentration and their remarkable qualities as people. He tells how, in one of the rehearsals of the Schubert quintet, Norbert stopped right in the middle of the slow movement, which is so intensely beautiful, and said, "Have you heard about the guy in New York who asked a violinist what violin he had? He said – I have a 1699 Stradivarius – Boy, that's cheap!" This joke, right in the middle of that slow movement,' Robert said, 'just shows the sort of mentality. They have such seriousness and such dedication and yet that's never overpowering.'

Their loyalty and devotion to their chosen career was a major factor in keeping them together. The Quartet came first. When Peter was invited to play the Walton viola concerto on the last night of the Proms, his immediate reaction was to turn it down and say, 'I'm sorry, I'm busy with the Quartet.' It might have been possible for them to change their schedule, but it did not enter his head to ask them to do so.

Another important factor was the feeling that they were continuing to make progress, improving their playing and adding to their experience. 'I thought our best playing came in the last five years,' Norbert said. When Peter died, Martin was sixty and Norbert, Sigi and Peter were only a few years older. Despite Sigi's heart attack in 1981, they were in good shape mentally and physically. In a radio interview not long before he died, Peter described how they still sometimes practised like beginners: 'We are very demanding on ourselves, even at this stage. We have to be very critical. Otherwise there is no progress. We don't want to sound like an old gramophone record. We want to find something fresh every time we play.' Norbert agreed and explained that they had never stopped learning and developing: 'Had we been stagnating we wouldn't still be playing together.' Bill Pleeth marvelled at their continuing intuitive and spontaneous approach. 'One performance,' he said, 'was never the thumb-print of the next performance, or the next performance. During rehearsals they would argue out different points and would settle what it was going to be like – but in the evening it was more likely to be a variation of that particular thing.'

Throughout their career, a distinguishing mark of the Amadeus Quartet, which was commented upon by Mariedi Anders when she first became their agent in North America, was the variety in their programming. When they went on tour, they took with them a group of works for which they suggested various programme combinations. The people putting on concerts could then choose. Inevitably, some of the works, particularly the contemporary ones, were less likely to be selected but the approach enabled them to keep fresh.

The quartet repertoire is a bottomless well of variety and intense musical experience. The greatest composers reserved their most intimate and profound thoughts for the quartet and exploring the heights and depths is a never-ending adventure. If, after forty years, anyone had asked the Amadeus whether they were bored, or stale, or had nowhere further to go, they would vehemently have denied it. In his interview in December 1981, Bernard Levin posed this question, and Martin replied: 'Every time we play a Beethoven cycle, we go through every quartet from beginning to end and every time we find something new. I look and I suddenly see that a passage is marked "piano": I had never noticed it before.' Norbert then went on to add that such an unexpected discovery could lead them to new ideas and improvements in their interpretation of the music. This continuous search for the truth – the composer's truth – showed itself in their performances. One performance was never quite like the next.

However good a quartet may be, it will not achieve international acclaim unless there is an audience to hear it. The Amadeus were very fortunate in that they came together at a time when, after the war had disrupted teaching and training, there were few good groups around – the Griller were shortly to leave for a residency in the United States – and audiences were clamouring for music. In Britain, the wartime Council for the Encouragement of Music and the Arts (CEMA), which preceded the Arts Council, had created a climate for classical music and the large refugee population in Britain had brought with them a longing for the Central European musical culture they had had to leave behind. Musical life in Berlin and Vienna had been destroyed, and in France and Italy it had been severely disrupted. Germany especially was crying out for music. The Amadeus thus had eager audiences and they never had to search for work.

Another element in their favour was the BBC, which became one of the great patrons of serious music, particularly from 1958 onwards when Sir William Glock became its Controller of Music. Its influence helped to establish London as the musical capital of the world and as a place where all musicians aspired to achieve recognition. From their first years together the Amadeus were in constant demand for live broadcasts, and they regularly appeared on Thursday evenings at the concert hall in Broadcasting House. The recordings made from their performances became a core feature of the BBC library of classical music which was then being built up. Not only did the BBC give the Amadeus a live platform for performance, but their broadcasts brought them widespread publicity. Similar developments were taking place in the rest of Europe, above all in Germany where the Amadeus were in much demand for radio broadcasts and the recordings derived from them.

Record companies, too, were wanting to build up their collections and, in spite of the problems the Quartet encountered initially in making satisfactory arrangements with them, the thirst for records undoubtedly helped to establish their reputation.

The Amadeus themselves in their turn created new audiences for chamber music. Music clubs, who traditionally entertained people in small halls with recitals by pianists, violinists or singers, began to discover that other kinds of chamber music were no longer too elitist or too esoteric. Concert promoters also found that chamber groups in larger halls were becoming an acceptable alternative to the full orchestras which were now so expensive. The string quartet scene thus changed radically during the Amadeus years. In 1973 the Amadeus performed Haydn's *Emperor* quartet (Opus 76, no.3) at a Promenade Concert in the Albert Hall in London to an audience not far short of 6,000. Similar changes were occurring in North America. Quartets, like the Budapest and the Hungarian, were breaking down the barriers and fostering audiences for music that had not been regarded as popular before. The Amadeus were to benefit from this when they first toured the USA and Canada in 1953. In their later years they played there too in large concert halls, such as the Carnegie Hall in New York, as well as at smaller venues.

David Waterman, the cellist of the Endellion Quartet, said in a radio interview in 1988 when the Amadeus no longer existed that 'Probably one of the reasons there are so many English quartets at the moment is that a lot of people were inspired to want to play quartets because of their example. Another thing they have done, which is very important for us, is that they have helped to create an audience which I am sure, when they started, was limited to people who were very much in the know. There is unfortunately still a little bit of the feeling that string quartets are rather high-faluting and academic, which couldn't be further from the truth. That's beginning to fall by the wayside.' He went on to say that the Amadeus were not only wonderful players but had an aura of stardom about them that was important in attracting audiences. They were able 'to charm their audiences to come and listen to them,' thus creating an appetite for string quartets.

Young players today have a level of technique that would have been thought miraculous fifty years ago and there are an enormous number of high quality quartets tumbling over themselves to find audiences. The outpouring is so great that, for most of them, there is only a slim chance of their surviving as groups able to devote their lives to playing string quartets in the way the Amadeus could do.

Today, in 1998, some ten years after the life of the Amadeus Quartet abruptly came to an end, the surviving three members have aged and look rather different from how they did at that gathering which I remember so well at the Dorice restaurant in 1953. Norbert has a shock of white hair and is as round as a barrel. He occasionally goes to a health farm and comes back more like a shrunken or empty barrel, but in three months' time it is full once again. Sigi is balding and rather less round than Norbert. He looks young for his age. Martin, like Norbert, has a shock of white hair. He may be heavier than he used to be, but he is still very trim and retains his distinguished looks. All four wives, too, have thickened with age. Between us we have six children and eleven grandchildren.

In 'A Second Violin Speaks', Sigi described the special role of the second fiddle. He started with a possible advertisement for a vacancy for the post. 'The successful candidate will produce medical evidence of robust health and stamina; he/she will be capable of level-headed organization and tactful negotiation, will have imagination, vision and intuition and yet be enough of a realist to recognize the natural limitations of the possible; the candidate will not only have to love music but must also be musical and be a first-class violinist; a sense of humour is essential and some knowledge of travel schedules, accountancy and psychology is desirable. The candidate will produce references as to reliability, will have to work within an organization and yet will be capable of initiative and leadership of a department. Any short-listed candidate's spouse will be interviewed with a view to ascertaining that he/she has the qualities to support such a career.' Siegmund Nissel was of course 'the successful candidate', and I hope I would have qualified as a satisfactory spouse. Variations on such an advertisement could be created for each member of a quartet. But the basic qualities needed remain the same – a love of music combined with exceptional ability and devotion to a group. It is a dedicated life, a marriage between four people, and if there are spouses, a doubly dedicated one.

# Engagements of the Amadeus Quartet in their Silver Jubilee Year, 1972–3 *

**1972**

**August**

| | | | |
|---|---|---|---|
| 11 | UK | Aldeburgh | Haydn Op.54 no.2: Schumann Op.41 no.3: Mozart K465 |
| 13 | | Dartington | Haydn Op.55 no.2: Beethoven Op.59 no.3: Haydn Op.55 no.3 |
| 14 | | Dartington | Haydn Op.64 no.3: Beethoven Op.74: Haydn Op.77 no.2 |
| 16 | | Dartington | Haydn Op.64 no.4: Beethoven Op.59 No.2: Haydn Op.54 no.2 |
| 17 | | Dartington | Haydn Op.54 no.1: Haydn Op.33 no.3: Haydn Op.76 no.1 |
| 23 | France | Menton | not available |
| 24 | | Antibes | not available |
| 28 | | Sete | not available |
| 30 | | St Jean de Luz | not available |

**September**

| | | | |
|---|---|---|---|
| 12–16 | | Munich | Recording with DGG – Haydn Op.55 no.1 and Op.54 no.3 |
| 29 | Japan | Tokyo | Haydn Op.76 no.3: Mozart K458: Schubert D810 (*Death and the Maiden*) |

**October**

| | | | |
|---|---|---|---|
| 1 | | Tokyo | Mozart K285 and K298 (flute quartets): Mozart K465 |
| 8 | | Tokyo | Mozart K421: Smetana string quartet no.1 (*From my Life*): Beethoven Op.135 |
| 9 | | Tokyo | Mozart K421: Dvorak Op.96 (*The American*): Beethoven Op.59 no.3 |
| 11 | | Tokyo | Beethoven Op.18 no.3: Op.132: Op.18 no.1 |
| 12 | | Tokyo | Haydn Op.76 no.3: Beethoven Op.95: Schubert D810 (*Death and the Maiden*) |
| 14 | South Korea | Seoul | Haydn Op.76 no.3: Mozart K465: Smetana string quartet no.1 (*From my Life*) |
| 17 | Australia | Brisbane | Schubert D 87: D 173: D 804 |
| 19 | | Sydney | Haydn Op.76 no.3: Mozart K458: Brahms Op.51 no.1 |
| 20 | | Melbourne | Beethoven Op.18 no.2: Op.135: Op.59 no.3 |
| 21 | | Canberra | Beethoven Op.18 no.3: Op.95: Op.127 |

* The itinerary and the works played are based on Siegmund Nissel's diary of engagements and do not take account of any changes which may have been made later.

| 24 | New Zealand | Christchurch | Schubert D112: D703 (*Quartettsatz*): D810 (*Death and the Maiden*) |
| 25 | | Wellington | Schubert D112: D703 (*Quartettsatz*): D810 (*Death and the Maiden*) |
| 26 | | Auckland | Haydn Op.76 no.3: Brahms Op.67: Dvořák Op.96 (*The American*) |
| 28 | Australia | Sydney | Schubert D87: D173: D814 |
| 30 | | Newcastle | Beethoven Op.18 no.2: Op.135: Op.59 no.2 |

**November**

| 1 | | Melbourne | Haydn Op.76 no.3: Mozart K458: Brahms Op.51 no.1 |
| 2 | | Adelaide | Beethoven Op.18 no.2: Op.95: Op.127 |
| 6 | | Adelaide | Schubert D112; D703 (*Quartettsatz*) and D810 (*Death and the Maiden*) |
| 8 | | Perth | Haydn Op.76 no.3: Mozart K458: Brahms Op.51 no.1 |
| 13 | UK | London, St John's | Mendelssohn Op.12: Haydn Op.20 no.5 |
| 19 | | London (10 Downing Street) | not available |
| 24 | Germany | Berlin | Haydn Op.76 no.3: Beethoven Op.74: Schubert D810 (*Death and the Maiden*) |
| 25 | | Berlin (radio) | not available |
| 26 | | Frankfurt | Haydn Op.77 no.1: Beethoven Op.133: Brahms Op.51 no.1 |
| 28 | | Munich | Haydn Op.54 no.2: Mozart K421: Beethoven Op.59 no.3 |
| 29 | | Augsburg | Haydn Op.54 no.2: Mozart K421: Beethoven Op.59 no.3 |

**December**

| 1 | | Regensburg | Mozart K428: Schubert D703 (*Quartettsatz*): Beethoven Op.132 |
| 3 | | Stuttgart | Haydn Op.76 no.3: Mendelssohn Op.12: Beethoven Op.96 |
| 4 | | Karlsruhe | Haydn Op.76 no.3: Mendelssohn Op.12: Beethoven Op.18 no.1 |
| 6 | | Cologne | Haydn Op.76 no.2: Britten Op.36: Beethoven Op.96 |
| 7 | | Kaiserslauten | Mozart K387: Schubert D703 (*Quartettsatz*): Beethoven Op.131 |
| 9 | | Konstanz | Haydn Op.76 no.2: Smetana string quartet no.1 (*From my Life*): Beethoven Op.95 |
| 11 | Switzerland | Chaux de Fonds | Mozart K428: Beethoven Op.95: Schubert D810 (*Death and the Maiden*) |
| 12 | | Lausanne | Mozart K421: Bartók string quaret no.6: Beethoven Op.95 |
| 14–18 | Germany | Munich | Recording with DGG – Haydn, Op.55 nos.1, 2 and 3 |

**1973**

**January**

| 9 | Germany | Elmau | Haydn Op.54 no.2: Mozart K515: Brahms Op.111 |
| 11 | | Elmau | Verdi string quartet: Schumann Op.47 (piano quartet) |
| 12 | | Elmau | Mozart K516 |
| 13 | | Munich | Mozart K516: Verdi string quartet: Brahms Op.111 |

| 16 | UK | London, QEH | Mozart K421: Verdi string quartet: Beethoven Op.59 no.3 |
| 18 | Holland | Nijmegen | Mozart K465: Bartók string quartet no.6: Beethoven Op.130 |
| 19 | | Amsterdam | Mozart K458: Bartók string quartet no.6: Brahms Op.51 no.2 |
| 21 | | Vara (radio) | Mozart K458: Beethoven Op.135 |
| 22 | | Groningen | Mozart K465: Bartók string quartet no.6: Beethoven Op.59 no.2 |
| 23 | | Utrecht | Haydn Op.54 no.2: Seiber string quartet no.3 (*Quartetto Lyrico*): Beethoven Op.135 |
| 24 | | Rotterdam | Haydn Op.20 no.5: Seiber string quartet no.3 (*Quartetto Lyrico*): Beethoven Op.127 |
| 26 | | Enschede | Mozart K465: Beethoven Op.95: Schubert D810 (*Death and the Maiden*) |
| 28 | UK | London, QEH | Mozart K428: Brahms Op.51 no.1: Beethoven Op.18 no.1 |
| 30 | | Lancaster | Mozart K465: Beethoven Op.135: Schubert D810 (*Death and the Maiden*) |

**February**

| 1 | | Uttoxeter | Haydn Op.54 no.1: Mozart K370: Schubert D804 |
| 2 | | Cardiff | Mozart K499: Seiber string quartet no.3 (*Quartetto Lyrico*): Beethoven Op.130 |
| 3 | | Meon | Haydn Op.76 no.1: Mozart K581: Beethoven Op.59 no.3 |
| 4 | | Rhyl | Haydn Op.76 no.1: Mozart K581: Beethoven Op.59 no.3 |
| 10 | | Rosehill | Beethoven Op.18 no.3: Op.95: Op.132 |
| 11 | | Glasgow | Haydn Op.76 no.1: Schubert D703 (*Quartettsatz*): Schubert D596 |
| 12 | | Stirling | Haydn Op.76 no.1: Schubert D703 (*Quartettsatz*): Schubert D596 |
| 15 | | London, QEH | Haydn Op.103: Schumann Op.41 no.3: Beethoven Op.59 no.1 |
| 16 | France | Paris (TV) | Beethoven Op.18 no.1: Op.95: Op.127 |
| 19 | | Paris | Mozart K421: K428: K465 |
| 21 | | La Rochelle | Haydn Op.54 no.2: Bartók string quartet no.6: Beethoven Op.74 |
| 22 | | Bordeaux | Beethoven Op.18 no.3: Op.95: Op.127 |
| 24 | | La Hulpe | Schubert D87: D703 (*Quartettsatz*): D596 |
| 27 | UK | London, QEH | Mozart K465: Dvořák Op.96 (*The American*): Beethoven Op.59 no.2 |

**March**

| 3–6 | Germany | Munich | Recording with DGG – Haydn Op.64 nos.3 and 4 and Op.103 |
| 8 | | Bad Godesberg | Haydn Op.76 no.2: Mozart K387: Dvořák Op.44 (piano quintet) |
| 9 | | Baden Baden (radio) | Haydn Op.74 no.3: Seiber string quartet no.3 (*Quartetto Lyrico*) |
| 10 | | Baden Baden | Haydn Op.74 no.3: Mozart K499: Brahms Op.51 no.1 |
| 12 | | Hamburg | Haydn Op.76 no.3 |
| 13 | | Bremen | Haydn Op.55 no.3: Seiber string quartet no.3 (*Quartetto Lyrico*): Schubert D810 (*Death and the Maiden*) |

| | | | |
|---|---|---|---|
| 14 | | Hanover | Beethoven Op.59 no.1: Op.132 |
| 16 | | Hamburg | Haydn Op.55 no.3: Schumann Op.41 no.3: Beethoven Op.135 |
| 17 | | Hamburg | Haydn Op.55 no.3: Schumann Op.41 no.3: Beethoven Op.135 |
| 19 | | Lubeck | Haydn Op.20 no.5: Britten string quartet no.2: Beethoven Op.127 |
| 23 | UK | London (TV) | not available |

**April**

| | | | |
|---|---|---|---|
| 1 | | London, QEH | Haydn Op.77 no.1: Smetana string quartet no.1 (*From my Life*): Beethoven Op.74 |
| 5 | USA | New York, Met | Beethoven Op.18 no.5: Op.74: Op.130 |
| 6 | | Annapolis | Haydn Op.77 no.1: Mozart K421: Beethoven Op.135 |
| 8 | | Louisville | Haydn Op.76 no.2: Beethoven Op.95: Schubert D887 |
| 12 | | New York, Met | Beethoven Op.18 no.3: Op.132: Op.18 no.2 |
| 15 | Canada | Montreal | Mozart K499: Seiber string quartet no.3 (*Quartetto Lyrico*): Beethoven Op.130 |
| 16 | | Toronto | Schubert D87: Britten Op.36: Beethoven Op.127 |
| 19 | USA | New York, Met | Beethoven Op.18 no.6: Op.95: Op.131 |
| 26 | UK | London, QEH | Haydn Op.77 no.2: Beethoven Op.95 |

**May**

| | | | |
|---|---|---|---|
| 11 | Switzerland | Zurich | Haydn Op.76 no.1: Britten Op.36: Dvořák p.96 (*The American*) |
| 14 | Austria | Graz | Haydn Op.76 no.3: Schubert D703 (*Quartettsatz*): Beethoven Op.132 |
| 16 | | Linz | Mozart K499: Bartók string quartet no.6: Brahms Op.51 no.1 |
| 18 | | Salzburg | Beethoven Op.18 no.3: Op.59 no.3: Op.132 |
| 20 | | Vienna | Mozart K387: K421: K515 |
| 24 | | Vienna | Mozart K458: K465: K516 |
| 26 | Germany | Hamburg | Brahms Op.51 no.2: Brahms Op.115 (clarinet quintet) |
| 28 | UK | Bath | Mozart K421: Tippett string quartet no.2: Brahms Op.51 no.1 |
| 31 | | Cambridge | Shostakovitch Op.138 |

**June**

| | | | |
|---|---|---|---|
| 2 | | Bath | Mozart K458: Britten Op.36: Beethoven Op.135 |
| 4 | | London, St John's | Haydn Op.54 no.2: Mozart K581 |
| 10 | | London, Mill Hill | not available |
| 19 | | Aldeburgh | not available |
| 21 | | York | Mozart K387: Schubert D703 (*Quartettsatz*) and D956 (cello quintet) |
| 23 | France | Nohant | Mozart K458: Beethoven Op.18 no.4: Schubert D810 (*Death and the Maiden*) |
| 24 | | Nohant | Haydn Op.77 no.1: Schubert D703 (*Quartettsatz*) and D956 (cello quintet) |

**July**

| | | | |
|---|---|---|---|
| 24 | UK | Dartington | Mozart K458: Mozart K465 |
| 26 | | Dartington | Schubert D703 (*Quartettsatz*): Bartók quartet no.4: Beethoven Op.131 |
| 28 | | Dartington | Haydn Op.54 no.2: Op.76 no.6: Op.77 no.1 |
| 30 | | Dartington | Bartók string quartet no.5: Mozart K515 |

# Engagements of the Amadeus Quartet in their Last Season, 1986–7

## CONCERTS AND RECORDINGS

**August**

| 24 | Italy | Città di Castello | not available |
|----|-------|-------------------|---------------|

**September**

| 2 | Italy | Città di Castello | not available |
|----|-------|-------------------|---------------|
| 13 | Argentine | Buenos Aires | Brahms Op.51 no.1: Brahms Op.34 (piano quintet) |
| 15 | | Buenos Aires | Haydn Op.54 no.2: Beethoven Op.95: Schumann Op.41 no.3 |
| 17 | | Buenos Aires | Haydn Op.54 no.2: Beethoven Op.74: Schumann Op.41 no.3 |
| 19 | | Buenos Aires | Brahms Op.67: *Wolf Serenade*: Brahms Op.51 no.2 |
| 21 | Brazil | São Paulo | not available |
| 29 | UK | Windsor | Haydn Op.64 no.6: Mozart K581 (clarinet quintet): Beethoven Op.18 no.1 |

**October**

| 1 | | London, Hampstead | not available |
|----|-------|-------------------|---------------|
| 15 | | London, University Ceremony | Mozart K458 |
| 19 | | London, Mill Hill | Haydn Op.54 no.2: Mozart K464: Beethoven Op.18 no.1 |
| 31 | Germany | Ulm | Brahms Op.115 (clarinet quintet): Schubert D667 (*The Trout* quintet) |

**November**

| 1 | | Ulm | Brahms Op.34 (piano quartet) |
|----|-------|-------------------|---------------|
| 11 | | Munich | Beethoven Op.18 no.4: Op.95: Op.132 |
| 13 | | Munich | Beethoven Op.18 no.2: Op.131: Op.18 no.1 |
| 16 | | Munich | Beethoven Op.127: Op.59 no.1 |
| 19 | Italy | Turin | Beethoven Op.18 no.4: Op.95: Op.132 |
| 23 | | Turin | Beethoven Op.18 no.2: Op.131: Op.18 no.1 |
| 26 | | Turin | Beethoven Op.127: Op.59 no.1 |

**December**

| 14 | | Turin | Beethoven Op.18 no.3: Op.74: Op.130 |
|----|-------|-------------------|---------------|
| 17 | | Turin | Beethoven Op.18 no.5: Op.133: Op.59 no.2 |
| 21 | | Turin | Beethoven Op.18 no.6: Op.135: Op.59 no.3 |

**January**

| | | | |
|---|---|---|---|
| 19 | Germany | Munich | Beethoven Op.18 no.5: Op.133: Op.59 no.2 |
| 23 | | Munich | Beethoven Op.18 no.6: Op.135: Op.59 no.3 |

**February**

| | | | |
|---|---|---|---|
| 8 | UK | London, RFH | Schubert D810 (*Death and the Maiden*): D956 (cello quintet) |
| 15 | Germany | Würzburg | Haydn Op.76 no.3: Mozart K458: Brahms Op.51 no.2 |
| 17 | | Bonn | Haydn Op.76 no.3: Beethoven 95: Schubert D804 |
| 19 | | Karlsruhe | Schubert D87: Beethoven Op.95: Brahms Op.51 no.2 |
| 21 | | Hamburg | Haydn Op.76 no.3: Mozart K458: Brahms Op.51 no.2 |
| 23 | | Mannheim | Mozart K458: Beethoven Op.95: Dvořák Op.96 (*The American*) |

**March**

| | | | |
|---|---|---|---|
| 13 | USA | Boston | Haydn Op.76 no.1: Britten Op.94: Schubert D810 (*Death and the Maiden*) |
| 18 | | New York, Carnegie Hall | Haydn Op.76 no.3: Mozart K421: Brahms Op.34 (piano quintet) |
| 20 | | Seattle | Haydn Op.76 no.1: Britten Op.94: Schubert D810 (*Death and the Maiden*) |
| 24 | UK | London, QEH | Brahms Op.115 (clarinet quintet) |

**April**

| | | | |
|---|---|---|---|
| 25 | France | Strasbourg | Mozart K525 (*Eine kleine Nachtmusik*): Haydn Op.76 no.3: Schubert D667 (*The Trout* quintet) |
| 27 | | Metz | Dvořák Op.96 (*The American*): Schubert D703 (*Quartettsatz*): Schubert D88 |
| 29 | | St Etienne | Haydn Op.54 no.2: Britten Op.94: Beethoven Op.132 |

**May**

| | | | |
|---|---|---|---|
| 1 | Holland | Amsterdam | Schubert D87: D703 (*Quartettsatz*): D810 (*Death and the Maiden*) |
| 3 | | Amsterdam | Schubert D112: D87 |
| 11 | UK | Newbury | Mozart K458: K575: K516 (viola quintet) |
| 22 | | Chelmsford | Amadeus Trio concert |

**June**

| | | | |
|---|---|---|---|
| 29–30 | | London | Decca recording: Beethoven Op.59 no.3: Op.74 |

**July**

| | | | |
|---|---|---|---|
| 1–2 | | London | Decca recording: Beethoven Op.59 no.3: Op.74 |
| 5 | | Cheltenham | Beethoven Op.18 no.4: Britten string quartet no.3: Beethoven Op.74 |

# TEACHING*

**August**
18–31          Italy          Città di Castello

**September**
1–2                           Città di Castello
26, 30         UK             London, Royal Academy of Music (RAM)

**October**
3                              London, RAM
7–11           Germany        Cologne Conservatoire
13, 17, 21     UK             London, RAM

**November**
3–7            Germany        Cologne Conservatoire
28             UK             London, RAM

**December**
3–4                            London, RAM
8–12           Germany        Cologne Conservatoire

**January**
9, 12, 14      UK             London, RAM
26–30          Germany        Cologne Conservatoire

**February**
2, 5           UK             London, RAM
9–13           Germany        Cologne Conservatoire
25, 27         UK             London, RAM

**March**
6, 25                          London, RAM

**April**
22–23                          London, RAM

**May**
4–9            Germany        Cologne Conservatoire
13, 15, 18, 20 UK             London, RAM

**June**
1–5            Germany        Cologne Conservatoire
15, 17, 19     UK             London, RAM
22–26          Germany        Cologne Conservatoire

* The teaching days at the Royal Academy of Music in London are based on Siegmund Nissel's diary. The Quartet members each gave a total of twenty-seven days at the RAM but spread their teaching over different days.

# Earnings of the Amadeus Quartet
## in 1972–3 and 1986–7*

---

|  | *percentage of total earnings* | |
| --- | :---: | :---: |
|  | 1972–3 | 1986–7 |
| **Concerts** | 67 | 39 |
| of which: |  |  |
| United Kingdom | 15 | 7 |
| Germany | 19 | 12 |
| Other Europe | 15 | 12 |
| North America | 4 | 5 |
| Japan and Korea | 4 | 3 |
| Australia and New Zealand | 9 | – |
| South America | – | 3 |
| **Records** | 26 | 17 |
| **Radio/TV** | 7 | 1 |
| **Teaching** | – | 43 |
| of which: |  |  |
| London, RAM | – | 18 |
| Cologne, Musikhochschule | – | 22 |
| Other | – | 4 |
| **Total Earnings** | 100 | 100 |
| £ (= 100%) | 71,200 | 312,000 |

* The table has been compiled on a 'net' basis, i.e. expenses such as agents' fees, fares and hotel costs have been deducted from gross fees. Thus earnings from concerts in North America have been estimated at 60% of the gross fee and those in Europe at 75%. Fees for teaching overseas have similarly been reduced to take account of fares and living expenses. Income from records on the other hand has been included at 100% because DGG paid both travelling and hotel expenses.

# Discography of
# the Amadeus Quartet*

| Work | Key | Date of recording | Company | Other artists |
|------|-----|-------------------|---------|---------------|
| **Beethoven** | | | | |
| String quartets: | | | | |
| Opus 14 no.1 | F major | Jan. 1969 | DGG | |
| Opus 18 no.1 | F major | Sept. 1961 | DGG | |
| no.2 | G major | Sept. 1961 | DGG | |
| no.3 | D major | Sept. 1961 | DGG | |
| no.4 | C minor | Sept. 1961 | DGG | |
| no.5 | A major | Sept. 1961 | DGG | |
| no.6 | B flat major | Sept. 1961 | DGG | |
| Opus 59 no.1 | F major | May 1959 | DGG | |
| Opus 59 no.2 | E minor | May 1959 | DGG | |
| Opus 59 no.3 | C major | May 1959 | DGG | |
| | | Jan. 1983 (live) | DGG | |
| | | June/July 1987 | Decca | |
| Opus 74 | E flat major | June 1960 | DGG | |
| | | June/July 1987 | Decca | |
| Opus 95 | F minor | May/June 1960 | DGG | |
| Opus 127 | E flat major | Mar./Apr. 1963 | DGG | |
| | | Nov. 1978 | DGG | |
| Opus 130 | B flat major | Sept./Oct. 1962 | DGG | |
| | | Aug. 1980 | DGG | |
| Opus 131 | C sharp minor | June 1963 | DGG | |
| | | June/July 1981 | DGG | |
| Opus 132 | A minor | Apr. 1962 | DGG | |
| | | Jan. 1980 | DGG | |
| Opus 133 | B flat major | Sept./Oct. 1963 | DGG | |
| | | June 1977 | DGG | |
| Opus 135 | F major | Mar./Apr. 1963 | DGG | |
| | | June 1977 | DGG | |
| String quintet: | | | | |
| Opus 29 | C major | Jan. 1969 | DGG | C. Aronowitz |
| Piano quartet: | | | | |
| Wo 036 no.1 | E flat major | June 1969 | DGG | C. Eschenbach |
| Wo 036 no.2 | D major | June 1969 | DGG | C. Eschenbach |
| Wo 036 no.3 | C major | June 1969 | DGG | C. Eschenbach |

* This list is mainly based on the discography prepared by Jean-Michel Molkhou in September 1987.

**Brahms**

String quartets:
| | | | | |
|---|---|---|---|---|
| Opus 51 no.1 | C minor | 1951 | Westminster | |
| | | Sept. 1959 | DGG | |
| Opus 51 no.2 | A minor | Feb. 1955 | HMV/DGG | |
| | | Sept. 1959 | DGG | |
| Opus 67 | B flat major | Mar./Apr. 1957 | HMV/DGG | |
| | | Jan. 1960 | DGG | |

String quintets:
| | | | | |
|---|---|---|---|---|
| Opus 88 | F major | Apr. 1968 | DGG | C. Aronowitz |
| Opus 111 | G major | May 1967 | DGG | C. Aronowitz |

String sextets:
| | | | | |
|---|---|---|---|---|
| Opus 18 | B flat major | Dec. 1966 | DGG | C. Aronowitz W. Pleeth |
| Opus 36 | G major | Mar. 1968 | DGG | C. Aronowitz W. Pleeth |

Piano quartet:
| | | | | |
|---|---|---|---|---|
| Opus 25 | G minor | Dec. 1970 | DGG | E. Gilels |
| | | June/July 1986 | CBS | M. Perahia |

Piano quintet:
| | | | | |
|---|---|---|---|---|
| Opus 34 | F minor | May 1969 | DGG | C. Eschenbach |

Clarinet quintet:
| | | | | |
|---|---|---|---|---|
| Opus 115 | B minor | Mar. 1967 | DGG | K. Leister |

**Britten**

String quartets:
| | | | |
|---|---|---|---|
| no.2 Opus 36 | C major | Jan. 1963 | Decca/Argo |
| no.3 Opus 94 | | Mar. 1978 | Decca |

**Bruckner**

| | | | | |
|---|---|---|---|---|
| String quintet | F major | Nov. 1964 | DGG | C. Aronowitz |

**Dvořák**

String quartet:
| | | | |
|---|---|---|---|
| Opus 96 | F major | Sept. 1959 | DGG |

**Fricker**

String quartet:
| | | |
|---|---|---|
| Opus 20 | Jan. 1963 | ARGO |

**Haydn**

String quartets:
| | | | |
|---|---|---|---|
| Opus 3 no.5 | F major | May 1950 | HMV |
| | | Jan. 1951 | Westminster |
| Opus 20 no.6 (finale) | A major | May 1954 | HMV |
| Opus 51 (*The Seven Last Words of Christ on the Cross*) | | Jan. 1951 | Westminster/Vega |
| | | May 1971 | DGG |
| Opus 54 no.1 | G major | Jan. 1957 | HMV/DGG |
| | | Oct. 1971 | DGG |
| no.2 | C major | May 1954 | HMV |

|  |  |  | Oct. 1971 | DGG |
|---|---|---|---|---|
|  | no.3 | E major | Sept. 1972 | DGG |
| Opus 55 no.1 |  | A major | Sept., Dec. 1972 | DGG |
|  | no.2 | F minor | Sept., Dec. 1972 | DGG |
|  | (*The Razor*) |  |  |  |
|  | no.3 | B flat major | Sept., Dec. 1972 | DGG |
| Opus 64 no.1 |  | C major | Dec. 1973 | DGG |
|  | no.2 | B minor | Dec. 1973 | DGG |
|  | no.3 | B flat major | Jan. 1957 | DGG |
|  |  |  | Mar. 1973 | DGG |
|  | no.4 | G major | Mar. 1973 | DGG |
|  | no.5 | D major | Mar. 1974 | DGG |
|  | (*The Lark*) |  |  |  |
|  | no.6 | E flat major | Mar. 1974 | DGG |
| Opus 71 no.1 |  | B flat major | June 1977 | DGG |
|  | no.2 | D major | June 1977 | DGG |
|  | no.3 | E flat major | Jan., Dec. 1978 | DGG |
| Opus 74 no.1 |  | C major | Oct. 1957 | DGG |
|  |  |  | Jan., Dec. 1978 | DGG |
|  | no.2 | F major | Jan., Dec. 1978 | DGG |
|  | no.3 | G minor | Oct. 1957 | DGG |
|  | (*The Rider*) |  | Jan., Dec. 1978 | DGG |
| Opus 76 no.1 |  | G major | Mar. 1970 | DGG |
|  | no.2 | D minor | Apr./May 1966 | DGG |
|  | (*The Fifths*) |  | Jan. 1983 (live) | DGG |
|  | no.3 | C major | Jan./Feb. 1951 | DGG |
|  | (*The Emperor*) |  | Sept. 1963 | DGG |
|  |  |  | Nov. 1982 | DGG |
|  | no.4 | B flat major | Mar. 1970 | DGG |
|  | (*The Sunrise*) |  |  |  |
|  | no.5 | D major | May 1970 | DGG |
|  | no.6 | E flat major | May 1970 | DGG |
| Opus 77 no.1 |  | G major | May 1956 | HMV |
|  |  |  | Mar. 1964 | DGG |
|  | no.2 | F major | Mar. 1965 | DGG |
| Opus 103 |  | D minor | Jan. 1951 | Westminster |
|  |  |  | Mar. 1973 | DGG |

## MacMillan

| String quartet no.2 | C minor | 1967 | CBS |
|---|---|---|---|
| *Two Sketches on French Canadian Airs* | 1967 | CBS |

## Mendelssohn

| Opus 81 (*Capriccio*) | E minor | Feb. 1955 | HMV |
|---|---|---|---|

## Mozart

String quartets:

| no.1 K80 | G major | Sept. 1976 | DGG |
|---|---|---|---|
| no.2 K155 | D major | Dec. 1975 | DGG |
| no.3 K156 | G major | Dec. 1975 | DGG |
| no.4 K157 | C major | Dec. 1975 | DGG |
| no.5 K158 | F major | Dec. 1975 | DGG |
| no.6 K159 | B flat major | June 1976 | DGG |
| no.7 K160 | E flat major | June 1976 | DGG |
| no.8 K168 | F major | June 1976 | DGG |

| | | | | |
|---|---|---|---|---|
| no.9 K169 | A major | June 1976 | DGG | |
| no.10 K170 | C major | Sept. 1976 | DGG | |
| no.11 K171 | E flat major | Sept. 1976 | DGG | |
| no.12 K172 | B flat major | Sept. 1976 | DGG | |
| no.13 K173 | D minor | Sept. 1976 | DGG | |
| no.14 K387 | G major | May 1950 | HMV | |
| | | June 1963 | DGG | |
| no.15 K421 | D minor | May 1954 | HMV | |
| | | May 1966 | DGG | |
| no.16 K428 | E flat major | Jan. 1951 | Westminster | |
| | | May 1957 | DGG | |
| | | May 1966 | DGG | |
| no.17 K458 | B flat major | Jan. 1951 | Westminster | |
| (The Hunt) | | May 1956 | HMV | |
| | | June 1963 | DGG | |
| | | Nov. 1982 | DGG | |
| no.18 K464 | A major | 1951 | Westminster | |
| | | Mar. 1964 | DGG | |
| no.19 K465 | C major | Sept. 1954 | HMV | |
| (The Dissonance) | | May 1966 | DGG | |
| no.20 K499 | D major | June 1955 | HMV | |
| (The Hoffmeister) | | Mar. 1967 | DGG | |
| no.21 K575 | D major | Sept. 1954 | HMV | |
| (The Prussian) | | Apr. 1969 | DGG | |
| no.22 K589 | B flat major | June 1955 | HMV | |
| (The Prussian) | | May 1966 | DGG | |
| no.23 K590 | F major | 1951 | Westminster | |
| (The Prussian) | | May 1957 | DGG | |
| **Divertimenti:** | | | | |
| K136 | D major | Sept. 1974 | DGG | |
| K137 | B flat major | Sept. 1974 | DGG | |
| K138 | F major | Sept. 1974 | DGG | |
| **Divertimento for string trio:** | | | | |
| K563 | E flat major | Feb. 1982 | DGG | |
| **Flute quartets:** | | | | |
| no.1 K285 | D major | July 1977 | DGG | A. Blau |
| no.2 K285a | G major | July 1977 | DGG | A. Blau |
| no.3 Anh.171 | C major | July 1977 | DGG | A. Blau |
| no.4 K298 | A major | July 1977 | DGG | A. Blau |
| **Oboe quartet:** | | | | |
| K370 | F major | Dec. 1975 | DGG | L. Koch |
| **Piano quartets:** | | | | |
| no.1 K478 | G minor | Sept. 1952 | Decca | C. Curzon |
| | | Feb. 1981 | DGG | W. Klien |
| no.2 K493 | E flat major | Sept. 1952 | Decca | C. Curzon |
| | | Feb. 1981 | DGG | W. Klien |
| **Adagio and Fugue:** | | | | |
| K456 | C minor | Nov. 1978 | DGG | |
| **String quintets:** | | | | |
| no.1 K174 | B flat major | Sept. 1974 | DGG | C. Aronowitz |
| no.2 K406 | C minor | May 1968 | DGG | C. Aronowitz |
| no.3 K515 | C major | Oct. 1953 | HMV | C. Aronowitz |
| | | May 1967 | DGG | C. Aronowitz |

| | | | | | |
|---|---|---|---|---|---|
| no.4 K516 | G minor | 1951 | Westminster | C. Aronowitz | |
| | | Nov. 1957 | HMV | C. Aronowitz | |
| | | Sept. 1969 | DGG | C. Aronowitz | |
| no.5 K593 | D major | Apr. 1957 | HMV | C. Aronowitz | |
| | | Mar. 1975 | DGG | C. Aronowitz | |
| no.6 K614 | E flat major | Mar./Apr. 1957 | HMV | C. Aronowitz | |
| | | Apr. 1968 | DGG | C. Aronowitz | |

Clarinet quintet:

| | | | | |
|---|---|---|---|---|
| K581 | A major | Dec. 1975 | DGG | G. de Peyer |

Horn quintet:

| | | | | |
|---|---|---|---|---|
| K407 | E flat major | Apr. 1969 | DGG | G. Seifert |

| | | | | |
|---|---|---|---|---|
| *Eine kleine* | | | | |
| *Nachtmusik* K525 | G major | Apr./May 1979 | DGG | R. Zepperitz |
| *A Musical Joke* | | | | |
| K522 | | Apr./May 1979 | DGG | R. Zepperitz |
| | | | | G. Seifert |
| | | | | M. Klier |

**Rainier**

| | | | |
|---|---|---|---|
| String quartet no.1 | | Mar. 1949 | Decca |

**Schubert**

String quartets:
no.8 D112

| | | | | |
|---|---|---|---|---|
| Opus posth. 168 | B flat major | Feb. 1955 | HMV | |
| | | May 1957 | HMV | |
| (minuet and trio) | | Sept. 1977 (live) | CBS | |
| | | Aug. 1980 | DGG | |
| no.9 D173 Opus posth. | G minor | May 1966 | DGG | |
| no.10 D87 | E flat | May 1954 | HMV | |
| Opus 125 | | Aug. 1980 | DGG | |
| no.12 D703 | C minor | 1951 | Westminster | |
| (*Quartettsatz*) | | Apr. 1959 | DGG | |
| | | Sept. 1977 (live) | CBS | |
| | | Nov. 1981 | DGG | |
| no.13 D804 | A minor | May 1954 | HMV | |
| Opus 29 | | May 1966 | DGG | |
| no.14 D810 | D minor | May 1953 | HMV | |
| (*Death and the Maiden*) | | Apr. 1959 | DGG | |
| | | Nov. 1981 | DGG | |
| no.15 D887 | G major | Sept. 1951 | DGG | |
| Opus 161 | | Mar. 1965 | DGG | |

Cello quintet:

| | | | | |
|---|---|---|---|---|
| D936 Op.163 | C major | Apr. 1953 | HMV | W. Pleeth |
| | | May/June 1965 | DGG | W. Pleeth |
| (2nd and 3rd movements) | | Sept. 1977 (live) | CBS | W. Pleeth |
| | | Mar. 1986 | DGG | R. Cohen |

Piano quintet:

| | | | | |
|---|---|---|---|---|
| D667 Opus 114 | A major | Aug. 1958 | HMV | H. Menuhin |
| (*The Trout*) | | | | J. E. Merret |
| | | Aug./Sept. 1965 | DGG | G. Gilels |
| | | | | R. Zepperitz |
| (4th and 5th movements) | | Sept. 1977 (live) | CBS | C. Curzon |
| | | | | R. Slatford |

**Seiber**

| | | | |
|---|---|---|---|
| String quartet no.3 (*Quartetto Lyrico*) | | May 1954 | HMV |

**Smetana**

| | | | |
|---|---|---|---|
| String quartet no.1 (*From my Life*) | E minor | June 1977 | DGG |

**Tchaikovsky**

| | | | |
|---|---|---|---|
| String quartet no.1 Opus 11 | D major | Oct. 1979 | DGG |

**Tippett**

| | | | |
|---|---|---|---|
| String quartet no.2 | | May 1954 | HMV |

**Verdi**

| | | | |
|---|---|---|---|
| String quartet | E minor | Oct. 1979 | DGG |

# Quartets Attending the Amadeus International Summer Course[1]

**1989**
Arg Argentine
UK Auriol
UK Bingham
Den Danish
G La Fleur
UK Maggini
G Orpheus
Fr Parisii
G Ruttiger

**1990**
Pol Camerata
Den *Danish*
UK Delos
It Egmont
Jap Erdödy
It Galiano
G Henschel
Fr Lalo
G New Leipzig
Pol Silesian
Fr Simon
Cz Skampa
Cz Waulin

**1991**
Fr Arpeggione
Rus Baku
G Berthold
UK Bridge
It Borciani
Pol *Camerata*
G Da Capo
Jap *Erdödy*
G *Henschel*
G *New Leipzig*
NZ New Zealand
It Rosamundae
G Werethina

**1992**
G Achat
Hun Amabile
G Ameral
Hun Auer
Fr *Arpeggione*
Y Belgrad
Fr Danel
Jap *Erdödy*
UK Lyric
USA Meridian
G Minguet
Fin New Helsinki
Fin Selin
Cz *Skampa*
G *Werethina*

**1993**
G Arioso
Hun *Auer*
Swit Bazin
UK *Bridge*
G Capriccio
Fr *Danel*
Hol Dufy
G *Henschel*
Fin Kerava
Fr *Lalo*
G Peterson
Ven Rios Reyna
Is Rubin
Jap Sawa

**1994**
G *Arioso*
G *Capriccio*
Rus Eleonora
Est Estonian
UK Hengrave
G *Henschel*
UK Mansbridge
Aus Mentis
UK Nossek
Ch Orient
Rom Silvestri

**1995**
Den Arki
UK Belasco
Pol Crakovia
It David
Pol Elsner
Est *Estonian*
Jap Kisa
Aus Koehne
Fr *Lalo*
Aus *Mentis*
Fr Rassaert
USA Round Top
Rus Talan
Fr Vuillaume

**1996**
G *Arioso*
USA Chagall
Pol *Crakovia*
Pol *Elsner*
Rom Gaudeamus
UK Kim
Jap *Kisa*
G Klenke
Pol Le Stagioni
Jap Lotus
Fr *Rassaert*
Ch South
Ch Tang gu la
Is Young
    Jerusalem

**1997**
G Armando
UK *Cosmos*
    (previously
    Kim)
USA Cypress
Fr Diotima
Pol *Elsner*
D Helios
Is Johannes
Jap *Kisa*
G Kreuzer
Pol *Le Stagioni*
Rom Lipatti
It Ludwig
Rus Quinten
Jap Sunrise
Fin Tempera

Quartets attending for the second or third time are shown in italics.

| *Number of quartets attending*[2] | | | *Nationality*[3] | |
|---|---|---|---|---|
| 1989 | 9 | | Argentine (Arg) | 1 |
| 1990 | 13 | | Austria (Aus) | 2 |
| 1991 | 13 | | China (Ch) | 3 |
| 1992 | 15 | | Czechoslovakia (Cz) | 2 |
| 1993 | 14 | | Denmark (Den) | 2 |
| 1994 | 11 | | Estonia (Est) | 1 |
| 1995 | 14 | | Finland (Fin) | 4 |
| 1996 | 14 | | France (Fr) | 8 |
| 1997 | 15 | | Germany (G) | 17 |
| | | | Holland (Hol) | 1 |
| | | | Hungary (Hun) | 2 |
| | | | Israel (Is) | 3 |
| | | | Italy (It) | 6 |
| | | | Japan (Jap) | 5 |
| | | | New Zealand (NZ) | 1 |
| | | | Poland (Pol) | 5 |
| | | | Romania (Rom) | 2 |
| | | | Russia (Rus) | 4 |
| | | | Switzerland (Swit) | 1 |
| | | | United Kingdom (UK) | 11 |
| | | | United States (USA) | 4 |
| | | | Venezuela (Ven) | 1 |
| | | | Yugoslavia (Y) | 1 |

1 Of those who attended the course in the first year, 1989, the Danish, the Orpheus and the Parisii Quartets are well established. The second year likewise included many who have since become very successful, in particular the Camerata, the Henschel, the Lalo, the New Leipzig and the Skampa. All five quartets joined the course again in later years. 1993 included the Auer, the Danel, the Petersen and the Sawa. In the most recent years, 1996 and 1997, there were an exceptional number of gifted quartets who have not yet had time to become established. Some groups, such as the Petersen, have changed personnel but have successfully managed the transition. Others, such as the Emperor, the Henschel and the Danel, have gone on to win first prizes at international competitions, and the Werethina were voted 'most promising young quartet' at the London International Competition in 1994. The Nossek have been quartet in residence at the University of York in the north of England, and the Skampa is now quartet in residence at the Wigmore Hall in London. Many others are teaching as well as playing – the Camerata at the Warsaw Conservatoire, and the Danish in Copenhagen.

2 The course lasts for two weeks and quartets may attend either for one week only or for the full fortnight.

3 The nationality indicated is that by which they describe themselves, although individuals within quartets are frequently of mixed nationality.

# Index